THE CLAY SANSKRIT LIBRARY

FOUNDED BY JOHN & JENNIFER CLAY

www.claysanskritlibrary.org

www.nyupress.org

Artwork by Robert Beer.
Typeset in Adobe Garamond at 10.25 : 12.3+pt.
XML-development by Stuart Brown.
Editorial input from Dániel Balogh, Ridi Faruque,
Chris Gibbons, Tomoyuki Kono & Eszter Somogyi.
Printed and bound in Great Britain by
T.J. International, Cornwall, on acid-free paper.

"HOW THE NĀGAS WERE PLEASED"

by HARṢA

&

"THE SHATTERED THIGHS"

by BHĀSA

TRANSLATED BY

Andrew Skilton

NEW YORK UNIVERSITY PRESS

JJC FOUNDATION

2009

First Edition 2009

The Clay Sanskrit Library is co-published by
New York University Press
and the JJC Foundation.

Further information about this volume
and the rest of the Clay Sanskrit Library
is available at the end of this book
and on the following websites:
www.claysanskritlibrary.org
www.nyupress.org

ISBN-13: 978-0-8147-4066-8 (cloth : alk. paper)
ISBN-10: 0-8147-4066-9 (cloth : alk. paper)

Library of Congress Cataloging-in-Publication Data
Harṣavardhana, King of Thānesar and Kanauj, fl. 606–647.
[Nāgānanda. English & Sanskrit]
"How the nagas were pleased" by Harsha ; &
"The shattered thighs" by Bhasa
/ translated by Andrew Skilton. – 1st ed.
p. cm.
Plays.
In English and Sanskrit (romanized) on facing pages.
Includes bibliographical references and index.
ISBN-13: 978-0-8147-4066-8 (alk. paper)
ISBN-10: 0-8147-4066-9 (alk. paper)
1. Sanskrit drama–Translations into English. I. Skilton, Andrew.
II. Bhāsa. Ūrubhaṅga. English & Sanskrit. III. Title.
IV. Title: Shattered thighs.
PK3794.H3N3313 2008
891'.2208–dc22
2008023122

CONTENTS

CSL CONVENTIONS

Sanskrit Alphabetical Order

Vowels:	*a ā i ī u ū ṛ ṝ ḷ ḹ e ai o au ṃ ḥ*
Gutturals:	*k kh g gh ṅ*
Palatals:	*c ch j jh ñ*
Retroflex:	*ṭ ṭh ḍ ḍh ṇ*
Dentals:	*t th d dh n*
Labials:	*p ph b bh m*
Semivowels:	*y r l v*
Spirants:	*ś ṣ s h*

Guide to Sanskrit Pronunciation

a	b*u*t
ā, â	f*a*ther
i	s*i*t
ī, î	f*ee*
u	p*u*t
ū, û	b*oo*
ṛ	vocalic *r*, American p*ur*dy or English p*re*tty
ṝ	lengthened *ṛ*
ḷ	vocalic *l*, ab*le*
e, ê, ē	m*a*de, esp. in Welsh pronunciation
ai	b*i*te
o, ô, ō	r*o*pe, esp. Welsh pronunciation; Italian s*o*lo
au	s*ou*nd
ṃ	*anusvāra* nasalizes the preceding vowel
ḥ	*visarga*, a voiceless aspiration (resembling the English *h*), or like Scottish lo*ch*, or an aspiration with a faint echoing of the last element of the preceding vowel so that *taiḥ* is pronounced *taih*^{i}
k	lu*ck*
kh	blo*ckh*ead
g	*g*o
gh	bi*gh*ead
ṅ	a*n*ger
c	*ch*ill
ch	mat*chh*ead
j	*j*og
jh	aspirated *j*, he*dgeh*og
ñ	ca*ny*on
ṭ	retroflex *t*, *t*ry (with the tip of tongue turned up to touch the hard palate)
ṭh	same as the preceding but aspirated
ḍ	retroflex *d* (with the tip

	of tongue turned up to touch the hard palate)	*b*	*b*efore
ḍh	same as the preceding but aspirated	*bh*	a*bh*orrent
ṇ	retroflex *n* (with the tip of tongue turned up to touch the hard palate)	*m*	*m*ind
t	French *t*out	*y*	*y*es
th	ten*t h*ook	*r*	trilled, resembling the Italian pronunciation of *r*
d	*d*inner	*l*	*l*inger
dh	guil*dh*all	*v*	*w*ord
n	*n*ow	*ś*	*sh*ore
p	*p*ill	*ṣ*	retroflex *sh* (with the tip of the tongue turned up to touch the hard palate)
ph	u*ph*eaval	*s*	hi*ss*
		h	*h*ood

CSL Punctuation of English

The acute accent on Sanskrit words when they occur outside of the Sanskrit text itself, marks stress, e.g., Ramáyana. It is not part of traditional Sanskrit orthography, transliteration, or transcription, but we supply it here to guide readers in the pronunciation of these unfamiliar words. Since no Sanskrit word is accented on the last syllable it is not necessary to accent disyllables, e.g., Rama.

The second CSL innovation designed to assist the reader in the pronunciation of lengthy unfamiliar words is to insert an unobtrusive middle dot between semantic word breaks in compound names (provided the word break does not fall on a vowel resulting from the fusion of two vowels), e.g., Maha·bhárata, but Ramáyana (not Rama·áyana). Our dot echoes the punctuating middle dot (·) found in the oldest surviving samples of written Indic, the Ashokan inscriptions of the third century BCE.

The deep layering of Sanskrit narrative has also dictated that we use quotation marks only to announce the beginning and end of every direct speech, and not at the beginning of every paragraph.

CSL Punctuation of Sanskrit

The Sanskrit text is also punctuated, in accordance with the punctuation of the English translation. In mid-verse, the punctuation will not alter the sandhi or the scansion. Proper names are capitalized. Most Sanskrit meters have four "feet" (*pāda*); where possible we print the common *śloka* meter on two lines. In the Sanskrit text, we use French *Guillemets* (e.g., *«kva saṃcicīrṣuḥ?»*) instead of English quotation marks (e.g., "Where are you off to?") to avoid confusion with the apostrophes used for vowel elision in sandhi.

SANDHI

Sanskrit presents the learner with a challenge: *sandhi* (euphonic combination). Sandhi means that when two words are joined in connected speech or writing (which in Sanskrit reflects speech), the last letter (or even letters) of the first word often changes; compare the way we pronounce "the" in "the beginning" and "the end."

In Sanskrit the first letter of the second word may also change; and if both the last letter of the first word and the first letter of the second are vowels, they may fuse. This has a parallel in English: a nasal consonant is inserted between two vowels that would otherwise coalesce: "a pear" and "an apple." Sanskrit vowel fusion may produce ambiguity.

The charts on the following pages give the full sandhi system.

Fortunately it is not necessary to know these changes in order to start reading Sanskrit. All that is important to know is the form of the second word without sandhi (pre-sandhi), so that it can be recognized or looked up in a dictionary. Therefore we are printing Sanskrit with a system of punctuation that will indicate, unambiguously, the original form of the second word, i.e., the form without sandhi. Such sandhi mostly concerns the fusion of two vowels.

In Sanskrit, vowels may be short or long and are written differently accordingly. We follow the general convention that a vowel with no mark above it is short. Other books mark a long vowel either with a bar called a macron (*ā*) or with a circumflex (*â*). Our system uses the

VOWEL SANDHI

Final vowels: (columns) / *Initial vowels:* (last column)

a	ā	i	ī	u	ū	ṛ	e	ai	o	au	*Initial vowels:*
' â	" â	y a	y a	v a	v a	r a	e '	ā a	o '	āv a	a
' ā	" ā	y ā	y ā	v ā	v ā	r ā	a ā	ā ā	a ā	āv ā	ā
' ê	" ê	' î	" î	v i	v i	r i	a i	ā i	a i	āv i	i
' ē	" ē	' ī	" ī	v ī	v ī	r ī	a ī	ā ī	a ī	āv ī	ī
' ô	" ô	y u	y u	' û	" û	r u	a u	ā u	a u	āv u	u
' ō	" ō	y ū	y ū	' ū	" ū	r ū	a ū	ā ū	a ū	āv ū	ū
a' r	a" r	y ṛ	y ṛ	v ṛ	v ṛ	' ṝ	a ṛ	ā ṛ	a ṛ	āv ṛ	ṛ
' âi	" âi	y e	y e	v e	v e	r e	a e	ā e	a e	āv e	e
' āi	" āi	y ai	y ai	v ai	v ai	r ai	a ai	ā ai	a ai	āv ai	ai
' âu	" âu	y o	y o	v o	v o	r o	a o	ā o	a o	āv o	o
' āu	" āu	y au	y au	v au	v au	r au	a au	ā au	a au	āv au	au

CONSONANT SANDHI

Permitted finals: *(Except āḥ/aḥ)*

k	ṭ	t	p	ṅ	n	m	ḥ/r	āḥ	aḥ	*Initial letters:*
k	ṭ	t	p	ṅ	n	ṃ	ḥ	āḥ	aḥ	k/kh
g	ḍ	d	b	ṅ	n	ṃ	r	ā	o	g/gh
k	ṭ	c	p	ṅ	ṃś	ṃ	ś	āś	aś	c/ch
g	ḍ	j	b	ṅ	ñ	ṃ	r	ā	o	j/jh
k	ṭ	ṭ	p	ṅ	ṃṣ	ṃ	ṣ	āṣ	aṣ	ṭ/ṭh
g	ḍ	ḍ	b	ṅ	ṇ	ṃ	r	ā	o	ḍ/ḍh
k	ṭ	t	p	ṅ	ṃs	ṃ	s	ās	as	t/th
g	ḍ	d	b	ṅ	n	ṃ	r	ā	o	d/dh
k	ṭ	t	p	ṅ	n	ṃ	ḥ	āḥ	aḥ	p/ph
g	ḍ	d	b	ṅ	n	ṃ	r	ā	o	b/bh
ṅ	ṇ	n	m	ṅ	n	ṃ	r	ā	o	*nasals* (n/m)
g	ḍ	d	b	ṅ	n	ṃ	r	ā	o	y/v
g	ḍ	d	b	ṅ	n	ṃ	*zero*[1]	ā	o	r
g	ḍ	l	b	ṅ	l̃[2]	ṃ	r	ā	o	l
k	ṭ	c ch	p	ṅ	ñ ś/ch	ṃ	ḥ	āḥ	aḥ	ś
k	ṭ	t	p	ṅ	n	ṃ	ḥ	āḥ	aḥ	ṣ/s
gg h	ḍḍ h	dd h	bb h	ṅ	n	ṃ	r	ā	o	h
g	ḍ	d	b	ṅ/ṅṅ[3]	n/nn[3]	m	r	ā	a[4]	*vowels*
k	ṭ	t	p	ṅ	n	m	ḥ	āḥ	aḥ	*zero*

[1] ḥ or r disappears, and if a/i/u precedes, this lengthens to ā/ī/ū. [2] e.g. tān+lokān=tāl̃ lokān.
[3] The doubling occurs if the preceding vowel is short. [4] Except: aḥ+a=o '.

macron, except that for initial vowels in sandhi we use a circumflex to indicate that originally the vowel was short, or the shorter of two possibilities (*e* rather than *ai*, *o* rather than *au*).

When we print initial *â*, before sandhi that vowel was *a*

î or *ê*,	*i*
û or *ô*,	*u*
âi,	*e*
âu,	*o*
ā,	*ā*
ī,	*ī*
ū,	*ū*
ē,	*ī*
ō,	*ū*
ai,	*ai*
āu,	*au*
’, before sandhi there was a vowel *a*	

When a final short vowel (*a*, *i*, or *u*) has merged into a following vowel, we print ’ at the end of the word, and when a final long vowel (*ā*, *ī*, or *ū*) has merged into a following vowel we print ” at the end of the word. The vast majority of these cases will concern a final *a* or *ā*. See, for instance, the following examples:

What before sandhi was *atra asti* is represented as *atr’ âsti*

atra āste	*atr’ āste*
kanyā asti	*kany” âsti*
kanyā āste	*kany” āste*
atra iti	*atr’ êti*
kanyā iti	*kany” êti*
kanyā īpsitā	*kany” ēpsitā*

Finally, three other points concerning the initial letter of the second word:

(1) A word that before sandhi begins with *ṛ* (vowel), after sandhi begins with *r* followed by a consonant: *yatha” rtu* represents pre-sandhi *yathā ṛtu*.

(2) When before sandhi the previous word ends in *t* and the following word begins with *ś*, after sandhi the last letter of the previous word is *c*

and the following word begins with *ch*: *syāc chāstravit* represents pre-sandhi *syāt śāstravit*.

(3) Where a word begins with *h* and the previous word ends with a double consonant, this is our simplified spelling to show the pre-sandhi form: *tad hasati* is commonly written as *tad dhasati*, but we write *tadd hasati* so that the original initial letter is obvious.

COMPOUNDS

We also punctuate the division of compounds (*samāsa*), simply by inserting a thin vertical line between words. There are words where the decision whether to regard them as compounds is arbitrary. Our principle has been to try to guide readers to the correct dictionary entries.

Exemplar of CSL Style

Where the Devanagari script reads:

कुम्भस्थली रक्षतु वो विकीर्णसिन्धूररेणुर्द्विरदाननस्य ।
प्रशान्तये विघ्नतमश्छटानां निष्ठ्यूतबालातपपल्लवेव ॥

Others would print:

kumbhasthalī rakṣatu vo vikīrṇasindūrareṇur dviradānanasya /
praśāntaye vighnatamaśchaṭānāṃ niṣṭhyūtabālātapapallaveva //

We print:

kumbha|sthalī rakṣatu vo vikīrṇa|sindūra|reṇur dvirad'|ānanasya
praśāntaye vighna|tamaś|chaṭānāṃ niṣṭhyūta|bāl'|ātapa|pallav" êva.

And in English:

May Ganésha's domed forehead protect you! Streaked with vermilion dust, it seems to be emitting the spreading rays of the rising sun to pacify the teeming darkness of obstructions.

("Nava·sáhasanka and the Serpent Princess" I.3)

Wordplay

Classical Sanskrit literature can abound in puns (*śleṣa*). Such paronomasia, or wordplay, is raised to a high art; rarely is it a *cliché*. Multiple meanings merge (*śliṣyanti*) into a single word or phrase. Most common are pairs of meanings, but as many as ten separate meanings are attested. To mark the parallel senses in the English, as well as the punning original in the Sanskrit, we use a *slanted* font (different from *italic*) and a triple colon (⁝) to separate the alternatives. E.g.

yuktaṃ Kādambarīṃ śrutvā kavayo maunam āśritāḥ
Bāṇa|dhvanāv an|adhyāyo bhavat' îti smṛtir yataḥ.

It is right that poets should fall silent upon hearing the Kadámbari, for the sacred law rules that recitation must be suspended when *the sound of an arrow ⁝ the poetry of Bana* is heard.

(Soméshvara·deva's "Moonlight of Glory" I.15)

Gwendoline Barbara Skilton
(1927–2006)

PREFACE

TRANSLATING "HOW THE Nagas were Pleased" fulfills a personal ambition of almost twenty years, since the day I bought from my favorite Bristol bookshop (now long gone) a battered copy of an anonymous text and translation from Bangalore. When in 2004 ISABELLE ONIANS invited me to offer my translation to the CSL the question arose of what to pair it with to make up a volume. SOMADEVA VASUDEVA astutely suggested "The Shattered Thighs." I had never placed the two together in my own mind, but as I worked on both I became ever more pleased with the conjunction.

Here we have two plays that break the rules: both show the hero dying on stage, a scenario forbidden in Sanskrit dramaturgy. From widely different ideological and social backgrounds, each evokes intense emotion in an exploration of love and heroism, conflict and peace, idealism and pragmatic accommodation. Each portrays the reconciliation of hate and retaliation in love and mercy.

Harsha's play, composed in the seventh century, reexamines the tale of a Magician prince who makes the ultimate sacrifice to save a sacrificial serpent (*nāga*). "How the Nagas were Pleased" places this Buddhist "birth story" concerning spiritual love in the context of the complexities of human affection. Sometimes misinterpreted as a tragedy, the play offers pathos, wonder, beauty, terror, love in its many aspects and spiritual idealism.

"The Shattered Thighs" transforms a crucial episode of the Maha·bhárata war. Bhasa shows us the Kuru leader

Duryódhana as he dies from a foul blow received in his duel with Bhima. Overturning the epic's depiction of Duryódhana as ambitious and transgressive, Bhasa depicts him as a noble and reconciling leader amidst the wreckage of the fearsome battle scene. An ignoble man is ennobled in death.

Both plays combine in good measure the typical pleasures of great Sanskrit literature (*kāvya*) with the most serious issues of living and dying. Whatever the merits of my own efforts herein, I wholeheartedly commend to the reader these two wonderful pieces of literature. All faults herein are mine; all virtues belong to the authors and the cultures that nurtured them.

It gives me satisfaction to record my indebtedness to a number of people in my work on this volume. To Isabelle Onians, who saw what I needed and cajoled me into working on "How the Nagas were Pleased" for the CSL. To Kate Crosby, who helped me gather the materials and generously read several drafts, offering suggestions for improvement. To Naomi Appleton, who also read a draft and to Dániel Balogh, who as copy editor read my text with meticulous attention to detail prompting a number of improvements. To Rath Borei, whose absence informed many words in this volume. To my mother who departed part way through. This volume is dedicated to them all.

Andrew Skilton
Llanishen, 2006

HOW THE NAGAS WERE PLEASED

INTRODUCTION

Nagananda is justly regarded as one of the best plays in Sanskrit literature. (KARMARKAR 1923: xxxi)

One of the most interesting pieces of Indian literature although it is a total failure as a drama... (WINTERNITZ 1998: 253)

"HOW THE NAGAS WERE Pleased" (*Nāgānanda*) is a five-act play written by the seventh-century Indian monarch, Harsha. He is also credited with two plays in four acts, "The Lady who Shows her Love" (*Priyadarśikā*) and "The Lady of the Jewel Necklace" (*Ratnāvalī*),[1] and two hymns in praise of the Buddha. "How the Nagas were Pleased" itself says it is based on a Buddhist story, and it is thus one of only two "Buddhist" plays to have survived in full.[2]

The story concerns the issue of personal sacrifice by substitution. A prince of the divine magicians (*vidyādharas*), called Jimúta·váhana, substitutes himself for a serpent (*nāga*) who has been designated as the tithe given by the snake community for consumption that day by Gáruda, the king of the birds. The same motif and narrative structure is to be found in another *jātaka* story,[3] in the Buddhist Pali canon. In the "Birth Story of Nigródha the Deer" (*Nigrodhamiga-jātaka*), the chief of the deer makes an agreement to present to the king on a regular basis a single subject for his consumption, rather than allow his fellow deer to suffer the random terror of the royal hunt.[4] The bodhisattva, or Buddha-to-be, substitutes himself for a doe whose turn it is, and as a result, out of respect for this altruism, the king bans the hunting of deer thereafter. In "How the Nagas were Pleased" the outcome is that Gáruda gives up eating snakes.

The story is derived explicitly from the "Birth Story of Jimúta·váhana" (*Vidyādharajātaka*), a text not known from surviving canonical Buddhist sources, where the designation *jātaka* suggests it should be found, but which is well-known in other narrative collections including the somewhat later "Emperor of the Sorcerers" (*Bṛhatkathāślokasaṅgraha*) and the "Magical Vine of the Bodhisattva's Many Lives" (*Avadānakalpalatā*).[5] Bosch has analyzed the influence and development between known versions of this story, but did not have the benefit of the recent discovery of a Pali version, albeit non-canonical and perhaps itself rather late.[6] Based on Bosch's work we must suppose that Harsha derived his source from Gunádhya's *Bṛhatkathā* itself, he suggests, based on a lost Buddhist exemplar. The other extant versions of this story are also derived from Gunádhya, but not via "How the Nagas were Pleased."

The substitution story of the deer proved popular in Buddhist circles, with a number of versions preserved in the textual record, whereas the *Vidyādhara* version appears to have appealed more to non-Buddhist authors. We can only speculate why Harsha chose the *Vidyādhara* story. Nevertheless his version of the *Vidyādharajātaka* became famous in its own time, as we know from the testament of the Chinese pilgrim I-Tsing who traveled in India in the last quarter of the seventh century and commented on the popularity of "How the Nagas were Pleased" at the time.

Whether this popularity was because of its Buddhist content or its literary quality, or both, we cannot say. Literary critics have disagreed on the dominant mood (*rasa*) of the play, opinion being divided between the "calm" (*śānta*) and the "heroic" (*vīrya*), both obviously well represented. This aside, all the *rasa*s are shown in the play, and, as WARDER points out in his excellent summary of critical appreciation of "How the Nagas were Pleased," Shiva·rama (fourteenth century) thought that Harsha had realized here all the aims of Sanskrit drama! Of a number of criticisms leveled at our play we can note the depiction, as in "The Shattered Thighs," of the hero's death on stage, something expressly forbidden in the dramaturgical literature (*Nāṭyaśāstra*).

Apologists reason that the death is admissible here insofar as the same character is soon brought back to life. More serious is an argued disjunction between the first three acts, containing a love story that is the invention of Harsha, and the last two, which correspond to the "original" Buddhist story. There is most certainly a change of mood between the two, but Harsha took great pains both to presage the latter in the former, and to release the tension of the latter by the reassertion of a happy status quo at the end of Act Five. Such a critique also fails to see that Harsha has constructed a panorama of the emotions that we commonly designate "love" across its broadest spectrum, through the wonderfully achieved juxtaposition of passionate personal love, erotic infatuation and despair, comic flirtation and jealousy, love as familial and social duty, parental love, and an impersonal, altruistic or spiritual love, as exemplified by Jimúta·váhana's sacrifice in the last two acts. Even the inherent contradictions of the last are highlighted by his father's complaint in Act Five:

Knowing, "this one's mine, this a stranger," in truth
isn't there actually a proper order for compassion?
How come you did not think, "Shall I save one or many?"
Giving your own life to save a snake from Tarkshya,
You have destroyed this entire family—yourself,
your parents and your wife! (5.109 [21])

A number of commentators have taken issue with the timeline of "How the Nagas were Pleased," expressing some dissatisfaction with its realism. How much time has passed between each act, or indeed, in the case of Act Three, within the act? Yet we should not forget that dramatic performance itself provides opportunity and means for the non-verbal indication of the passage of time and change of place. Over and above this, we should recall that all participation in narrative relation in any form involves some suspension of disbelief.

Much seems to be made, usually by literary critics, of this being a Buddhist story in a brahmanical context, although that is to ignore the universal accommodation—to be found in all traditional Buddhist societies—of "worldly" goals with the "transcendental" values of Buddhism. The gods of the world, here the devotional Hindu gods, deal with worldly matters, while Buddhist soteriology addresses a release or awakening beyond worldly values that is as remote from the gods as from human beings. We may not be far wrong in seeing this same distinction reflected in our play. The hero pursues the altruistic ideal of total self-sacrifice upheld in Buddhism but thereby creates utter havoc among those towards whom he feels compassion but who do not share his values. I have in mind here, as examples, the destruction of the hero's family by his religious suicide, and the devastating effect on Shankha·chuda when his own role, as the sacrifice that saves his people for a day, is "stolen" by the bodhisattva! While "worldly" characters, human and divine, universally admire and love the hero for this very idealism, the resultant mess in the world has to be sorted out by the gods of the world, herein Gauri, who restores life to Jimúta·váhana. The outcome, the final achievement for the hero, who desires solely to sacrifice himself for others and thus exemplify the model of spiritual sovereignty, is worldly happiness and political sovereignty. This paradox is noted also by WARDER, and possibly reflects an actual conflict between political duty and personal spirituality in Harsha's own life.

It may then be that we have in "How the Nagas were Pleased" a courtly assimilation of the radical altruism of Buddhist narrative literature, making it psychologically authentic and implicitly showing it to be a rather problematic theoretical ideal. It seeks to resolve those problems through the characters' interaction with the deities of this world in the brahmanical context of divine grace and favor. If this interpretation is valid, then "How the Nagas were Pleased" joins a body of other Buddhist narrative that explores some of these same tensions. The difference here is, I suggest, that a Buddhist narrative that like many others has highly emotive if not devastating implications for human relationships in society, is now masterfully portrayed with full attention given to those psychological and emotional realities. By contrast we are often given rather summary not to say bland relations of these stories in the *jātaka* and *avadāna* collections.

The skeptical reader might also ask what has happened to the hero's overwhelming concern to sacrifice himself when, at the end of the play, he delightedly accepts the total worldly success bestowed by Gauri. This issue is perhaps clouded by the frequent assumption that Buddhist monastics, like their Christian counterparts, undertook a vow of poverty. This is not so, and there is plenty of evidence that in all Buddhist societies some monks, at least, accumulated considerable wealth and moved in the circles of power and influence. A positive reading of what might thus erroneously be seen as a paradox, is that spiritual and political sovereignty are not necessarily mutually exclusive. Jimúta·váhana is not a monk, of course, and there is a further implicit message of Harsha's play that can be identified.

The clue to understanding Jimúta·váhana's apparent happiness with this outcome is perhaps best seen on comparison with the narrative structure as revealed in the *Nigrodhamiga* story. There the bodhisattva's personal sacrifice by substitution results not just in the saving of one single life (in fact, in both versions, of two lives: a pregnant doe in one, and an only *nāga* son with a dependent mother in the other) but in the king's decision to ban not only the hunting and consumption of all deer, but of all creatures, birds and fish included. This is the outcome that validates the bodhisattva's personal sacrifice, which if it remained a single act of substitution would be thus circumscribed and insignificant. What, we could reasonably ask, would happen when the next sacrifice comes due? Shankha·chuda himself argues:

Oh, noble-souled man, you have shown this sincere compassion for me through your resolve to give your self, but do not persist. For,

Inferior creatures like me are born and they die.
Where do people like you come from,
Who are ready to do anything to help others?

(4.93–94)

If the compassionate concede to the less noble the world is depleted of good people.

Harsha's treatment suggests not just the potential futility of Jimúta·váhana's personal sacrifice as an isolated gesture, but also its destructive character since it results initially in the imminent death of everyone whom Jimúta·váhana loves, namely his parents, his wife and the very person for whom he substituted himself in order thereby to "save." His actions are redeemed through the responses of the worldly figures of power, who either reward the good (Gauri) or are shamed into being better themselves (Gáruda).

Textual Sources for this Text and Translation

Readers unfamiliar with the problems that can beset the publication of texts reproduced before the mechanical age may be dismayed to discover that the *Nāgānanda* has survived in as many as five distinct recensions.[7] These are identified regionally—as from South India, the Deccan, Bengal, Nepal, and Tibet (in a translation)—and this means that the *Nāgānanda* circulated in each of these regions in a distinct form and wording. These differences include individual words, sentences, and verses, variously missing, added or transposed, affecting stage directions, banter and dialogue as well as the exalted language of the verses, and are overall so frequent that I shall not be recording them.

Scholars have so far suggested that these recensions are independent, i.e. none can be derived from any other, which in turn means that none can be held up as especially distant from or close to a putative original written by the hand of Harsha. This situation is normal for any text that has been copied for centuries in manuscript, and arises partly through the combination of scribal error plus scholarly correction and "improvement," and partly through the demands of performance in the case of a drama. Of course, it could be that Harsha produced several versions of his own play, but we have no other reason to assume this. The critical, or analytical, process by which an editor compares these recensions and whittles the variants down to as close an account as possible of Harsha's original text has not yet been performed, and may not be for some time to come. The situation is further complicated by the plethora of texts and editions printed in India since 1863, the date of the first.

"How the Nagas were Pleased" has a rich and fertile publishing history—STEINER's bibliography of fifty-eight texts and translations can be supplemented by even more in this age of electronic library catalogs (STEINER 1991 and 1997). Many of these titles contain texts prepared by eminent pandits, some of whom have approached it without the same text-genealogical intent as an editor trained in the Western Classical milieu, and have taken readings from one recension or another on aesthetic, stylistic or grammatical grounds, occasionally recording the other variants but rarely their source.[8] Add to these a number of less careful texts, plus others that are anonymous and the sources for which are unrecorded, and we have a potentially confusing and perhaps misleading situation in which we can read a published text of the *Nāgānanda* that neither acknowledges the diversity of its recensions nor shows us how that text has been preserved in any traditional community in South Asia. Readers particularly sensitive to these matters describe such texts as modern fictions given undue currency by virtue of the printing press and would claim that they are inauthentic both to Harsha and to the communities that have preserved and transmitted the *Nāgānanda*.

Valid or not, such critiques beg the question of what we shall read in this volume. The preparation of a critical edition is inappropriate for these purposes and so the simplest and most appropriate solution is to take the text of just one recension and present that. For this purpose I have chosen GANAPATI SHASTRI's edition of what STEINER calls the Southern recension. I translate the text as it is, making only very minor changes, amounting to correcting the rare typographic errors and occasionally the sandhi in the Sanskrit translation of the Prakrit, and changing the punctuation of the text to conform to CSL house style. Where there is a questionable reading in the Prakrit, I have usually left it unchanged. Translating this edition is appropriate for several reasons, which I shall only briefly outline. Firstly, we will be dealing with a single recension that has been published by an eminent scholar in a fairly critical edition based on six manuscripts, that does not conflate the text of this recension with that of others. This text is accompanied by a splendid fourteenth-century commentary by Shiva·rama, which takes the state of the text back to that date, thus sidestepping the manuscript vagaries of the intervening seven centuries. Secondly, despite the reprinting of GANAPATI SHASTRI's work in 1989 with a new introduction by UNNI, I have not found either edition easy to locate or acquire and it appears effectively to be out of print and held in few libraries. Thirdly, the quality of GANAPATI SHASTRI's text is very high and rather better on comparison than that of the other recensions available. HAHN concludes, "The quality of Ganapati Śāstri's [sic] own work and the inclusion of the *Nāgānandavimarśinī* make his book so far the best edition for students and scholars who wish to enjoy the literary qualities of the *Nāgānanda*" (HAHN 1991: iii). (Shiva·rama's commentary cannot be included in this volume.) Finally, "How the Nagas were Pleased" has been a popular piece in the repertoire of the Keralan theater and so SHASTRI's southern text can be seen as an appropriate companion to the *Ūrubhaṅga*, preserved by the same community.

What of access to the other recensions I have mentioned? The Deccan or "Central" recension is represented in the edition published by BRAHME and PARANJAPE in Poona, in 1893, but that is, as far as I can tell, out of print. The Nepalese recension has not yet been published, although identified by HAHN as early as 1974. The Tibetan translation has been published in uncritical editions—BHATTACHARYA's edition (Calcutta, 1957) also contains an interlinear Sanskrit text. The "Northern" recension is represented by GHOSHA's 1864 edition (Calcutta), which on account of being long out of print and effectively unavailable, was reprinted in 1991 and is presently still in print. Hitherto, easy access has therefore been possible to only one of the identified recensions: the Northern recension in HAHN and STEINER's reprint of GHOSHA. Now, here, GANAPATI SHASTRI's "Southern recension" is available once again courtesy of the CLAY SANSKRIT LIBRARY.

Notes

1 Translated by WENDY DONIGER, Clay Sanskrit Library, New York: New York University Press & JJC Foundation, 2007.

2 The other is Chandra·gomin's *Lokānanda* and survives in a Tibetan translation only (see HAHN 1987).

3 A *jātaka* is a "Birth Story," a genre of narrative literature that relates an account of a previous life of the Buddha.

4 See COWELL, vol. 1, story number 12, p. 36ff.

5 This story is listed under the headword *"Jimutavāhana"* in L. GREY, "A Concordance of Buddhist Birth Stories," Oxford, 1994. For these two Sanskrit texts, see respectively "The Emperor of the Sorcerers," 2 vols., translated by SIR JAMES MALLINSON, Clay Sanskrit Library, New York: New York University Press & JJC Foundation, 2005 and "The Magical Vine of the Bodhisattva's Many Lives" (forthcoming) in the Clay Sanskrit Library.

6 Discovered by J. FILLIOZAT. Further information is available from the public archive of the *École française d'Extrême-Orient*, under the classmark, "EFEO DATA Filliozat file 403 Vijjadharajataka data." See also her "Sources for the Vijjādharajātaka Studies in Indochina" in *The South East Asian Review* (forthcoming).

7 My understanding of the basic distinction between these five recensions of the *Nāgānanda* is in large part indebted to the analytical work of STEINER and HAHN (see Bibliography, especially GHOṢA 1991 and STEINER 1997).

8 KALE and KARMARKAR also contain English translations and analytical commentaries on the text.

Bibliography

EDITIONS AND TRANSLATIONS

GAṆAPATI SĀSTRĪ, T.: *The Nāgānanda of Srī Harsha Deva with the Commentary Nāgānandavimarsinī by Sivarāma.* Trivandrum Sanskrit Series. Trivandrum, 1917. [G]

GHOṢA, M.C.: *Nāganandam,* Presidensi yantre mudritam: Calcutta, 1864; reprinted as, *The Recensions of the Nāgānanda by Harṣadeva, vol. 1, The North Indian Recension.* General Introduction, M. HAHN; Preface and bibliography of editions and translations of the Nāgānanda, R. STEINER. Aditya Prakashan: New Delhi 1991.

HAHN, M.: *Joy for the World, a Buddhist Play by Candragomin.* Berkeley: Dharma Publishing, 1987.

KALE, M.R.: *The Nāgānandam of Harsha-Deva,* Bombay 1919; reprinted as, A.V. TORASKAR, and N.A. DESHPANDE, *Nāgānand of Harshadev. Edited with a complete English Translation, Introduction, Exhaustive notes, Sanskrit commentary of Late M R Kale and useful Appendices.* Bombay: Booksellers' Publishing Co, 1953.

KARMARKAR, R.D.: *Nāgānanda of Śrīharṣa edited with an introduction, translation, notes critical and explanatory and appendices,* Vishvanath and Co: Bombay 1923.

SECONDARY LITERATURE

BOSCH, F.D.K.: *De legende van Jīmūtavāhana in de Sanskrit-Litteratuur*. Leiden, 1914.

COWELL, E.B.: *The Jātaka or Stories of the Buddha's Former Births*. Cambridge: Cambridge University Press, 1895.

HAHN, M.: "General Introduction" to GHOṢA, reprint 1991.

STEINER, R.: "Preface" to GHOṢA, reprint 1991.

STEINER, R.: *Untersuchungen zu Harṣadevas Nāgānanda und zum indischen Schauspiel*, Indica et Tibetica Verlag: Swisttal-Odendorf 1997.

WARDER, A.K.: *Indian Kāvya Literature, volume four, The Ways of Originality (Bāṇa to Dāmodaragupta)*, Delhi: Motilal Banarsidass, 1983 (reprinted 1994).

WINTERNITZ, M.: *History of Indian Literature, Volume* III, *Part One: Classical Sanskrit Literature*. Delhi: Motilal Banarsidass 1998 (originally published,1963).

Dramatis Personæ

Characters marked with ⌜corner brackets⌟ speak Prakrit.

MALE

HERO:	JIMÚTA·VÁHANA, a Magician prince
⌜COMPANION⌟:	ATRÉYA, a brahmin
SHANKHA·CHUDA:	a *naga* (serpent) whose turn it is to be eaten by GÁRUDA
GÁRUDA:	Lord of birds, semi-divine bird of prey
MITRA·VASU:	brother of the heroine, MÁLAYAVATI, and a prince of the Adept clan
JIMÚTA·KETU:	the hero's father, king of the Magician clan
⌜ROGUE⌟:	SHÉKHARAKA, member of the Adept household and beau of NAVA·MÁLIKA
BUTLER:	VASU·BHADRA, manager of the Adept household
DOORMAN:	SUNÁNDA, doorman of the same
MANSERVANT:	to SHÉKHARAKA
⌜RETAINER⌟:	to the king of the *nagas*
ASCETIC:	SHANDÍLYA, a hermit
PRODUCER:	in the court of Harsha, who mounts the play

FEMALE

⌜HEROINE⌟:	MÁLAYAVATI, a princess of the Adepts
⌜MAID⌟:	CHÁTURIKA, a maid to the heroine, MÁLAYAVATI
⌜MAID⌟:	MANO·HÁRIKA, a maid to the heroine, MÁLAYAVATI
⌜MAID⌟:	NAVA·MÁLIKA, a maid to the heroine, MÁLAYAVATI, girlfriend of SHÉKHARAKA
GAURI:	the Goddess, consort of Shiva, also called Párvati
⌜QUEEN⌟:	the mother of the HERO
⌜OLD WOMAN⌟:	the mother of SHANKHA·CHUDA
⌜ACTRESS⌟:	wife of the PRODUCER

PROLOGUE

1.1 «DHYĀNA|VYĀJAM upetya cintayasi kām?
unmīlya cakṣuḥ kṣaṇaṃ
paśy' Ânaṅga|śar'|āturaṃ janam imaṃ.
Trāt" âpi no rakṣasi!
mithyā|kāruṇiko 'si! nirghṛṇataras
tvattaḥ kuto 'nyaḥ pumān?»
s'|ērṣyaṃ Māra|vadhūbhir ity abhihito
bodhau Jinaḥ pātu vaḥ! [1]

api ca,

Kāmen' ākṛṣya cāpaṃ; hata|paṭu|paṭah'|ā-
valgibhir Māra|vīrair;
bhrū|bhaṅg'|ôtkampa|jṛmbhā|smita|lalitavatā
divya|nārī|janena;
Siddhaiḥ prahv'|ôttam'|âṅgaiḥ; pulakita|vapuṣā
vismayād Vāsavena
dhyāyan bodher avāptāv a|calita iti vaḥ
pātu dṛṣṭo Mun'|îndraḥ! [2]

nāndy|ante tataḥ praviśati SŪTRA|DHĀRAḤ.

1.5 SŪTRA|DHĀRAḤ: ady' âham Indr'|ôtsave sa|bahumānam āhūya nānā|dig|deś'|āgatena rājñaḥ Śrī|Harṣa|devasya pāda|padm'|ôpajīvinā rāja|samūhen' ôktaḥ. yathā, «yat

"Of what lady are you thinking under the pretext of meditation? 1.1
Open your eyes for a second,
Look at these people suffering the arrows of bodiless Cupid.* Some Protector! You do not protect us.
Your compassion is phony! How could anyone be more heartless than you are?"
The Conqueror, at the point of Awakening harassed maliciously like this by Mara's women, may he protect you!

And again,

By Cupid with his bow drawn; by Mara's champions leaping around to the beat of shrill war drums;
By the heavenly ladies, frowning, trembling, yawning, smiling, wanton;
By the Adepts with their heads bowed in respect; by Vásava, his glorious body prickling with dismay;
Beheld thus, unmoved as he meditates intent on Awakening, may the Lord of sages protect you!*

Thereupon at the conclusion of the invocation the PRODUCER *enters.*

PRODUCER: Today, on Indra's festival day, I've been very politely summoned by a gathering of chiefs who have arrived from lands in various directions round about, all of them subordinate to the lotus feet of the King Shri Harsha, and I've been informed as follows, "We have 1.5

tad asmat|svāminā Śrī|Harṣa|deven' â|pūrva|vastu|racan'|âlaṅkṛtaṃ Vidyādhara|jātaka|pratibaddhaṃ «Nāgānandaṃ» nāma nāṭakam kṛtam, ity asmābhiḥ śrotra|paramparayā śrutaṃ, na prayogato dṛṣṭam. tat tasy' âiva rājño bahu|mānād asmāsu c' ânugraha|buddhyā yathāvat prayogen' âdya tvayā nāṭayitavyam!» iti. tad yāvad idānīṃ nepathya|racanāṃ kṛtvā yath"|âbhilaṣitaṃ sampādayāmi. āvarjitāni ca sāmājika|jana|manāṃs' îti me niścayaḥ. kutaḥ,

Śrī|Harṣo nipuṇaḥ kaviḥ; pariṣad apy
  eṣā guṇa|grāhiṇī;
loke hāri ca bodhisattva|caritaṃ;
  nāṭye ca dakṣā vayam.
vastv ek'|âikam ap' îha vāñchita|phala|
  prāpteḥ padaṃ; kiṃ punar
mad|bhāgy'|ôpacayād ayaṃ samuditaḥ
  sarvo guṇānāṃ gaṇaḥ? [3]

tad yāvad gṛhiṇīm āhūya saṅgītakam anutiṣṭhāmi.

(parikramya, nepathy'|âbhimukham avalokya)

dvija|parijana|bandhu|hite,
  mad|bhavana|taṭāka|haṃsi, mṛdu|śīle,
para|puruṣa|candra|kamaliny,
  ārye, kāryād itas tāvat! [4]

heard rumor that there is a play called 'How the Nagas were Pleased' written by our master, Shri Harsha, based on the 'Birth Story of King of Magicians' but elaborated with a new plot and never before seen on the stage. So, out of respect for the king himself and to oblige us, please arrange for it to be properly staged today!" That is why, up till now I've been busy with arrangements in the dressing room, and I shall make it happen as requested. And I have no doubt that the minds of the audience have been won over, since,

> Shri Harsha is a pretty fine poet; this audience too
> can appreciate literary merit;
> The world is fascinated by the exploits of the
> bodhisattva;
> And we are skilled in dramatic performance.
> Any one single factor is occasion for achieving
> the goal I am after; how much more
> This entire collection of virtues brought together
> through the build up of my good fortune?

So I shall call my wife and set up the musical entertainment.

(walking around and looking towards the dressing room)

> O Good to the twice-born, to servants and to
> relatives, the golden goose on the pond that is
> my home, so gentle in character,
> A daytime lotus flower to the moon of other men,
> darling, just come here—it's business!

1.10 NAṬĪ: *(praviśya s'|âsrā)* ⌜ayya, iyamhi!⌟

SŪTRA | DHĀRAḤ: *(vilokya)* ārye, Nāg' | ānande nāṭayitavye kim idam a|kāraṇam eva rudyate?

NAṬĪ: ⌜ayya, kahaṃ ṇa rodissaṃ? jadā tādo ajjuā a thavira| bhāva | jāda | ṇivvedāo kuḍumba | bhār' | uvvahaṇa | joggo dāṇiṃ tuvaṃ ti hiae ārovia tavo|vaṇaṃ gadāo.⌟

SŪTRA|DHĀRAḤ: kathaṃ mām api parityajya vanaṃ prayātau pitarau? *(vicintya)* tat kim idānīṃ yujyate? atha vā, katham ahaṃ guru|caraṇa|paricaryā|sukhaṃ parityajya gṛhe tiṣṭhāmi? kutaḥ,

pitror vidhātuṃ śuśrūṣāṃ,
  tyaktv" āiśvaryaṃ kram'|āgatam
vanaṃ yāmy aham apy eṣa
  yathā Jīmūtavāhanaḥ [5]

1.15 *niṣkrāntau.*

āmukham.

ACTRESS: *(entering the stage in tears)* Darling, here I am! 1.10

PRODUCER: *(seeing her)* Darling, why this unnecessary weeping when we're staging "How the Nagas were Pleased"?

ACTRESS: Darling, how could I not weep? Your father and his courtesan are feeling disillusioned through his old age, and have gone off to an ascetic's grove, convinced at heart that you are now ready to bear the burden of the household.

PRODUCER: How can my parents abandon me and go off to the wilderness? *(reflecting)* What should I do now? In fact, can I really stay at home and give up the pleasure of waiting on the feet of my parents? Rather,

> Abandoning hereditary authority in order to offer
> eager care to my parents,
> Let me go the wilderness, too, just like Jimúta·váhana!

They go out together. 1.15

Prologue concludes.

ACT ONE

tataḥ praviśati NĀYAKO VIDŪṢAKAŚ *ca.*

NĀYAKAḤ:

rāgasy' āspadam ity avaimi. na hi me
dhvaṃs' îti na pratyayaḥ.
kṛty'|âkṛtya|vicāraṇāsu vimukhaṃ
ko vā na vetti kṣitau?
evaṃ nindyam ap' îdam indriya|vaśaṃ
prītyai bhaved yauvanaṃ
bhaktyā yāti yad' îttham eva pitarau
śuśrūṣamāṇasya me. [6]

VIDŪṢAKAḤ: *(sa|roṣam)* ⌜bho vaassa, ṇa ṇivviṇṇo eva tuvaṃ ettiaṃ kālaṃ edāṇam jīvanta|mudāṇaṃ vuḍḍhāṇaṃ kide īdisaṃ vaṇa|vāsa|dukkhaṃ aṇuhavanto? tā pasīda! dāṇim pi dāva guru|jaṇa|sussūsā|nibbandhādo nivvattia icchā|paribhoa|ramaṇijjaṃ rajja|sokkham aṇubhavīadu.⌟

1.20 NĀYAKAḤ: sakhe, na samyag abhihitam! kutaḥ,

tiṣṭhan bhāti pituḥ puro bhuvi yathā
siṃhāsane kiṃ tathā?
kiṃ saṃvāhayataḥ sukhāni caraṇau
tātasya, kiṃ rājakam?
kiṃ bhukte bhuvana|traye dhṛtir asau
bhukt'|ôjjhite yā guror?
āyāsaḥ khalu rājyam ujjhita|guros.
ten' âsti kaś cid guṇaḥ? [7]

The HERO *and his* COMPANION *enter.*

HERO:

I understand that it is the abode of passion.
I believe full well that it will perish.
On the face of this earth who does not know how it
scorns the distinction between right and wrong?
Though reprehensible in these ways when controlled
by the senses, this youthfulness should be
pleasurable
If it passes just like this, while with devotion I am
eagerly caring for my parents.

COMPANION: *(irritated)* Old friend, aren't you fed up experiencing the unpleasantness of life in the wilderness because of these two old folks more dead than alive? Cheer up! You should leave off this dogged eagerness to care for your parents now, and enjoy the fun of being king. You can do what you like!

HERO: You did not put that very well, my friend! Why, 1.20

Does one cut as good a figure on the Lion's Throne
as when one stands on the ground before
one's father?
What are pleasures, what the company of kings
while massaging one's father's feet?
Is there the satisfaction in the enjoyments of the
threefold world as there is in one's parents'
leftovers?
Certainly kingship is trouble for the person who has
put aside his parents. Is there any virtue in it?

VIDŪṢAKAḤ: *(ātma|gatam)* ⌜aho! se guru|jaṇa|sussūs"|âṇurāo!⌟ *(vicintya)* ⌜bhodu, evvaṃ dāva bhaṇissaṃ.⌟ *(prakāśam)* ⌜bho vaassa, ṇa khu ahaṃ kevalaṃ rajja|sokkhaṃ uddisia evvaṃ bhaṇāmi. aṇṇam pi de karaṇijjam atthi evva.⌟

NĀYAKAḤ: vayasya, nanu kṛtam eva karaṇīyam. paśya,

nyāyye vartmani yojitāḥ prakṛtayaḥ;
santaḥ sukhaṃ sthāpitā;
nīto bandhu|janas tath" ātma|samatāṃ;
rājye 'pi rakṣā kṛtā;
datto datta|manorath'|âdhika|phalaḥ
kalpa|drumo 'py arthine;
kiṃ kartavyam ataḥ paraṃ? kathaya vā
yat te sthitaṃ cetasi. [8]

1.25 VIDŪṢAKAḤ: ⌜bho vaassa! accanta|sāhasio Madaṅga|deva|hadao de paḍivakkho. tassiṃ ca samāsaṇṇa|ṭṭhide pahāṇ'|âmacca|samahiṭṭhidaṃ pi ṇa tue viṇā rajjaṃ su|tthidaṃ ti me paḍibhādi.⌟

NĀYAKAḤ: kiṃ Mataṅgo rājyaṃ grahīṣyat' îty āśaṅkase? yady evaṃ, tataḥ kim? sva|śarīrataḥ prabhṛti par'|ârtham eva sarvaṃ mayā paripālyate. yat tu svayam na dīyate, tat tāt'|ânurodhāt. tat kim anen'|âvastunā cintitena? varaṃ tāt'|ājñ" âiv' ânuṣṭhitā! ājñāpito 'smi tātena, yathā: «vatsa Jīmūtavāhana, bahu|divasa|paribhogena dūrī|kṛtaṃ

COMPANION: *(to himself)* Ooh! His obsession with looking after his parents! *(thinking)* OK. This is what I'll say. *(out loud)* Old chap, I don't speak in this way solely on account of the pleasure of kingship. There really is something else which you should do.

HERO: Surely I've already done what's needed, my friend? Look,

> The ordinary folk have been employed in proper
> ways; good people have been made happy;
> My relations have been raised to the same status
> as me; the kingdom has also been made safe;
> I have given the wish-fulfilling tree, that gives
> more than one has wished for, to those in need;
> What more should be done than this?
> Just say what you have in mind.

COMPANION: My dear friend, that cursed King Matánga is 1.25
ambitious beyond all bounds and he's your enemy; and it's not clear to me that, while he advances, the kingdom is secure without you, even though managed by the chief minister.

HERO: Are you worried that Matánga will take the kingdom? Even if that were so, what of it? I have protected everything, even my body, solely for the benefit of others. It is only to oblige my father that I have not given it away myself. So what is the point of worrying about this minor matter? It is more important to follow father's instructions! Father instructed me as follows: "My dear child Jimúta·váhana, here is exhausted of firewood, sacred grass and flowers through many days' usage, and

samit | kuśa | kusumam. upayukta | mūla | phala | kanda | nīvāra | prāyam idaṃ sthānaṃ vartate. tan Malaya | parvataṃ gatvā nivāsa|yogyam āśrama|padaṃ nirūpay'» êti. tad yāvan Malayam eva gacchāvaḥ.

ubhau parikrāmataḥ.

VIDŪṢAKAḤ: ⌜bho vaassa, pekkha pekkha! eso khu sara | saghaṇa | siṇiddha | candaṇa | vaṇ' | ucchaṅga | parimilaṇa | lagga | bahala | parimalo visama | taḍa | paḍaṇa | jajjarijjanta | ṇijjhar' | uccalia | sisira | sīar' | āsāra | vāhī paḍama | saṅgam' | ukkaṇṭhia | piā | kaṇṭha | ggaho via magga | parissamaṃ avaṇaanto romañcedi pia|vaassaṃ Malaya|māruo.⌟

NĀYAKAḤ: *(vilokya)* aye! kathaṃ, prāptā eva Malaya | parvatam! *(sarvato datta|dṛṣṭiḥ)* aho! rāmaṇīyakam asya. tathā hi,

1.30 mādyad|dig|gaja|gaṇḍa|bhitti|kaṣaṇair
bhagna|sravac|candanaḥ;
krandat|kandara|gahvaro, jala|nidher
āsphālito vīcibhiḥ;
pād'|âlaktaka|rakta|mauktika|śilaḥ
siddh'|âṅganānāṃ gataiḥ;
sevyo 'yaṃ Malay'|âcalaḥ. kim api me
cetaḥ karoty utsukam. [9]

its roots, fruit, bulbs and wild rice are almost used up. Therefore go to the Málaya mountain and look for a hermitage site that is good for habitation." With this in mind, let's go straight to the Málaya mountain.

Both walk about.

COMPANION: Look, look my friend! It must be the breeze from Málaya that's causing goose-flesh for my dear companion. It relieves the fatigue of the journey just like a lover's embrace of his beloved at their first rendezvous. It's heavily fragrant from caressing the flanks of pungent, dense, moist sandalwood forests, and wafts showers and cool mists up through waterfalls broken and scattered by their rough banks.

HERO: *(looking closely)* Ah! We certainly have reached the Málaya mountain! *(looking all about)* Gosh! The loveliness of the place. For,

> Its sandalwood broken and oozing from the rubbing 1.30
> of the cheekbones of the lusting elephants
> from the four quarters;*
> Lashed by the ocean's waves, its glens and caverns
> roaring;
> Its pearly rocks reddened by carmine dye from the
> feet of the Adept women as they go about;
> This immovable Málaya is the place to stay.
> It makes my mind yearn for something.

tad ehy, āruhya nivāsa|yogyam āśramaṃ nirūpayāvaḥ.

ārohaṇam nāṭayataḥ.

NĀYAKAḤ: *(nimittaṃ sūcayan)* sakhe,

spandate dakṣiṇaṃ cakṣuḥ,
phala|kāṅkṣā na me kva cit;
na ca mithyā muni|vacaḥ;
kathayiṣyati kin nv idam? [10]

1.35 VIDŪṢAKAḤ: ⌜bho vaassa, āsaṇṇaṃ de piaṃ ṇivededi!⌟

NĀYAKAḤ: evam nāma, yathā bhavān bravīti.

VIDŪṢAKAḤ: *(sa|harṣam)* ⌜bho vaassa, edaṃ khu sa|visesa|ghaṇa|siṇiddha|pādav'|ôvasohidaṃ surabhi|havig|gaṃdha|gabbhiṇ'|uddāma|dhūma|ṇiggamaṃ aṇ|uvvigga|magga|suha|ṇisaṇṇa|sāvaa|gaṇaṃ tavo|vaṇaṃ via lakkhīadi.⌟

NĀYAKAḤ: sakhe, samyag upalakṣitam. tapo|vanam ev' âitat. kutaḥ,

vāso|'rthaṃ dayay" âiva n' âtipṛthavaḥ
kṛttās tarūṇāṃ tvaco;
bhagn'|ālakṣya|jarat|kamaṇḍalu nabhaḥ|
svacchaṃ payo nairjharam;
dṛśyante truṭit'|ôjjhitāś ca vaṭubhir
mauñjyaḥ kva cin mekhalā;
nity'|ākarṇanayā śukena ca padaṃ
sāmnām idaṃ paṭhyate. [11]

Come on then, now that we have arrived, let's look for a hermitage site that is good for habitation.

Miming, they ascend.

HERO: *(indicating an omen)* Friend,

> My right eye is trembling, but there is nothing that I want;
> And yet the words of the sages are not wrong; what will this foretell?

COMPANION: It indicates that something pleasant for you is 1.35
due, old chap!

HERO: Yes indeed, as you say!

COMPANION: *(with excitement)* I say old chap, for sure it looks like a penance grove over here. It's graced with unusually dense and verdant trees and groups of wild animals sitting happy and fearless on the path. Prodigious clouds of smoke laden with the fragrant scent of oblations drift out.

HERO: Well spotted, my friend. This really is a penance grove. For,

> It is out of kindness that the tree bark has not been peeled too much for clothing;*
> In the sky-clear water of the brook ancient, broken water pots are visible;
> Here and there can be seen broken sacred grass braids cast off by young brahmin boys;
> And through hearing it all the time a parrot recites a line of verse from the "Sama Veda."*

1.40 tad ehi, praviśy' âvalokayāvaḥ.

praveśanaṃ nāṭayataḥ.

NĀYAKAḤ: *(sarvato vilokya)* aho nu khalu mudita|muni|jana|pravicāryamāṇa|sandigdha|veda|vākya|vistarasya, paṭhad|vaṭu|jan'|ācchidyamān'|ārdra|samidhaḥ, tāpasa|kumārik"|āpūryamāṇa|bāla|vṛkṣa|kālavālasya praśānta|ramyatā tapo|vanasya! iha hi,

madhuram iva vadanti svāgataṃ bhṛṅga|śabdair.
natim iva phala|namraiḥ kurvate 'mī śirobhiḥ.
mama dadata iv' ârghyaṃ puṣpa|vṛṣṭīḥ kirantaḥ.
katham, atithi|saparyāṃ śikṣitāḥ śākhino 'pi? [12]

tan nivāsa|yogyaṃ tapo|vanam. manye bhaviṣyat' îha nivasatām asmākaṃ nirvṛtiḥ.

1.45 VIDŪṢAKAḤ: ⌜bho vaassa, kiṃ ṇu khu ede īsi|valia|kandharā ṇiccala|muh'|osaraṃta|daradalia|dabbha|gabbha|kabalā samuṇṇamia|diṇṇ'|ekka|kaṇṇā ṇimīlida|loaṇā āaṇṇaaṃto via hariṇā lakkhiaṃti.⌟

NĀYAKAḤ: *(karṇaṃ dattvā)* sakhe, samyag upalakṣitaṃ bhavatā! tathā hi,

Come on then, let's go in and have a look. 1.40

They mime entering.

HERO: *(looking around)* Ah, but the tranquil delight of the ascetic grove! Here the particulars of ambiguous statements in the Veda are investigated by happy sages, green firewood is being cut by the brahmin boys as they recite, and the water basins of the young trees are filled by the young ascetic girls. For in this place,

> By the buzzing of bees they seem to speak a sweet
> welcome.
> By the hanging of their heads heavy with fruit
> they seem to bow down.
> Scattering a rain of blossoms they seem to make me
> the guest offering.
> What's this, are even the trees trained in the protocol
> for a guest?

Now we know that this ascetic grove is good for a dwelling. I think we will be more than happy living here.

COMPANION: I say old boy, what is it these deer appear to listen to, their necks turned a little, half-chewed mouthfuls of darbha grass* dropping from inside their unmoving mouths, one ear pricked and attentive, their eyes closed? 1.45

HERO: *(listening)* Well observed, my friend! For,

sthāna|prāptyā dadhānaṃ
prakaṭita|gamakāṃ mandra|tāra|vyavasthāṃ
nirhrādinyā vipañcyā
militam ali|ruten' êva tantrī|svanena,
ete dant'|ântarāla|
sthita|tṛṇa|kabala|ccheda|śabdaṃ niyamya
vyājihm'|âṅgāḥ kuraṅgāḥ
sphuṭa|lalita|padaṃ gītam ākarṇayanti [13]

VIDŪṢAKAḤ: ⌜bho vaassa, ko ṇu khu eso tavo|vaṇe gāadi?⌟

NĀYAKAḤ: yathā komal'|âṅguli|tal'|âbhihanyamānā n'|âti-sphuṭaṃ kvaṇanti tantryaḥ, kākalī|pradhānaṃ ca gīyate, tathā tarkayāmi *(aṅguly|agreṇ'|âgrato nirdiśan)* asminn āyatane devatām ārādhayantī kā cid divya|yośid upavīṇayat' îti.

1.50 VIDŪṢAKAḤ: ⌜bho vaassa, edaṃ dev'|āadaṇaṃ pekkhamha.⌟

NĀYAKAḤ: sādh' ûktam. vandyāḥ khalu devatāḥ. *(upasarpan, sahasā sthitvā)* vayasya, kadā cid draṣṭum an|arho 'yam jano bhaviṣyati. tad anena tāvat tamāla|gulmen' ântaritau devatā|darśan'|âvasaraṃ pratipālayāvaḥ.

tathā kurutaḥ. tataḥ praviśati bhūmāv upaviṣṭā vīṇāṃ vādayantī MALAYAVATĪ CEṬĪ *ca.*

As they hold back the noise of chewing a mouth of
grass between their teeth,
These antelope are listening, their bodies awry,
to a song of clear and melodious words,
Harmonized with the sounding of lyre strings*
like the humming of bees,
Containing an arrangement of low and high notes
the ornaments* of which are displayed
according to the register.

COMPANION: I say old man, who's this singing in the ascetic grove?

HERO: As the strings are being struck indistinctly with the tips of tender fingers and the singing is dominated by the gentle *kákali* mode,* I deduce that *(indicating in front with his pointing finger)* it is some heavenly young lady that's playing on the lyre while courting the deity at this altar.

COMPANION: Well, let's look at the deity's altar, old boy. 1.50

HERO: Good suggestion. The gods really should be worshipped. *(approaching softly, but suddenly halting)* It may be that it's not appropriate to look on this person, my friend. So, let's wait for a chance to see the deity, hiding inside this clump of *tamála* trees.*

They do so. Thereupon appears MÁLAYAVATI *seated on the ground playing her lute, and her* MAIDSERVANT.

NĀYIKĀ: *(vīṇayā saha gāyati)*

utphulla|kamala|kesara|
parāga|gaura|dyute, mama hi, Gauri,
abhivāñchitaṃ prasidhyatu,
bhagavati, yuṣmat|prasādena! [14]

1.55 NĀYAKAḤ: *(karṇaṃ dattvā)* vayasya, aho gītam! aho vāditram!

vyaktir vyañjana|dhātunā daśa|vidhen'
âpy atra labdh" âmunā.
vispaṣṭo druta|madhya|lambita|pari-
cchinnas tridh" âyaṃ layaḥ.
gopucchā|pramukhāḥ krameṇa yatayas
tisro 'pi saṃvāditāḥ.
tattv'*|âugh'|ânugatāś ca vādya|vidhayaḥ
samyak trayo darśitāḥ. [15]

CEṬĪ: ⌜bhaṭṭi|dārie! ciraṃ khu vāidaṃ. ṇa khu de parissamo agga|hatthāṇaṃ?⌟

NĀYIKĀ: ⌜hañje Caürie! bhaavadīe purado vādayantīe kudo mama parissamo?⌟

CEṬĪ: *(s'|âdhikṣepam)* ⌜bhaṭṭi|dārie, ṇaṃ bhaṇāmi, kiṃ edāe ṇikkaruṇāe purado vāideṇa? ettiaṃ kālaṃ kaṇṇaā|jaṇa|dukkhareḥiṃ ṇiam'|ôpavāsehiṃ ārāhaantīe ṇa de pasādaṃ daṃsedi!⌟

1.60 VIDŪṢAKAḤ: ⌜bho vaasya, kaṇṇaā khu esā! kīsa ṇa pekkhamha?⌟

HEROINE: *(singing, accompanied by her lute)*

> Golden Gauri! Lustrous as golden pollen on the threads in an open lotus flower!*
> May my longing, my Lady, be by your grace fulfilled!

HERO: *(lending ear)* What a song, my friend! What music! 1.55

> Clarity is achieved here by using the tenfold elements of syllabic articulation.*
> The threefold tempo, differentiated as fast, medium and slow, is clear.
> Even the three rhythmic variations are played in order, beginning with the "cow tail,"*
> And the three modes of instrumental accompaniment, essence, flood and sequential,* are exhibited correctly!

MAIDSERVANT: Miss! This music has gone on for a while. Aren't your fingers tired?

HEROINE: Maid Cháturika! How can I get tired playing for the goddess?

MAIDSERVANT: *(dismissively)* I tell you, Miss, there's no point in playing for this pitiless lady. She shows you no grace though you've courted her for ages with vows and fasts that are really difficult for young ladies!

COMPANION: Well old man, she's actually an unmarried girl! 1.60
Why don't we look?

NĀYAKAḤ: ko doṣaḥ? nir|doṣa|darśanā hi kanyakāḥ. kin tu kadā cid asmān dṛṣṭvā bāla|bhāva|sulabha|lajjā|sādhvasān na ciram iha tiṣṭhet. tad anen' âiva tāval latā|jāl'|ântareṇa paśyāvaḥ.

ubhau paśyataḥ.

VIDŪṢAKAḤ: *(dṛṣṭvā sa|vismayam)* ⌜bho vaassa, pekkha, pekkha! esā ṇa kevalaṃ vīṇāe kaṇṇāṇaṃ evva suhaṃ uppādedi. imiṇā vīṇā|viṇṇāṇ'|âṇurūveṇa rūveṇa akkhīṇaṃ pi suhaṃ uppādedi. kā vuṇa esā? kiṃ dāva devī? ādu ṇāa|kaṇṇaā? āho vijjāhara|dāriā? udāho siddha|ula|saṃbhava tti?⌟

NĀYAKAḤ: *(sa|spṛham avalokayan)* vayasya, k" êyam iti n' âvagacchāmi. etat punar ahaṃ jāne,

1.65 svarga|strī yadi, tat kṛt'|ârtham abhavac
cakṣuḥ|sahasraṃ Harer.
nāgī cen, na rasātalaṃ śaśa|bhṛtā
śūnyaṃ mukhe 'syāḥ sati.
jātir naḥ sakal'|ânya|jāti|jayinī,
vidyādharī ced iyaṃ.
syāt siddh'|ânvaya|jā yadi, tribhuvane
siddhāḥ prasiddhās tataḥ [16]

VIDŪṢAKAḤ: *(NĀYAKAM avalokya, sa|harṣam ātma|gatam)* ⌜diṭṭhiā cirassa dāva kālassa paḍido khu eso goare Vammahassa.⌟ *(ātmānaṃ nirdiśya)* ⌜aha vā mama evva bamhaṇassa.⌟

HERO: No problem. There's no fault in looking at young ladies. But once she's seen us she might not stay long here, being alarmed and timid as young ladies commonly are. So let's watch for the meanwhile through this network of creepers.

The two of them observe.

COMPANION: *(seeing with admiration)* I say dear boy, have a look at this! She doesn't only please the ear with her lyre. She pleases the eye with her looks, which complement her playing. So, who is she? A goddess, perhaps? Or a young Naga lady? Or could she be a Magician's daughter? Or even born to the Adept clan?

HERO: *(looking on, longingly)* I cannot tell who she is, my friend. At least this I do know,

> If a heavenly lady, then Hari's thousand eyes 1.65
> have been satisfied.
> If she's a Naga girl, then while her face is round,
> the dank nether region will not lack a moon.
> If this is a Magician girl then our race wins out
> over all races.
> If she has been born in the lineage of the Adepts
> then the Adepts should be celebrated in the
> three worlds.*

COMPANION: *(looking at the* HERO, *to himself with delight)* What luck! At last he's actually fallen within the range of the passionate god of love. *(pointing to himself)* Or just of me, a brahmin!

CEṬĪ: *(sa|praṇayam)* ⌜bhaṭṭi|dārie, ṇaṃ bhaṇāmi, kiṃ edāe ṇik|karuṇāe purado vāideṇa?⌟ *(iti vīṇām ākṣipati.)*

NĀYIKĀ: ⌜hañje! mā mā bhaavadiṃ Gauriṃ ahikkhiva! ajja kido me bhaavadīe pasādo.⌟

CEṬĪ: *(sa|harṣam)* ⌜bhaṭṭi|dārie! kahehi dāva kīriso so pasādo.⌟

1.70 NĀYIKĀ: ⌜hañje, ajja jāṇāmi siviṇae evvaṃ evva vīṇaṃ vādaantī bhaavadīe Gaurīe bhaṇida mhi. «vacche, parituṭṭha mhi tuha ediṇā vīṇā|viṇṇāṇ'|âdisaeṇa, imāe bāla|jaṇa|dullahāe a|sāhāraṇāe mam' ôvari bhattīe a. tā vijjāhara|cakkavaṭṭī a|ireṇa de pāṇi|ggahaṇaṃ ṇivvaṭṭaïssidi» tti.⌟

CEṬĪ: ⌜bhaṭṭi|dārie, jaï evvaṃ, kissa siviṇae tti bhaṇāsi? ṇaṃ hia'|êcchido evva devīe *varo* diṇṇo.⌟

VIDŪṢAKAḤ: ⌜bho vaassa, avasaro khu amhāṇaṃ *devī*|daṃsaṇassa. tā ehi, pavisamha.⌟ *(upasarpataḥ. an|icchantam iva* NĀYAKAṂ *balād ākṛṣya...)* ⌜hodi! saccaṃ evva esā bhaṇādi. *varo evva eso* devīe diṇṇo.⌟

NĀYIKĀ: *(sa|sādhvasam uttiṣṭhantī)* ⌜hañje, ko ṇu khu eso?⌟

CEṬĪ: *(*NĀYAKAṂ *nirūpya)* ⌜imāe aṇṇoṇṇa|sarisīe ākidīe eso so bhaavadīe prasāda tti takkemi.⌟

MAIDSERVANT: *(beseeching)* I tell you, for sure, there's no point in playing in front of this pitiless lady. *(She snatches away the lyre.)*

HEROINE: Maid! Don't insult the Lady Gauri! My Lady graced me today.

MAIDSERVANT: *(delighted)* Miss! Tell me at once what kind of grace it is.

HEROINE: Today, in a dream, maid, while I was playing the 1.70
lyre just like this, I believe the Lady Gauri spoke to me. "I am really pleased with this wonderful skill on the lyre of yours, my child, and with your unusual devotion to me, which is so difficult for young people. So, before long, the emperor of the Magicians will take your hand!"

MAIDSERVANT: If it happened like that, Miss, why say it was in a dream? Surely the goddess has given a *treat : husband* after your heart's desire?

COMPANION: Well old chap, now's the time for us to see our *goddess : queen*! Come on then, let's go in. *(The two approach softly. Dragging the* HERO *by force as if he was unwilling...)* Lady! What she's said is really true. *This really is a treat : Here's the husband* given by the goddess!

HEROINE: *(getting up in alarm)* Maid, who's this?

MAIDSERVANT: *(pointing at the* HERO*)* With those looks so well suited, each for the other, I guess he must be the grace from the Lady.*

1.75 NĀYIKĀ *sa/spṛhaṃ sa/lajjaṃ* NĀYAKAM *avalokayantī tiṣṭhati.*

NĀYAKAḤ:

tanur iyaṃ, taral'|āyata|locane,
  śvasita|kampita|pīna|ghana|stani,
śramam alaṃ tapas" âiva gatā punah.
  kim iti, saṃbhrama|kāriṇi, khidyase? [17]

NĀYIKĀ: ⌜hañje, adisakkhaseṇa ṇa sakkuṇomi edassa saṃmuhe ṭhāduṃ!⌟

NĀYAKAṂ *tiryak sa/lajjaṃ paśyantī, kiñ cit parāvṛtta/mukhī tiṣṭhati.*

VIDŪṢAKAḤ: ⌜bhodi, kiṃ ettha tumhāṇaṃ tavo|vaṇe īriso āāro, jeṇa adihi|jaṇo āado vāā|matteṇa vi ṇa saṃbhāvaṇīo?⌟

1.80 CEṬĪ: *(*NĀYIKĀṂ *dṛṣṭv" ātma/gatam)* ⌜aṇurajjadī via ettha edāe diṭṭhī! tā evvaṃ dāva bhaṇissaṃ.⌟ *(prakāśam)* ⌜bhaṭṭi|dārie, juttaṃ bhaṇādi bamhaṇo. uido khu de adihi|jaṇa|sakkāro. tā kīsa edassiṃ mah"|âṇubhāve paḍipatti|mūḍhā via ciṭṭhasi? aha vā ciṭṭha tuvaṃ! ahaṃ evva jah"|âṇurūvam karissaṃ.⌟ *(*NĀYAKAM *uddiśya)* ⌜sāadaṃ ayyassa. āsaṇa|pariggaheṇa alaṃ|karodu imaṃ padesaṃ ayyo.⌟

VIDŪṢAKAḤ: ⌜bho vaassa, sobhaṇaṃ esā bhaṇādi! upavisia muhuttaaṃ vissamamha.⌟

NĀYAKAḤ: yuktam āha bhavān.

The HEROINE *stands looking at the* HERO *shyly and with longing.* 1.75

HERO:

You, with large fluttering eyes,
Your full but firm bosom heaving!
Your body is already tired from enough penance.
So why are you distressed, you girl in a whirl?

HEROINE: Maid, I'm so nervous I can't bear to stay in front of him!

She stands with her face turned back, looking shyly and obliquely at the HERO.

COMPANION: Lady, is this how you behave here in the ascetic's grove? When a guest comes he isn't greeted with even a single word?

MAIDSERVANT: *(observing the* HEROINE, *and to herself)* Her 1.80
gaze seems entranced with him! I know what to say. *(out loud)* Princess, the brahmin has made a good point. You should welcome a guest. So why are you hanging about at a loss how to behave towards this gentleman? Oh well, you stand there! I'll do the form. *(addressing the* HERO*)* Welcome, Sir. Would Sir adorn this place by accepting a seat?

COMPANION: Good friend, she said that nicely! Let's take a seat and rest for a moment.

HERO: That's a good suggestion.

ubhāv upaviśataḥ.

NĀYIKĀ: *(sa|lajjam)* ⌜haddhi parihāsa|sīle! mā evvaṃ karohi. kadā i ko vi tāvaso maṃ pekkhe, tado maṃ a|viṇīda tti saṃbhāvaïssidi.⌟

1.85 *tataḥ praviśati* TĀPASAḤ.

TĀPASAḤ: ājñāpito 'smi kula|patinā Kauśikena yathā, «vatsa Śāṇḍilya, pitur ājñayā yuva|rājo Mitrāvasur bhaviṣyad| vidyādhara|cakravartinaṃ kumāraṃ Jīmūtavāhanam ih' âiva Malaya|parvate kv' âpi vartamānaṃ bhaginyā Malayavatyā vara|hetor draṣṭum adya gataḥ. taṃ ca pratīkṣamāṇāyāḥ kadā cin madhyan|dina|savana|vidhir atikrāmet. tad enām āhūy' āgacch'» êti. tad yāvad Gaurī|gṛhaṃ gacchāmi. *(parikrāman bhuvaṃ nirūpya)* aye, kasya punar iyaṃ pāṃsula|pradeśe prakāśita|cakravarti|cihnā pada|paṅktiḥ? *(agrato* JĪMŪTAVĀHANAṂ *nirūpya)* nūnam asy' âiv' êyaṃ mahā|puruṣasya. api ca,

uṣṇīṣaḥ sphuṭa eṣa mūrdhani, vibhāty
ūrṇeyam antar bhruvoś,
cakṣus tāmaras'|ânukāri, hariṇā
vakṣaḥ|sthalaṃ spardhate.
cakr'|âṅkaṃ ca yathā kara|dvayam idaṃ,
manye tathā ko 'py ayaṃ,
no vidyādhara|cakravarti|padavīm
a|prāpya viśrāmyati. [18]

They both sit down.

HEROINE: *(shyly)* No! You teaser! Don't do this. As soon as some ascetic sees me, he'll think me lacking in decorum.

At that point an ASCETIC *enters.* 1.85

ASCETIC: I've been instructed as follows by Káushika, the head of the hermitage, "My dear boy Shandílya, by order of his father, Mitra·vasu the crown prince has today gone to see the young prince Jimúta·váhana, the future emperor of the Magicians, who is somewhere here on Málaya mountain, about being a husband for his sister Málayavati. And while she is waiting for him, the time for her midday ablutions might perhaps run out. So, call her and come back." That's why I am off to the temple of Gauri. *(walking about and noticing the ground)* Ah, whose is this track of footprints in this dusty spot displaying the sign of an emperor? *(pointing to* JIMÚTA·VÁHANA *ahead)* It must belong to this great person. And,

The crown* of his head is distinct.
The hair between his eyebrows catches the eye.
His eyes resemble a red lotus. His chest rivals a lion's.
And since this pair of feet have the mark of the wheel,
  I guess this chap, whoever he may be,
Will not rest without achieving the status of emperor
  of the Magicians.

atha vā kṛtaṃ sandehena. su|vyaktam anena Jīmūtavāhanena bhavitavyam. *(*MALAYAVATĪṂ *nirūpya)* aye, iyam api rāja|putrī. *(ubhau vilokya)* cirāt khalu yukta|kārī vidhiḥ syād, yadi yugalam idam anyony'|ânurūpaṃ ghaṭayet. *(upasṛtya* NĀYAKAM *uddiśya)* svasti bhavate.

NĀYAKAḤ: *(utthāya)* bhagavan! Jīmūtavāhano 'ham abhivādaye. *(āsanaṃ dātum icchati.)*

1.90 TĀPASAḤ: alam alam abhyutthānena! nanu «sarvasy' âbhyāgato gurur» iti bhavān ev' âsmākaṃ pūjyaḥ. tad yathā|sukhaṃ sthīyatām.

NĀYAKAḤ: bāḍham.

NĀYIKĀ: ⌜ayya! paṇamāmi.⌟

TĀPASAḤ: bhadre, anurūpa|bhartṛ|bhāginī bhūyāḥ! rājaputri, āha tvāṃ kulapatiḥ Kauśikaḥ, «atikrāmati madhyan|dina|savana|velā. tvaritam āgamyatām» iti.

NĀYIKĀ: ⌜jaṃ gurū āṇavedi.⌟

1.95 *utthāya niḥśvasya sa|lajjaṃ, s'|ânurāgaṃ ca* NĀYAKAṂ *paśyantī,* TĀPASA*|sahitā niṣkrāntā* NĀYIKĀ CEṬĪ *ca*

NĀYAKAḤ: *(s'|ôtkaṇṭhaṃ niḥśvasya, nāyikāṃ gacchantīṃ paśyan)*

anayā jaghan'|ābhoga|bhara|manthara|yānayā
anyato 'pi vrajantyā me hṛdaye nihitaṃ padam. [19]

In fact, there's no need to speculate further. It's absolutely clear that this is Jimúta·váhana. *(noticing* MÁLAYAVATI*)* Ah, and here is the king's daughter. *(looking at the pair)* Destiny would be doing the right thing, at last, if it united this couple who are so suited for one another. *(approaching and addressing the* HERO*)* Good health, sir.

HERO: *(getting up)* Reverend! I am Jimúta·váhana and I salute you. *(He offers his seat.)*

ASCETIC: No, no need to get up! Surely it's you who should be honored by us, since "the guest is important to everyone." So you stay at your leisure. 1.90

HERO: Thank you.

HEROINE: Sir! I bow to you.

ASCETIC: Lucky girl, may you be wedded to a suitable husband! Káushika, the head of the hermitage, tells you, Miss, "The time for your midday ablution is running out. Come back quickly."

HEROINE: As my teacher instructs!

Getting up and sighing, looking at the HERO *shyly and entranced, the* HEROINE, *along with her* MAIDSERVANT, *leaves in the company of the* ASCETIC. 1.95

HERO: *(sighing longingly, and watching the heroine leaving)*

> A footprint is laid on my heart, even though
> she's going off the other way,
> By this lady, slow stepping on account of the burden
> of her broad hips.

VIDŪṢAKAḤ: ⌜diṭṭhaṃ jaṃ pekkhidavvaṃ! dāṇiṃ majjh'|aṇṇa|sūra|saṃdāva|viuṇio via me jaṭhar'|aggī damadamāyadi. tā ṇikkamamha. jeṇa adihī bhavia muṇi|jaṇa|saāsādo laddhehiṃ kaṃda|mūla|phalehiṃ pi dāva pāṇa|dhāraṇaṃ karissaṃ.⌟

NĀYAKAḤ: *(ūrdhvam avalokya)* aye, madhyam adhyāste nabhastalasya bhagavān sahasra|dīdhitiḥ. tathā hi,

1.100 tāpāt tat|kṣaṇa|ghṛṣṭa|candana|ras'|ā-
pāṇḍū kapolau vahan,
saṃsaktair nija|karṇa|tāla|pavanaiḥ
saṃvījyamān'|ānanaḥ
saṃpraty eṣa viśeṣa|sikta|hṛdayo
hast'|ôjjhitaiḥ śīkarair
gāḍh'|āyallaka|dussahām iva daśāṃ
dhatte gajānāṃ patiḥ [20]

niṣkrāntau.

COMPANION: He's seen what he should have been looking for! Now, the fire in my belly is roaring as if doubled by the heat of the midday sun. So, let's go off. Now that I'm a guest, I shall sustain my breath with bulbs, roots and fruit received from the sage folk.

HERO: *(looking above)* Ah, the Lord, the thousand-rayed sun, has entered upon the middle of the sky. So it is that,

Due to the heat, bearing his two cheeks whitened 1.100
from the just-crushed sandalwood juice,
His face fanned by the continual breeze from his
flapping ears,
Now his heart in particular sprayed with jets of water
squirted from his trunk,
The elephant lord endures a state that seems
unbearable from profound yearning.

The two leave.

INTRODUCTORY SCENE

2.1 *tataḥ praviśati* CEṬĪ.

CEṬĪ: ⌜āṇatta mhi bhaṭṭi|dāriāe Malaavadīe, «hañje Maṇoharie, ajja cirāadi bhāduo me ayya|Mittāvasū. tā gadua jāṇāhi, kiṃ āado ṇa vetti.»⌟ *(parikrāmati. nepathy' âbhimukham ālokya)* ⌜kā uṇa esā ido evva āacchadi?⌟ *(nirūpya)* ⌜kahaṃ, Caüriā!⌟

tataḥ praviśati CATURIKĀ.

MANOHARIKĀ: *(upasṛtya)* ⌜hañje Caürie! kiṃ ṇimittaṃ puṇa tumaṃ evvaṃ turia|turiaṃ āacchasi?⌟

2.5 CATURIKĀ: ⌜āṇatta mhi bhaṭṭi|dāriāe Malaavadīe, «hañje Caürie, kusum'|âvacaa|parissama|ṇissahaṃ me sarīraṃ sarad|ādava|jaṇido via sandāvo ahiadaraṃ bāhei. tā gaccha tuvaṃ, bāla|kadalī|patta|parikkhitte candaṇa|ladā|gharae canda|maṇi|silā|dalaṃ sajjī|karehi» tti. aṇuṭṭhiaṃ ca mae jah"|āṇattaṃ. tā jāva gadua bhaṭṭi|dāriāe ṇivedemi.⌟

PRATHAMĀ: ⌜jaï evvaṃ, tā lahuaṃ ṇivedehi, jeṇa se tahiṃ gadāe sandāvo uvasamaṃ gamissadi.⌟

DVITĪYĀ: *(vihasy', ātma|gatam)* ⌜ṇa eriso sandāvo evvaṃ uvasamaṃ gamissadi! aṇṇañ ca vivitta|ramaṇijjaṃ candaṇa|ladā|gharaaṃ pekkhantīe ahiadaraṃ bhavissadi tti takkemi.⌟ *(prakāśam)* ⌜tā gaccha tuvaṃ. ahaṃ pi sajjaṃ silā|dalaṃ tti bhaṭṭi|dāriāe ṇivedemi.⌟

niṣkrānte.

praveśakaḥ.

Thereupon a MAIDSERVANT *enters.* 2.1

MAIDSERVANT: I've been instructed by the Princess Málaya·vati, "Miss Mano·hárika, my brother the honorable Mitra·vasu is taking such a long time today. So go and find out whether or not he has come." *(She walks about. Looking at the curtain...)* Now who's this woman coming right this way? *(noticing)* What's this? It's Cháturika!

At that point CHÁTURIKA *enters.*

MANO·HÁRIKA: *(coming over)* Maid Cháturika! Why are you hurrying back like this?

CHÁTURIKA: I've been instructed by the Princess Málaya- 2.5
vati, "Maid Cháturika, a fever torments my body more and more. It's like the autumnal swelter and it's unbearable because I'm tired from picking flowers! So go and prepare the moonstone bench in the sandal vine bower that's overspread with young banana leaves." And I've done as I was instructed. So, I'm off to tell the princess.

THE FIRST: In that case, you'd better tell her quickly, so that she can go there and her fever will calm down!

THE SECOND: *(chuckling, to herself)* This isn't the kind of fever that will calm down that way! I reckon it will get worse with her looking at a bower of sandal vine that's all lovely and lonely! *(out loud)* You go, then, and I'll let the princess know that the bench is ready.

They both leave.

End of the introductory scene.

ACT TWO

2.10 *tataḥ praviśati s'|ôtkaṇṭhā* MALAYAVATĪ CEṬĪ *ca.*

NĀYIKĀ: *(niḥśvasy', ātma|gatam)* ⌜hiaa! taha ṇāma tadā tassiṃ jaṇe lajjāe maṃ param|muhī|karia dāṇiṃ appaṇā tahiṃ evva gaaṃ si tti aho de appambharittaṇaṃ.⌟ *(prakāśam)* ⌜hañje, ādesehi me bhaavadīe āadaṇassa maggaṃ.⌟

CEṬĪ: ⌜ṇaṃ candaṇa|ladā|gharaaṃ bhaṭṭi|dāriā patthidā!⌟

NĀYIKĀ: *(sa|lajjam)* ⌜suṭṭhu tue sumarāvidaṃ. tā ehi, tahiṃ evva gacchamha.⌟

CEṬĪ: ⌜edu edu bhaṭṭi|dāriā.⌟ *(agrato gacchati.)*

2.15 NĀYIK" *âpy anyato gacchati.*

CEṬĪ: *(pṛṣṭhato dṛṣṭvā, ātma|gataṃ s'|ôdvegam)* ⌜aho se suṇṇa-hiaattaṇaṃ! kahaṃ, taṃ evva devīe bhavaṇaṃ patthiā.⌟ *(prakāśam)* ⌜bhaṭṭi|dārie, ṇaṃ ido candaṇa|ladā|gharaaṃ. tā ido ehi.⌟

NĀYIKĀ *sa|vilakṣaṃ sa|lajjaṃ ca tathā karoti.*

CEṬĪ: ⌜bhaṭṭi|dārie, edaṃ candaṇa|ladā|gharaaṃ. tā pavisia canda|maṇi|silā|dale uvavisadu bhaṭṭi|dāriā.⌟

ubhe upaviśataḥ.

2.20 NĀYIKĀ: *(niḥśvasy', ātma|gatam)* ⌜bhaavaṃ kusum'|āuha, jeṇa tuvaṃ rūva|sohāe ṇijjido si, tassiṃ ṇa kiñ ci tue kidaṃ. maṃ puṇa aṇ|avaraddhaṃ *abala* tti karia paharanto kahaṃ ṇa lajjasi?⌟ *(ātmānaṃ nirdiśya, madan'|âvasthāṃ*

Thereupon enters MÁLAYAVATI, *lovesick, and her* MAIDSERVANT. 2.10

HEROINE: *(sighing, to herself)* Oh my heart! You made me turn away from that man out of embarrassment then, but now of your own accord you go right to him. You are so selfish. *(out loud)* Maid, show me the way to the altar of Her Ladyship.

MAIDSERVANT: Actually, Miss, you were going to the sandal vine bower!

HEROINE: *(shyly)* Thank you for reminding me. Come then, we may as well go straight there.

MAIDSERVANT: Come on, Miss, come along. *(She goes ahead.)*

The HEROINE *goes in another direction.* 2.15

MAIDSERVANT: *(looking back, surprised, to herself)* Oh, she's so absent-minded! Look how she's started off for that place of the goddess. *(out loud)* Miss, actually the sandal vine bower is over here. So come this way.

The HEROINE *does so, shy and embarrassed.*

MAIDSERVANT: Here is the sandal vine bower, Miss. May the princess go in and take a seat on the moonstone bench.

They sit down.

HEROINE: *(sighing, to herself)* Lord armed with flowers, 2.20
though he has surpassed you in bodily beauty, you have done nothing to him.* But me, who has not offended you, how come you feel no shame striking me, presumably because I'm *weak : a woman*? *(observing herself,*

nāṭayantī, prakāśam) ⌜hañje, kīsa uṇa edaṃ ghaṇa|pallava|ṇiruddha|sūra|kiraṇaṃ tādisaṃ eva candaṇa|ladā|gharaaṃ ṇa me ajja sandāva|dukkhaṃ avaṇedi?⌟

CEṬĪ: *(sa|smitam)* ⌜jāṇāmi ahaṃ ettha kāraṇaṃ! kin tu a|sambhāvaṇīaṃ ti bhaṭṭi|dāriā ṇa taṃ paḍivajjadi.⌟

NĀYIKĀ: *(ātma|gatam)* ⌜ālakkhida mhi imāe! taha vi pucchissaṃ dāva.⌟ *(prakāśam)* ⌜hañje, kiṃ tava ediṇā? kahehi dāva, kiṃ taṃ kāraṇaṃ?⌟

CEṬĪ: ⌜eso de hia'|acchido *varo.*⌟

NĀYIKĀ: *(sa|harṣaṃ sa|sambhramaṃ c' ôtthāy' âgrato dvi|trāṇi padāni gatvā)* ⌜kahiṃ, kahiṃ so?⌟

2.25 CEṬĪ: *(utthāya sa|smitam)* ⌜bhaṭṭi|dārie, ko «so?»⌟

NĀYIKĀ *sa|lajjam upaviśy' âdho|mukhī tiṣṭhati.*

CEṬĪ: ⌜bhaṭṭi|dārie, ṇaṃ edamhi vattu|kāmā, eso de hia'|acchido *varo* devīe diṇṇa tti siviṇae patthāvide jo tak|khaṇaṃ evva vimutta|kusuma|cāvo via bhaavaṃ maara|ddhao bhaṭṭi|dāriāe diṭṭho. so de imassa sandāvassa kāraṇaṃ. jeṇa evaṃ sahāva|sīdalaṃ pi candaṇa|ladā|gharaaṃ ṇa de ajja sandāva|dukkhaṃ avaṇedi.⌟

acting a state of infatuation, out loud) Maid, how come this very same bower of sandal vines, where the sun's rays are blocked by these thick shoots, isn't taking away my horrid fever today?

MAIDSERVANT: *(with a smile)* I know what's going on here! But the princess wouldn't agree, and she'd say it's impossible.

HEROINE: *(to herself)* She's seen through me! Even so, I'll just ask. *(aloud)* What are you on about, maid? Just say, what is the reason?

MAIDSERVANT: It's this *treat : husband* after your heart's desire!

HEROINE: *(with delight and agitation she gets up and takes two or three steps)* Where, where is he?

MAIDSERVANT: *(getting up with a smirk)* Who's "he," Miss? 2.25

The HEROINE *sits down shyly and remains with her face cast down.*

MAIDSERVANT: Actually I was going to say this, Miss, that the chap who was described in the dream as a *treat : husband* given by the goddess after your heart's desire, was His Lordship with the *mákara* banner, but as if minus his bow and arrows, that the princess saw at that very moment.* He's the cause of this fever of yours. That's why even this naturally cool bower of sandal vine isn't taking away your horrid fever today.

NĀYIKĀ: (CATURIKĀYĀ *alakāni sajjayantī)* ⌜hañje, *Caüriā* khu tuvaṃ. kiṃ de avaraṃ pacchādīadi. tā kahaïssaṃ.⌟

CEṬĪ: ⌜bhaṭṭi|dārie, ṇaṃ dāṇiṃ eva kahidaṃ imiṇā *var'*|ālāva|matta|jaṇideṇa sambhameṇa. tā mā santappa. jaï ahaṃ *Caüriā*, tado so vi bhaṭṭi|dāriaṃ a|pekkhanto ṇa muhūttaaṃ pi aṇṇahiṃ ahiramissadi tti, edaṃ pi mae ālakkhidaṃ eva.⌟

2.30 NĀYIKĀ: *(s'|âsram)* ⌜hañje, kudo me ettiāṇi bhāa|dheāṇi?⌟

CEṬĪ: ⌜bhaṭṭi|dārie, mā evaṃ bhaṇa. kiṃ Mahu|mahaṇo vaccha|tthaleṇa Lacchiṃ an|uvvahanto ṇivvudo hoi?⌟

NĀYIKĀ: ⌜kiṃ vā su|aṇo piaṃ vajjia aṇṇaṃ bhaṇiduṃ jāṇādi? sahi, ado vi sandāvo ahiadaraṃ maṃ bāhei, jaṃ so mah"|âṇubhāvo vāā|mettaeṇa vi a|kida|paḍivattiṃ a|dakkhiṇa tti maṃ sambhāvaïssidi.⌟ *(iti roditi)*

CEṬĪ: ⌜bhaṭṭi|dārie, mā roda.⌟ *(utthāya candana|pallavaṃ gṛhītvā niṣpīḍya hṛdaye dadāti.)* ⌜ṇam bhaṇāmi mā roda tti. aaṃ khu thaṇa|paṭṭa|diṇṇo candaṇa|pallava|raso imehi avirala|paḍantehi assu|bindūhi uṇhī|kido ṇa de hiaa|sandāva|dukkhaṃ avaṇedi.⌟ *(kadalī|patram ādāya vījati.)*

HEROINE: *(touching* CHÁTURIKA*'s curly locks)* Maid, you certainly are *Cháturika : a clever girl.* Why hide any more from you? I will tell you.

MAIDSERVANT: Actually, Miss, you told it just now by your flurry at the mere mention of your *treat : husband.* So don't distress yourself. If I am *Cháturika : a clever girl,* then it's also clear to me that, while he's not seeing the princess, he isn't interested in anything else either, not for a moment.

HEROINE: *(tearfully)* Maid, how can I be so lucky? 2.30

MAIDSERVANT: Don't speak like that, Miss. Can the slayer of Madhu rest easy without carrying home Lakshmi on his chest?*

HEROINE: Don't nice people know how to say anything other than pleasant things? My dear, even this makes the fever torment me more. That gentleman will think that I was rude, not behaving properly towards him with even a word. *(Saying this she starts to weep.)*

MAIDSERVANT: Don't weep, Miss. *(Getting up and taking a sandal shoot and crushing it, she drips the sap over* MÁLAYAVATI*'s heart.)* Really, I tell you, don't weep. Hmm. This juice from the sandal shoot that I've put on your bodice is actually warmed up by the endless rain of tear drops. It's not going to take away the horrid fever in your heart. *(Taking a banana leaf, she fans her.)*

NĀYIKĀ: *(hastena nivārayantī)* ⌜sahi, mā vījehi. uṇho khu eso kadalī|dala|māruo.⌟

2.35 CEṬĪ: ⌜bhaṭṭi|dārie, mā imassa dosaṃ karehi.⌟

⌜kuṇasi ghaṇa|candaṇa|laā|
  pallava|saṃsagga|sīdalaṃ pi imaṃ
ṇīsāsehi tumaṃ cia
  kadalī|dala|māruaṃ uṇhaṃ.⌟ [1]

NĀYIKĀ: ⌜sahi, atthi ko vi imassa dukkhassa uvasam'|ôvāo?⌟

CEṬĪ: ⌜bhaṭṭi|dārie, atthi, jadi so iha āacche.⌟

tataḥ praviśati NĀYAKO VIDŪṢAKAŚ *ca.*

NĀYAKAḤ:

2.40 vyāvṛty' âiva sit'|āsit'|êkṣaṇa|rucā
  tān āśrame śākhinaḥ
kurvatyā viṭap'|âvasakta|vilasat|
  kṛṣṇ'|âjin'|âughān iva
yad dṛṣṭo 'smi tayā muner api puras,
  ten' âiva mayy āhate,
puṣp'|êṣo, bhavatā mudh" âiva kim iti
  kṣipyanta ete śarāḥ? [2]

VIDŪṢAKAḤ: ⌜bho vaassa, kahiṃ khu gaaṃ de dhīrattaṇaṃ?⌟

NĀYAKAḤ: vayasya, nanu dhīra ev' âsmi! kutaḥ,

HEROINE: *(warding her off with her hand)* My dear, don't fan me. The breeze from this banana leaf is so hot.

MAIDSERVANT: You can't blame this leaf, Miss.

It's you heating the breeze from this banana leaf
with your sighs,
Even though its cooled from passing through
the dense shoots of the sandal vines.

HEROINE: My dear, is there any remedy for this unhappiness?

MAIDSERVANT: If he were to come here, there is, Miss.

Thereupon the HERO *and his* COMPANION *enter.*

HERO:

I was seen by her too in front of the sage,
just when she turned back,
Her eyes shining light and dark, making the trees
in the hermitage
Look like a flood of dappled deer flashing amid
the undergrowth.
Since I've been stricken by that, flower-arrowed Lord,
why do you fire these arrows without point?

COMPANION: Old chap, just where has your firmness gone?

HERO: I'm firm alright, my friend! Because,

nītāḥ kiṃ na niśāḥ śaśāṅka|rucayo?
n' āghrātam indīvaraṃ?
kim n' ônmīlita|mālatī|surabhayaḥ
soḍhāḥ pradoṣ'|ânilāḥ?
jhaṅkāraḥ kamal'|ākare madhulihāṃ
kiṃ vā mayā na śruto?
nirvyājaṃ vidhureṣv a|dhīra iti māṃ
ken' âbhidhatte bhavān? [3]

atha vā, na samyag ahaṃ bravīmi! vayasy' Ātreya,

2.45 strī|hṛdayena na soḍhāḥ
kṣiptāḥ kusum'|êṣavo 'py Anaṅgena
yen' âdy' âiva puras tava,
vadāmi dhīra iti sa katham aham? [4]

VIDŪṢAKAḤ: *(ātma|gatam)* ⌜evaṃ ahīrattaṇaṃ paḍivajjanteṇa ācakkhido ṇeṇa hiaassa mahanto āveo. tā evaṃ ācakkhāmi.⌟ *(prakāśam)* ⌜bho vaassa, kīsa tuvaṃ ajja lahu eva guru|jaṇaṃ sussūsia iha āado?⌟

NĀYAKAḤ: vayasya! sthāne khalv eṣa praśnaḥ. kasya v" ânyasy' âitat kathanīyam? adya khalu svapne jānāmi s" âiva priyatamā *(aṅgulyā nirdiśan)* atra candana|latā|gṛhe candrakānta|maṇi|śilāyām upaviṣṭā praṇaya|kupitā kim api mām upālabhamān" êva rudatī mayā dṛṣṭā. tad icchāmi svapn'|ânubhūta|dayitā|samāgama|ramye 'sminn eva pradeśe divasam ativāhayitum. tad ehi, gacchāvaḥ.

Have I not passed whole nights bright with the moon?
Have I not sniffed a blue lotus?
Have I not had to put up with evening breezes
scented by blossoming *málati* flowers?
And have I not had to listen to the honey-suckers
buzzing over a mass of lotuses?
How can you say, without qualification, that of all
love-sick people, I'm not firm in public?*

Actually, what I said isn't true! Atréya, my friend,

With my heart on a woman, I cannot bear 2.45
the flower darts shot by limbless Cupid,
So how can I claim to you today that I am firm?

COMPANION: *(to himself)* By admitting his want of firmness like this, he reveals the great agitation in his heart. So this is how I'll speak to him. *(out loud)* Haven't you come rather quickly from seeing to your parents today, old man?

HERO: That's a well-placed question, my friend. And who else could I speak to about it? Today, in a dream, I believe I saw that same most beloved woman *(pointing with his finger)* there in a bower of sandal vines seated on a moonstone bench, love-lorn, reproaching me over something and weeping. So I want to spend the day right there on that spot that's so lovely because I met my beloved there in the dream. Come on, let's go.

parikrāmataḥ.

CEṬĪ: *(karṇaṃ dattvā sa|sambhramam)* ⌜bhaṭṭi|dārie, pada|saddo via suṇīadi!⌟

2.50 NĀYIKĀ: *(sa|sambhramam ātmānaṃ paśyantī)* ⌜hañje, mā īdisaṃ āāraṃ pekkhia ko vi hiaaṃ me tulīadu. tā uṭṭhehi. imiṇā ratt'|âsoa|pādaveṇa ovāridāo pekkhamha ko eso tti.⌟

tathā kurutaḥ.

VIDŪṢAKAḤ: ⌜bho vaassa, edaṃ candaṇa|ladā|gharaaṃ. tā pavisamha.⌟

nāṭyena praviśataḥ.

NĀYAKAḤ: *(praviśya)*

2.55 candana|latā|gṛham idaṃ
sa|candra|maṇi|śilam api priyaṃ na mama
candr'|ānanayā rahitaṃ,
candrikayā mukham iva niśāyāḥ. [5]

CEṬĪ: *(nāyakaṃ dṛṣṭvā)* ⌜bhaṭṭi|dārie, diṭṭhiā vaḍḍhasi! so evva de hiaa|vallaho.⌟

NĀYIKĀ: *(dṛṣṭvā sa|harṣaṃ sa|sādhvasaṃ ca)* ⌜hañje, imaṃ pekkhia ṇa sakkuṇomi iha accāsaṇṇe ṭhāduṃ. kadā i eso maṃ pekkhe. tā ehi. aṇṇado gacchamha.⌟ *(s'|ōrukampaṃ pada|dvayaṃ dadāti.)*

CEṬĪ: *(vihasya)* ⌜adikādare! iha ṭṭhidaṃ pi ko tumaṃ pekkhadi? ṇaṃ visumarido antare ratt'|âsoa|pādavo? tā iha eva ciṭṭhamha.⌟

They both move about.

MAIDSERVANT: *(listening with agitation)* I think I can hear footsteps, Miss!

HEROINE: *(looking at herself with agitation)* Maid, whoever it is mustn't see me in such a state and gauge my heart. So get up. Let's hide behind this red *ashóka* tree* and see who it is.

They both do so.

COMPANION: Here's a bower of sandal vines, old chap. Let's go in then.

They both act entering.

HERO: *(having entered)*

> This bower of sandal vines, even with a moonstone bench, is not pleasant to me
> Bereft as it is of her moon-like face, like the gloaming without the face of the moon.

MAIDSERVANT: *(seeing the hero)* Miss, you are in luck! It's him, your favorite.

HEROINE: *(looking with delight and anxiety)* Maid, I can't stay here watching him, it's too close. It's possible he might see me. Come on, let's go somewhere else. *(She takes a couple of steps with her thigh shaking.*)*

MAIDSERVANT: *(laughing aloud)* You're so timid! Who'll see you right here? Have you forgotten the red *ashóka* tree between us? So, let's stay right where we are.

tathā kurutaḥ.

2.60 VIDŪṢAKAḤ: *(nirūpya)* ⌜bho vaassa, esā sā canda|maṇi|silā!⌟

NĀYAKAḤ *sa|bāṣpaṃ niśvasiti.*

CEṬĪ: ⌜bhaṭṭi|dārie, «esā s" êtti» ālāvo suṇīadi. tā avahidā suṇamha.⌟

ubhe ākarṇayataḥ.

VIDŪṢAKAḤ: *(hastena cālayan)* ⌜bho vaassa, ṇaṃ bhaṇāmi esā sā canda|maṇi|sila tti.⌟

2.65 NĀYAKAḤ: vayasya, samyag upalakṣitam. *(hastena nirdiśan)*

śaśi|maṇi|śilā s" êyaṃ, yasyāṃ
vipāṇḍuram ānanaṃ
kara|kisalaye kṛtvā vāme
ghana|śvasit'|ôdgamā,
cirayati mayi vyakt'|ākūtā
manāk|sphuritair bhruvor
niyamita|mano|manyur dṛṣṭā
mayā rudatī priyā. [6]

tad asyām eva candra|kānta|maṇi|śilāyām upaviśāvaḥ.

NĀYIKĀ: *(vicintya)* ⌜kā uṇa «esā» bhavissadi?⌟

CEṬĪ: ⌜bhaṭṭi|dārie, jaha amme ovārida|sarīrāo edaṃ pekkhamha, taha tuvaṃ pi edeṇa diṭṭhā bhave.⌟

2.70 NĀYIKĀ: ⌜jujjaï edaṃ. kiṃ puṇa paṇaa|kuvidaṃ pia|jaṇaṃ hiae karia mantedi?⌟

They do so.

COMPANION: *(noticing)* Here she is, old chap, that moonstone bench!

The HERO *sighs, in tears.*

MAIDSERVANT: Miss, I heard someone say, "Here she is." So we must pay attention and listen.

They both listen.

COMPANION: *(shaking him with his hand)* I say, old chap! I said, "Here she is … the moonstone bench!"

HERO: Well spotted, my friend. *(pointing with his hand)*

> Here is the moonstone bench whereon I saw her weeping, my beloved,
> Holding her wan face in the left of her tender hands, heaving deep sighs.
> When I was late her emotions were clear on her brow.
> It trembled a little, as she suppressed the anger in her mind.

Let's sit together then, right here on the moonstone bench.

HEROINE: *(thoughtfully)* Who can "she" be?

MAIDSERVANT: Just as we've seen him while we've been hiding, maybe he's seen you as well, Miss.

HEROINE: That's possible. But then why's he fallen in love with her and why's he talking about her as a lover who's love-lorn?

CEṬĪ: ⌜mā īdisaṃ āsaṅkaṃ karehi. puṇo vi dāva suṇamha.⌟

VIDŪṢAKAḤ: *(ātma|gatam)* ⌜ahiramadi eso edāe kahāe. bhodu, edaṃ eva se vaḍḍhāvaïssaṃ.⌟ *(prakāśam)* ⌜bho vaassa, taha paruṇṇā tue kiṃ bhaṇidā?⌟

NĀYAKAḤ: vayasya, idam uktā,

nisyandata iv' ânena
  mukha|candr'|ôdayena te
etad bāṣp'|âmbunā siktaṃ
  candra|kānta|śilā|talam. [7]

2.75 NĀYIKĀ: *(sa|roṣam)* ⌜sudaṃ edaṃ, Caürie. atthi kiṃ pi ado varaṃ sodavvaṃ?⌟ *(s'|âsram)* ⌜ehi, gacchamha.⌟

CEṬĪ: *(hastena gṛhītvā)* ⌜bhaṭṭi|dārie, mā evaṃ. jeṇa tuvaṃ diṭṭhā, so aṇṇaṃ uddisia evaṃ bhaṇissadi tti ṇa me hiaaṃ pattiāadi. tā kah"|âvasāṇaṃ dāva paḍivālamha.⌟

NĀYAKAḤ: vayasya, tām ev' âsyāṃ śilāyām ālikhya tayā citra|gatay" ātmānaṃ vinodayeyam. tad ita eva giri|taṭān manaś|śilā|śakalāny ānaya.

VIDŪṢAKAḤ: ⌜jaṃ bhavaṃ āṇavedi.⌟ *(niṣkramya, praviśya)* ⌜bho vaassa, tue ekko vaṇṇo āṇatto, mae uṇa iha pavvadādo pañca vaṇṇā āṇīdā. tā ālihadu bhavaṃ.⌟

NĀYAKAḤ: vayasya, sādhu kṛtam. *(gṛhītvā, śilāyām ālikhan sa|romāñcam)* sakhe, paśya paśya.

MAIDSERVANT: Don't fret like this. Let's listen a bit more.

COMPANION: *(to himself)* He's enjoying this discussion. Very well, I'll drag it out for him. *(out loud)* My dear friend, what did you say while she was crying?

HERO: This is what I said, my friend,

> As if weeping* on account of this rising moon
> of your face,
> This moonstone bench is splashed by a flood of tears.

HEROINE: *(angrily)* You heard that, Cháturika. Is there any- 2.75
thing more we need to hear? Come on, let's go.

MAIDSERVANT: *(taking her hand)* Don't speak like that, Miss. I don't believe in my heart that the man who saw you would speak like that about another woman. We might as well wait until the end of the conversation.

HERO: Friend, I'll draw her on this stone and while away the time with her in the picture. So fetch bits of red pigment from the mountain slope.*

COMPANION: As you request. *(going off and coming back)* You've asked for one color from the mountain, old chap, but I've brought five. You can get drawing.

HERO: You have done well, my friend. *(taking them, drawing on the stone with a delightful thrill)* Look, dear friend, look.

2.80 *akliṣṭa|bimba|śobh"|â-*
*dharasya** nayan'|ôtsavasya śaśina iva
dayitā|mukhasya sukhayati
rekh" âpi *prathama|dṛṣṭ"* êyam. [8]

ālikhati.

VIDŪṢAKAḤ: *(sa|kautukaṃ nirvarṇya)* ⌈bho vaassa, a|ppaccakkhaṃ vi evaṃ ālihīadi tti acchariaṃ.⌋

NĀYAKAḤ: vayasya,

priyā sannihit" âiv' êyaṃ
saṅkalpaiḥ sthāpitā puraḥ.
dṛṣṭvā dṛṣṭvā likhāmy enāṃ
yadi, tat ko 'tra vismayaḥ? [9]

2.85 NĀYIKĀ: *(niḥśvasya s'|âsram)* ⌈Caürie, jādaṃ khu kah"|âvasāṇaṃ. tā ehi, ayya|Mittāvasuṃ dāva pekkhamha.⌋

CEṬĪ: *(sa|viṣādam, ātma|gatam)* ⌈haṃ. jīvia|ṇirapekkho via se ālāvo.⌋ *(prakāśam)* ⌈bhaṭṭi|dārie, gadā eva tahiṃ Maṇohariā. ado kadā i bhaṭṭi|dārao Mittāvasū iha eva āacche.⌋

tataḥ praviśati MITRĀVASUḤ.

MITRĀVASUḤ: ājñāpito 'smi tātena yathā, «vatsa Mitrāvaso, kumāro Jīmūtavāhano 'smābhir ih' āsanna|vāsāt su|parīkṣitaḥ, tad yogyo 'yaṃ varaḥ. tasmai vatsā Malayavatī

A celebration to my eyes, my beloved's face 2.80
gives pleasure like the moon *when it's new,*
its disc free from clouds, even this outline
seen for the first time, lower lip like a perfect
bimba fruit.

He draws.

COMPANION: *(observing with curiosity)* I say old chap, it's extraordinary that she can be drawn like this without even being present before your eyes.

HERO: My friend,

My beloved really is present here,
stored in my imagination.
If I keep looking and then draw her,
what is there to wonder at?

HEROINE: *(sighing, with tears)* Cháturika, the end of the 2.85
discussion is pretty apparent. Come then, we'll first see Mitra·vasu.

MAIDSERVANT: *(dejected, to herself)* Hmm. Her words suggest an indifference to life. *(out loud)* Mano·hárika has just gone to him, Miss. So perhaps Prince Mitra·vasu may be coming straight here.

At that point MITRA·VASU *enters.*

MITRA·VASU: I've been instructed by my father as follows, "My dear boy Mitra·vasu, we've had a good look at the young prince Jimúta·váhana because he's been staying near us, and he will make a good husband. My dear girl Málayavati should be presented to him." But because

pratipādyatām» iti. ahaṃ tu sneha|parādhīnatay" ânyad eva kim apy avasth"|ântaram anubhavāmi. kutaḥ,

yad vidyādhara|rāja|vaṃśa|tilakaḥ,
prājñaḥ, satāṃ sammato,
rūpeṇ' â|pratimaḥ, parākrama|dhano,
vidvān, vinīto, yuvā,
yac c' âsūn api santyajet karuṇayā
satv'|ârtham abhyudyatas,
ten' âsmai dadataḥ svasāram atulā
tuṣṭir viṣādaś ca me. [10]

2.90 śrutaṃ ca mayā yathā, asau Jīmūtavāhano 'tr' âiva Gaury|āśrama|sambaddhe candana|latā|gṛhe vartata iti. tad etac candana|latā|gṛham. yāvat praviśāmi. *(praviśati.)*

VIDŪṢAKAḤ: *(sa|sambhramam avalokya)* ⌜bho vaassa, imiṇā pacchādehi kadalī|patteṇa imaṃ citta|gadaṃ kamma.* eso khu siddha|juarāo Mittāvasū iha eva āado. kadā i eso pekkhe.⌟

NĀYAKAḤ *kadalī|patreṇa pracchādayati.*

MITRĀVASUḤ: *(upasṛtya)* kumāra, Mitrāvasuḥ praṇamati.

NĀYAKAḤ: *(dṛṣṭvā)* Mitrāvaso, svāgatam. iha sthīyatām.

2.95 CEṬĪ: ⌜bhaṭṭi|dārie, āado khu eso Mittāvasū.⌟

NĀYIKĀ: ⌜hañje, piaṃ me.⌟

I am overcome with affection for her I feel otherwise. Because,

> Since he is an ornament to the royal lineage of the Magicians, wise, esteemed by the good,
> Without a peer in looks, well-endowed with valor, knowledgeable, young and well-behaved,
> And since he is ready to renounce his life altogether out of pity for another creature,
> Offering him my sister gives me both incomparable satisfaction and dismay.

And I've heard that Jimúta·váhana has been hanging around the bower of sandal vines near the hermitage of Gauri. This must be the bower. I'll go in then. *(He enters.)* 2.90

COMPANION: *(looking with agitation)* I say old boy, cover your drawing with this banana leaf. Here's the crown prince of the Adepts, Mitra·vasu, coming this way. He might see it.

The HERO *covers it with the banana leaf.*

MITRA·VASU: *(approaching)* Young prince, Mitra·vasu bows to you!

HERO: *(seeing him)* Mitra·vasu, welcome. Be seated here.

MAIDSERVANT: See, Miss, Mitra·vasu has just arrived. 2.95

HEROINE: Maid, I'm glad.

NĀYAKAḤ: Mitrāvaso, api kuśalī siddha|rājo Viśvāvasuḥ?

MITRĀVASUḤ: kuśalī tātaḥ. tāta|sandeśen' âiv' âsmi tvat|sakāśam ih' āgataḥ.

NĀYAKAḤ: kim āha tatra|bhavān?

2.100 NĀYIKĀ: ⌜suṇissaṃ dāva kiṃ tādeṇa sandiṭṭhaṃ tti.⌟

MITRĀVASUḤ: idam āha tātaḥ, «asti me duhitā Malayavatī nāma. jīvitam iv' âsya sarvasy' âiva siddha|rāj'|ânvayasya. sā mayā tubhyaṃ pratipāditā. pratigṛhyatām» iti.

CEṬĪ: *(vihasya)* ⌜bhaṭṭi|dārie, kiṃ ṇa kuppasi dāṇiṃ?⌟

NĀYIKĀ: *(sa|spṛhaṃ sa|lajjaṃ c' âdho|mukhī sthitvā)* ⌜hañje, mā tussa. kiṃ visumaridaṃ de edassa aṇṇa|hiaattaṇaṃ?⌟

NĀYAKAḤ: *(apavārya)* vayasya, saṅkaṭe patitāḥ smaḥ.

2.105 VIDŪṢAKAḤ: *(apavārya)* ⌜bho, jāṇāmi bhavado ṇa taṃ vajjia aṇṇahiṃ cittaṃ ahiramadi tti. taha vi jaṃ kiñ ci bhaṇia visajjīadu eso.⌟

NĀYIKĀ: *(sa|roṣam ātma|gatam)* ⌜had'|āsa! ko vā edaṃ ṇa jāṇādi?⌟

NĀYAKAḤ: Mitrāvaso, ka iha* n' êcched bhavadbhiḥ saha ślāghyam imam sambandham? kin tu na śakyate cittam anyataḥ pravṛttam anyato nivartayitum. ato n' âham enāṃ pratigrahītum utsahe.

HERO: Mitra·vasu, does Vishva·vasu, the king of the Adepts, prosper?

MITRA·VASU: My father prospers. In fact, it's on an errand of father's that I have come here to you.

HERO: What says his honor?

HEROINE: Now I'll hear what father's errand is. 2.100

MITRA·VASU: This is what father said, "I have a daughter called Málayavati. It's as if she is the life of the entire royal lineage of the Adepts. I present her to you. Accept her."

MAIDSERVANT: *(laughing aloud)* Are you angry now, Miss?

HEROINE: *(longingly and bashfully, she stays down-faced)* Don't be pleased, maid. Why, have you forgotten that he's in love with another?

HERO: *(aside)* We are fallen in a dire strait, my friend.

COMPANION: *(aside)* I know your mind is occupied with no 2.105
one but her, so say something or other and send him away.

HEROINE: *(angrily, to herself)* The fraud! Who doesn't know that?

HERO: Mitra·vasu, who in the world would not desire this laudable connection with you? But it's not possible to turn the mind to one person when it's already turned to another. For that reason, I cannot bear to accept her.

NĀYIKĀ *mūrchāṃ nāṭayati.*

CEṬĪ: ⌜samassasadu, samassasadu bhaṭṭi|dāriā!⌟

2.110 VIDŪṢAKAḤ: ⌜bho! parāhīṇo khu eso. tā kiṃ edeṇa bhaṇanteṇa? guru|jaṇaṃ se gadua abbhatthehi.⌟

MITRĀVASUḤ: *(ātma|gatam)* sādh' ûktam. n' âyaṃ guru|vacanam atikrāmati. eṣa guru|jano 'py asminn eva Gaury|āśrame prativasati. tad yāvad gatv" âsya pitror Malayavatīṃ pratigrāhayāmi.

NĀYIKĀ *samāśvasiti.*

MITRĀVASUḤ: *(prakāśam)* evaṃ nivedit'|ātmano 'smān pratyācakṣāṇaḥ kumāra eva bahutaraṃ jānāti.

NĀYIKĀ: *(sa|roṣam)* ⌜kahaṃ paccakkhāṇa|lahuo Mittāvasū puṇo vi mantedi?⌟

2.115 *niṣkrānto* MITRĀVASUḤ.

NĀYIKĀ: *(s'|âsram ātmānaṃ paśyantī)* ⌜kiṃ mama ediṇā dobbhagga|kalaṅka|maliṇeṇa accanta|dukkha|bhāiṇā ajja vi sarīra|hadaeṇa? jāva iha eva ratt'|âsoa|pādave imāe adimutta|ladāe ubbandhia attāṇaṃ vāvādaïssaṃ. tā evaṃ dāva.⌟ *(prakāśaṃ sa|vilakṣa|smitam)* ⌜hañje, pekkha dāva, Mittāvasū dūraṃ gado ṇa v' êtti. jeṇa ahaṃ pi* ido gamissaṃ.⌟

CEṬĪ: ⌜jaṃ bhaṭṭi|dāriā āṇavedi.⌟ *(kati cit padāni gatvā)* ⌜aṇṇādisaṃ se hiaaṃ pekkhāmi. tā ṇa dāva gamissaṃ. iha eva ovāridā pekkhāmi kiṃ esā paḍivajjadi tti.⌟

The HEROINE *mimes a faint.*

MAIDSERVANT: Bear up, Miss, bear up!

COMPANION: Hey! He's actually a dependent. So there's no 2.110
point talking with him. Go to his parents and make your request to them.

MITRA·VASU: *(to himself)* He's made a good point. He should not act without his parents' consent. His parents also live right here in this Gauri hermitage. So I shall go to his parents and get them to accept Málayavati.

The HERONE *comes round.*

MITRA·VASU: *(out loud)* The young prince himself knows best why he rejects what we have conveyed.

HEROINE: *(angrily)* How come Mitra·vasu is still speaking when he has been insulted by a refusal?

MITRA·VASU *leaves.* 2.115

HEROINE: *(looking at herself tearfully)* There's no point to this wretched body of mine. It's dirtied by stains of misfortune. Its lot is excessive misery. I am going to kill myself here with this *atimúkta* vine* on the *ashóka* tree. I'll say this now. *(out loud, with a forced smile)* Maid, see whether or not Mitra·vasu has gone far yet. I'm going to leave here, too.

MAIDSERVANT: As the princess requests. *(taking a few steps)* I can see that she has something else in mind. So I'm not going. I'll hide right here and see what she does.

NĀYIKĀ: *(utthāya, diśo vilokya, pāśaṃ gṛhītvā, s'|âsram)* ⌜bhaavadi Gauri! iha tue ṇa kido pasādo. tā aṇṇassiṃ pi dāva jamme jaha ṇa īdisī dukkha|bhāiṇī homi, taha karehi.⌟ *(kaṇṭhe pāśam arpayati.)*

CEṬĪ: *(dṛṣṭvā sa|sambhramam)* ⌜parittāaha! parittāaha! esā bhaṭṭi|dāriā ubbandhia attāṇaṃ vāvādedi.⌟

2.120 NĀYAKAḤ: *(sa|sambhramam upetya)* kv' âsau? kv' âsau?

CEṬĪ: ⌜iaṃ asoa|pādave.⌟

NĀYAKAḤ: *(dṛṣṭvā sa|harṣam)* kathaṃ, s" âiv' êyam asman|manoratha|bhūmiḥ! *(NĀYIKĀṂ pāṇau gṛhītvā latā|pāśam ākṣipan)*

na khalu, na khalu, mugdhe, sāhasaṃ kāryam evaṃ.
vyapanaya karam etat pallav'|ābhaṃ latāyāḥ.
kusumam api vicetuṃ yo na, manye, samarthaḥ
kalayati sa kathaṃ te pāśam udbandhanāya? [11]

NĀYIKĀ: *(sa|sādhvasam)* ⌜haddhi! ko ṇu khu eso?⌟ *(NĀYAKAṂ nirūpya sa|roṣaṃ hastam ākṣeptum icchati.)* ⌜muñca! muñca me agga|hatthaṃ! ko tumaṃ ṇivāreduṃ? maraṇe vi kiṃ tumaṃ eva abbhatthaṇīo?⌟

2.125 NĀYAKAḤ: n' âhaṃ muñcāmi.

kaṇṭhe hāra|latā|yogye
yena pāśas tav' ârpitaḥ,
gṛhītaḥ s'|âparādho 'yaṃ.
sa kathaṃ mucyate karaḥ? [12]

HEROINE: *(getting up, looking all around, taking a noose, in tears)* My Lady Gauri! You've not graced me in this life. So in the next life, please make it so that my lot is not like this again. *(She places the noose around her neck.)*

MAIDSERVANT: *(seeing this, in alarm)* Help! Help! It's the princess. She's hanging herself.

HERO: *(approaching in agitation)* Where is she? Where is she? 2.120

MAIDSERVANT: She's by the *ashóka* tree.

HERO: *(seeing her, delighted)* Oh! She's right here! The object of my desire. *(taking her hand and throwing down the noose of vines)*

> You shouldn't do a violent thing like this,
> you silly girl, you shouldn't.
> Remove this tender hand from the vine.
> It's unsuited even to plucking flowers, I think, so
> How can it apply itself to your noose for a hanging?

HEROINE: *(fearfully)* Oh no! Who is this? *(Seeing the* HERO, *she angrily tries to put down his hand.)* Let go! Let go of my fingers! Who are you to stop me? Is it you one has to ask about dying too?

HERO: I'll not let go. 2.125

> How can this guilty hand that I have grasped
> be freed,
> With which was placed the noose on your neck
> fit for a vine of pearls?

VIDŪṢAKAḤ: ⌜bhodi, kiṃ puṇa se maraṇa|vavasāassa kāraṇaṃ?⌟

CEṬĪ: *(s'|ākūtam)* ⌜ṇaṃ eso eva de pia|vaasso!⌟

NĀYAKAḤ: *(s'|ânuśayam)* katham aham ev' âsyā maraṇa|kāraṇam? na khalv avagacchāmi.

2.130 VIDŪṢAKAḤ: ⌜bhodi, kahaṃ via?⌟

CEṬĪ: ⌜jā sā pia|vaasseṇa de kā vi hiaa|vallahā ālihidā, tāe pakkha|vādiṇā paccācikkhantassa Mittāvasuṇo «ṇ' âhaṃ paḍicchāmi» tti suṇia jāda|ṇivvedāe imāe evaṃ vavasidaṃ.⌟

NĀYAKAḤ: *(sa|harṣam ātma|gatam)* katham? iyam ev' âsau Viśvāvasor duhitā Malayavatī? atha vā, *ratn'|ākarād* ṛte kutaś candra|lekhā|prasūtiḥ. kaṣṭaṃ, manāg vañcito 'smi.

VIDŪṢAKAḤ: ⌜bhodi, jaï evaṃ, aṇ|avaraddho dāṇi pia|vaasso. aha va jaï ṇa pattiāadi, saaṃ eva gadua silā|dalaṃ pekkhadu hodī!⌟

NĀYIKĀ: *(sa|harṣaṃ, sa|lajjaṃ ca* NĀYAKAṂ *paśyantī hastam ākṣeptum icchati.)* ⌜muñca. muñca me agga|hatthaṃ.⌟

2.135 NĀYAKAḤ: *(sa|smitam)* na tāvan muñcāmi, yāvan mayā hṛdaya|vallabhāṃ śilāyām ālikhitāṃ na paśyasi.

COMPANION: Madam, what exactly was the reason for her determination to die?

MAIDSERVANT: *(pointedly)* Actually, it was him, your dear friend!

HERO: *(repentantly)* How could it be me who's the cause of her death? I really don't understand.

COMPANION: Madam, how, exactly? 2.130

MAIDSERVANT: She determined to do this because she was filled with despair hearing Mitra·vasu offering her in marriage and being turned down by your dear friend when he was so partial to some woman dear to his heart whom he had drawn!

HERO: *(delighted, to himself)* What? It's she who is Málaya·vati, the daughter of Vishva·vasu? But then, how could the outline of the moon arise but from the *ocean : mine of jewels*?* This is awful. I've made a bit of a blunder.

COMPANION: Madam, if that's the case, then my dear friend is now blameless. Or perhaps, if madam doesn't believe me, she can go to the stone bench and look for herself!

HEROINE: *(Happily, looking bashfully at the* HERO, *she tries to take away her hand.)* Let go. Let go of my fingers.

HERO: *(smiling)* I'll not let go yet, not until you look at the 2.135
woman dear to my heart whom I have drawn on the stone.

sarve parikrāmanti.

VIDŪṢAKAḤ: *(kadalī|patram apanīya)* ⌜esā se hiaa|vallahā!⌟

NĀYIKĀ: *(nirūpy', âpavārya sa|smitam)* ⌜Caürie, ahaṃ via ālihidā!⌟

CEṬĪ: *(citr'|ākṛtiṃ* NĀYIKĀṂ *ca nirvarṇya)* ⌜bhaṭṭi|dārie, kiṃ bhaṇāsi «ahaṃ via ālihida» tti? erisaṃ se sārikkhaṃ, jeṇa ṇa āṇīadi kiṃ dāva iha maṇi | silā | dale bhaṭṭi | dāriāe paḍibimbaṃ saṅkandaṃ, ādu tuvaṃ ālihida tti!⌟

2.140 NĀYIKĀ: *(vihasya)* ⌜dujjaṇī | kida mhi imiṇā idaṃ cittaṃ daṃsaanteṇa.⌟

VIDŪṢAKAḤ: ⌜bho, ṇivvutto dāṇi gāndhavvo vivāho! muñca idāṇiṃ se agga|hatthaṃ. esā kā vi turia|turiaṃ āacchadi.⌟

NĀYAKO *muñcati.*

CEṬĪ: *(praviśya, sa|harṣaṃ sahas" ôpasṛtya)* ⌜bhaṭṭi | dārie, paḍicchidā tuvaṃ Jīmūdavāhaṇassa gurūhi!⌟

VIDŪṢAKAḤ: *(nṛtyan)* ⌜sampuṇṇo maṇoraho pia | vaassassa; aha va atta|hodīe. aha va ṇa edāṇaṃ,⌟ *(bhojanam abhinayan)* ⌜mama eva bamhaṇassa!⌟

2.145 CEṬĪ: (NĀYIKĀM *uddiśya)* ⌜āṇatta mhi juvarāa|Mittāvasuṇā, jaha, «ajja eva Malaavadīe vivāho. tā lahu edaṃ geṇhia āaccha» tti. tā ehi, gacchamha.⌟

They all walk about.

COMPANION: *(removing the banana leaf)* Here's the lady of his heart!

HEROINE: *(looking, aside with a smile)* Cháturika, it's drawn like me!

MAIDSERVANT: *(looking very closely at the figure in the drawing and the* HEROINE*)* Miss, what do you mean, it's drawn like you? It's so like you, Miss, that I can't tell whether you've been drawn here on the stone surface or it's your reflection!

HEROINE: *(laughing aloud)* Showing this picture, he shows 2.140
me to be wrong.

COMPANION: Hey, now the marriage of mutual affection is completed!* You can let go of her fingers now. Some woman is coming here in great haste.

The HERO *lets go.*

MAIDSERVANT: *(entering, approaching in a rush, delighted)* Miss, you have been accepted by Jimúta·váhana's parents!

COMPANION: *(dancing)* My dear friend's delight is complete; or rather, the good lady's. Or maybe neither's, *(miming eating)* but just mine, the brahmin!

MAIDSERVANT: *(addressing the* HEROINE*)* I've been instructed 2.145
by the young prince Mitra·vasu as follows, "Málayavati is to be married this very day. So get her and come back quickly." Come on then, let's go.

VIDŪṢAKAḤ: ⌜gadā tuvaṃ, dāsīe dhīde, edaṃ gaṇhia? pia|vaassena uṇa iha eva accidavvaṃ?⌟

CEṬĪ: ⌜had'|āsa! mā tuvara! tumhāṇaṃ pi ṇhāvaṇaaṃ āadaṃ eva.⌟

NĀYIKĀ *s'|ânurāgaṃ sa|lajjaṃ* NĀYAKAṂ *paśyantī sa|parivārā niṣkrāntā.*

NEPATHYE:

2.150 vṛṣṭyā piṣṭātakasya
dyutim iha Malaye Meru|tulyāṃ dadhānaḥ,
sadyaḥ sindūra|dūrī|
kṛta|divasa|samārambha|sandhy"|ātapa|śrīḥ,
udgītair aṅganānāṃ
cala|caraṇa|raṇan|nūpura|hrāda|hṛdyair,
udvāha|snāna|velāṃ
kathayati bhavataḥ siddhaye siddha|lokaḥ. [13]

VIDŪṢAKAḤ: *(ākarṇya)* ⌜bho vaassa, āadaṃ ṇhāvaṇaaṃ.⌟

NĀYAKAḤ: *(sa|harṣam)* sakhe, yady evaṃ, kim idānīm iha sthīyate? tad āgaccha. tātaṃ namas|kṛtya snāna|bhūmim eva gacchāvaḥ.

COMPANION: Are you going off, you little skivvy, taking her with you? Is my dear friend supposed to just sit around here?

MAIDSERVANT: Fraud! Don't be impatient. The bathing things are on their way for you as well.

The HEROINE, *looking at the* HERO *with longing and affection, leaves with her entourage.*

BEHIND THE SCENE:

Giving to Málaya a splendor equal to Meru's 2.150
with a shower of perfumed powder,
At the same time dispelling with vermillion
the glorious sunshine of daybreak and evening,
With the lovely songs of ladies to the sound of
anklets tinkling on their moving feet,
The people of the Adepts announce the time of the
nuptial bath for your success!

COMPANION: *(listening)* I say old man, the bathing things are here.

HERO: *(delighted)* If that's the case, my dear friend, why wait any longer? Come on. We'll salute father and go the bathing place itself.

anyonya|darśana|kṛtaḥ
samāna|rūp'|ânurāga|kula|vayasām
keṣāñ cid eva, manye,
samāgamo bhavati puṇyavatām. [14]

niṣkrāntau.

2.155 *dvitīyo 'ṅkaḥ.*

Getting to see one another, so alike in beauty, love,
  family, and age,
Only a lucky few, I think, are then united.

The two leave.

End of the second act.

ACT THREE

3.1 *tataḥ praviśati matta, ujjvala|veṣaś, caṣaka|hasto* VIṬAŚ CEṬAŚ *ca.*

VIṬAḤ:

⌜ṇiccaṃ jo pibaï suraṃ,
janassa piya|saṅgamaṃ ca jo kuṇaï—
maha de do ccia devā
Baladevo Kāmadevo a.⌟ [1]

⌜sa|phalaṃ khu mama Seharaassa jīviaṃ,⌟

⌜vaccha|tthalammi daïā,
diṇṇ'|uppala|vāsiā muhe maïrā,
sīsammi a searao
ṇiccaṃ cia saṇṭhiā jassa.⌟ [2]

3.5 *(pariskhalan)* ⌜are! ko maṃ cālei?⌟ *(sa|hāsam)* ⌜avassaṃ Ṇomāliā maṃ parihasadi!⌟

CEṬAḤ: ⌜bhaṭṭakā, ṇa dāva āadā Ṇomāliā.⌟

VIṬAḤ: *(sa|roṣam)* ⌜paḍhama|ppadosa evva Malaavadī|vivāha| maṅgalaṃ ṇivvuttaṃ. tā kīsa idāṇiṃ pabhāde vi ṇa āacchadi.⌟ *(sa|harṣam)* ⌜aha va, imassi Malaavadīe vivāha| maṅgal'|ûsave savvo evva ṇia|ppaṇaïṇī|jaṇa|saṇāho siddha|vijjāhara|loo Kusum'|āar'|uyyāṇe āvāṇa|sokkhaṃ aṇuhodi. tā tahiṃ evva ṇomāliā maṃ udikkhamāṇā ciṭṭhaï. tā tahiṃ evva gamissaṃ. kīdiso *Ṇomāliāe* viṇā *Seharao*?⌟

skhalan parikrāmati.

There enters a drunken ROGUE *(*SHÉKHARAKA *"Crest") dressed* 3.1
up, liquor glass in hand, accompanied by his MANSERVANT.

ROGUE:

Two only are the gods for me,
He who makes lovers each other see,
He who drinks liquor normally,
Kama·dev and Bala·dev—ee!*

Me, Shékharaka, I'm really blessed,

With me lover lying on me chest,
The wine in me mouth lotus-scented,
A crest on me 'ead, always there.

(staggering) Eh! Who's shoving me? *(giggling)* It must be 3.5
Nava·málika having a laugh with me!

MANSERVANT: Master, Nava·málika hasn't arrived yet.

ROGUE: *(angrily)* Málayavati's wedding ceremony was over in the early evening. So how come she's not here at dawn already? *(happily)* But maybe, while the celebration of Málayavati's wedding ceremony is going on, every single Adept and Magician person is enjoying a drink in the Flower riot gardens, in company with their own lovers. So, that's where Nava·málika must be, waiting for me. What would happen to *Shékharaka : the crest* without his *Nava·málika : jasmine*?

He staggers about.

CEṬAḤ: ⌜edaṃ uyyāṇaṃ. pavisadu bhaṭṭao.⌟

3.10 *ubhau praviśataḥ.*

tataḥ praviśati skandha|nyasta|vastra|yugalo VIDŪṢAKAḤ.

VIDŪṢAKAḤ: ⌜sudaṃ mae, pia|vaasso Kusum'|āar'|ujjāṇaṃ gamissadi tti. tā jāva tahiṃ eva gamissaṃ.⌟ *(parikramya)* ⌜edaṃ ujjāṇaṃ. jāva pavisāmi.⌟ *(praviśya bhramara|sampātaṃ nāṭayan)* ⌜kīsa uṇa ede duṭṭha|mahuarā maṃ eva abhiddavanti.⌟ *(ātmānam āghrāya)* ⌜bhodu, jāṇidaṃ mae! jaṃ Malaavadīe bandhu|jaṇeṇa jāmāduassa pia|vaasso tti sa|bahumāṇaṃ vaṇṇaehi vilitto mhi. santāṇa|kusuma|seharaṃ ca piṇaddhaṃ. eso accādaro me aṇatthī|bhūdo. kiṃ dāṇiṃ ettha karissaṃ? aha va edeṇa eva Malayavadīe saāsādo laddheṇa ratt'|aṃsua|jualeṇa itthiā via laṃbaṃ laṃbaṃ parihia uttarīya|kid'|âvaguṇṭhaṇo gamissaṃ. pekkhāmi dāva dāsīe puttā duṭṭha|mahuarā kiṃ karissanti tti.⌟

tathā karoti.

VIṬAḤ: *(nirūpya sa|harṣam)* ⌜are, ceḍaa!⌟ *(aṅgulyā nirdiśya sa|hāsam)* ⌜esā khu Ṇomāliā, ahaṃ cirassa āado tti kuvidā avaguṇṭhaṇaṃ karia aṇṇado gacchadi. tā kaṇṭhe gaṇhia pasādemi ṇaṃ.⌟

3.15 *sahas" ôpasṛtya, kaṇṭhe gṛhītvā mukhena tāmbūlaṃ dātum icchati.*

MANSERVANT: Here's the garden. Let Master go in.

The two enter. 3.10

Thereupon enters the COMPANION *with two garments placed over his shoulder.*

COMPANION: I've heard that my dear friend will be going to the Flower riot gardens. So that's where I'm going. *(moving about)* This is the garden. I'll just go in. *(having gone in, acting an attack by bees)* Why is it me these bloody bees are going for? Of course, I know! I was smeared with a load of fragrant powders by Málayavati's relations because I was with my dear friend the son-in-law. And they stuck on a crest of *santána** flowers. This high honor has become a problem! What shall I do about it now? I know, I'll wrap around this pair of red shoulder wraps from Málayavati's, like a lady, so that it hangs a lot, and carry on enveloped in a cloak! Then I'll see what these bloody son-of-a-bitch drones will do!

He does so.

ROGUE: *(noticing, happily)* Oi, manservant! *(pointing with his finger and laughing)* Here's Nava·málika, all wrapped up. She's going in the other direction cos she's angry with me cos I'm late! I'll give her a cuddle and make up to her.

He rushes over, embraces her and tries to put betel in her mouth. 3.15

VIDŪṢAKAḤ: *(madya|gandhaṃ sūcayan nāsikāṃ gṛhītvā parā-vṛtta|mukhaḥ)* ⌜ahaṃ ekkāṇaṃ mahu|arāṇaṃ muhādo kahaṃ vi paribbhaṭṭho aṇṇassa duṭṭha|mahuarassa muhe paḍido mhi.⌟

VIṬAḤ: ⌜kahaṃ? koveṇa param|muhī|bhūdā?⌟ *(*VIDŪṢAKASYA *caraṇāv ātmanaḥ śirasi kurvan)* ⌜pasīda, Ṇomālie, pasīda!⌟

tataḥ praviśati CEṬĪ

CEṬĪ: ⌜āṇatta mhi bhaṭṭi|dāriāe mādāe, «hañje Ṇomālie! Kusum'|āar'|uyyāṇaṃ gacchia uyyāṇa|pāliaṃ Pallaviaṃ bhaṇāhi, ajja sa|visesaṃ tamāla|vīhiaṃ sajjī|karehi. Mala-yavadī|sahideṇa jāmādueṇa ettha āantavvaṃ» tti. āṇattā a mae Pallaviā. jāva raaṇī|virah'|ukkaṇṭhiaṃ pia|vallahaṃ Seharaaṃ aṇṇesāmi.⌟ *(dṛṣṭvā)* ⌜eso Seharao.⌟ *(sa|roṣam)* ⌜kahaṃ? aṇṇaṃ kaṃ pi itthiaṃ pasādedi!⌟

VIṬAḤ:

3.20 ⌜Hari|Hara|Pidāmahāṇaṃ
pi gavvido jo ṇa jāṇae ṇamiduṃ,
so Seharao calaṇe-
su tujjha, Ṇomālie, paḍaï.⌟ [3]

VIDŪṢAKAḤ: ⌜dāsīe putta! matta|pālaa! kudo ettha Ṇomāliā?⌟

COMPANION: *(indicating the smell of liquor and holding his nose, turning his face away)* How come I've escaped from the clutches of one lot of drones to fall into the hands of another bloody drone?

ROGUE: What's this? She's turned her face away in anger? *(placing his own head at the feet of the* COMPANION*)* Be nice, Nava·málika, please be nice!

At that point the MAIDSERVANT *enters.*

MAIDSERVANT: I've been instructed by the princess's mother, "Maid Nava·málika, go to the Flower riot gardens and tell Pállavika, the lady gardener, particularly to prepare the *tamála* avenue today. Málayavati and our son-in-law will be coming here," and I've instructed Pállavika. Now that's done I can look for my lovely bloke, Shékharaka, who's been hankering for me all night. *(seeing him)* Here's Shékharaka. *(angrily)* What's this? He's flirting with some other woman!

ROGUE:

> The Shékharaka who knows not how to bow to Hari, Hara or Pita·maha* 3.20
> Because he's proud, falls at your two feet, Nava·málika.

COMPANION: Son-of-a-bitch! Prince of drunks! Is Nava·málika here?

CEṬĪ: *(nirūpya sa|smitam)* ⌜kahaṃ? ahaṃ ti karia mada|paravaseṇa Seharaeṇa ayyo Atteo pasādīadi. jāva alia|kopaṃ karia duve vi ede parihasissaṃ.⌟

CEṬAḤ: *(*ŚEKHARAKAṂ *hastena cālayan)* ⌜bhaṭṭaka, muñca! muñca. edaṃ ṇa hoi Ṇomāliā. eśā khu Ṇomāliā lośa|lattehi ṇaaṇehi pekkhantī āadā.⌟

CEṬĪ: *(upasṛtya)* ⌜Seharaa! kā ṇu hu esā pasādīadi?⌟

VIDŪṢAKAḤ: *(avaguṇṭhanam apanīya)* ⌜ahaṃ manda|bhāae putto!⌟

VIṬAḤ: *(vidūṣakaṃ nirūpya)* ⌜are, kapila|makkaḍaa! tuvaṃ pi maṃ Seharaaṃ parihasasi? are ceḍaa! gaṇha imaṃ. jāva Ṇomāliaṃ pasādemi.⌟

CEṬAḤ: ⌜jaṃ bhaṭṭao āṇavedi.⌟

VIṬAḤ: *(*VIDŪṢAKAṂ *vimucya,* CEṬYĀḤ *pādayoḥ patan)* ⌜pasīda, Ṇomālie, pasīda!⌟

VIDŪṢAKAḤ: ⌜eso me apakkamiduṃ avasaro.⌟ *(palāyitum īhate.)*

CEṬAḤ: *(*VIDŪṢAKAM *yajñ'|ôpavīte gṛhṇāti. yajñ'|ôpavītaṃ truṭyati.)* ⌜kahiṃ, kahiṃ, kapila|makkaḍaa, palāaśi?⌟ *(tad|uttarīyeṇa gale baddhv" ākarṣati.)*

MAIDSERVANT: *(looking closely, with a smile)* What's this? Shékharaka, who is under the influence of drink, is flirting with the gentleman Atréya, thinking he's me. If that's the case I'll make out that I'm angry and have a laugh at the expense of the pair of them.

MANSERVANT: *(shaking* SHÉKHARAKA *with his hand)* Let go, Master! Let go. This isn't Nava·málika.* Here's Nava·málika, glaring with red and angry eyes!

MAIDSERVANT: *(coming up)* Shékharaka! Who on earth is this you're flirting with?

COMPANION: *(removing his cloak)* I'm the son of an unfor- 3.25
tunate mother!

ROGUE: *(looking at the companion closely)* Hey, you ginger ape!* You n'all are laughing at me, Shékharaka? Hey, manservant! Grab him, while I make up with Nava·málika.

MANSERVANT: As Master instructs.

ROGUE: *(letting go of the* COMPANION, *bowing at the* MAIDSERVANT*'s feet)* Be nice, Nava·málika, please be nice!

COMPANION: It's time for me to make my getaway. *(He tries to flee.)*

MANSERVANT: *(He grabs the* COMPANION *by his sacred thread.* 3.30
The sacred thread snaps.) Where, oh where are you running to, you ginger ape? *(Tying him up with the cloak around his neck, he drags him along.)*

VIDŪṢAKAḤ: ⌜hodi Ṇomālie, pasīda. moāvehi maṃ.⌟

CEṬĪ: *(vihasya)* ⌜jadi bhūmie sīsaṃ ṇivesia pādesu me paḍasi.⌟

VIDŪṢAKAḤ: *(sa|roṣam)* ⌜kahaṃ? rāa|mittaṃ bhavia, dāsīe dhīde, pādesu de paḍissaṃ?⌟

CEṬĪ: *(aṅgulyā tarjayantī, sa|smitam)* ⌜dāṇiṃ tumaṃ pāḍaïssaṃ! Seharaa, uṭṭhehi uṭṭhehi. pasaṇṇā khu ahaṃ.⌟ *(kaṇṭhe gṛhṇāti.)* ⌜eso jāmāduassa pia|vaasso tue khalī|kido. edaṃ suṇia kadā i bhaṭṭārao Mittāvasū kuppe. tā ādareṇa sammāṇehi ṇaṃ.⌟

3.35 VIṬAḤ: ⌜jaṃ Ṇomāliā āṇavedi.⌟ *(VIDŪṢAKAṂ kaṇṭhe gṛhītvā)* ⌜ayya! tumaṃ pia|sambandhia tti karia avahasido.⌟ *(ghūrṇayan)* ⌜kiṃ saccaṃ eva Seharao matto, kido parihāso?⌟ *(uttarīyaṃ vartulī|kṛty' āsanaṃ dadāti.)* ⌜iha uvavisadu sambandhio.⌟

VIDŪṢAKAḤ: ⌜diṭṭhiā avaado via se mada|veo.⌟ *(upaviśati.)*

VIṬAḤ: ⌜Ṇomālie, uvavisa tumaṃ edassa passado, jeṇa duve vi tumhe samaṃ sammāṇemi.⌟

CEṬĪ *vihasy' ôpaviśati.*

COMPANION: Madam Nava·málika, be nice. Make him let me go.

MAIDSERVANT: *(laughing aloud)* If you bow at my feet and put your head on the ground.

COMPANION: *(angrily)* What's this? As a friend of the king, I'm to bow down at your feet, you little bitch?

MAIDSERVANT: *(wagging her finger and smiling)* I'll make you bow down at my feet yet! Shékharaka, get yourself up, I'm rather pleased with you. *(She gives him an embrace.)* This dear friend of the son-in-law has been mistreated by you. Were Master Mitra·vasu to hear about this, he might get angry. You'd better show him some respect.

ROGUE: As Nava·málika requests. *(clasping the* COMPANION 3.35
round the neck) My dear chap, I was having a laugh, making you out as some kind of relation to our dear master. *(staggering)* What do you think, was Shékharaka drunk, or was he just joking about?* *(Making his cloak into a ball, he offers a seat.)* Please sit down, cousin!

COMPANION: Thank goodness, the worst of his drunkenness seems to be over. *(He takes the seat.)*

ROGUE: Nava·málika, please sit next to him so that I can honor the pair of you together.

The MAIDSERVANT *sits down laughing aloud.*

VIṬAḤ: ⌜ceḍaa, su|pūridaṃ khu edaṃ casaaṃ karehi accha|surāe.⌟

3.40 CEṬAḤ *caṣakam unnayan pūraṇaṃ nāṭyena karoti.*

VIṬAḤ: *(sva|śiraḥ|śekharāt puṣpāṇi gṛhītvā caṣake vinyasya jānubhyāṃ patitvā* NAVAMĀLIKĀYĀ *upanayan)* ⌜Ṇomālie, pibia cokkhia dehi edaṃ!⌟

CEṬĪ: *(sa|smitam)* ⌜jaṃ Seharao āṇavedi.⌟ *(tathā karoti.)*

VIṬAḤ: *(*VIDŪṢAKASYA *caṣakam upanayan)* ⌜edaṃ Ṇomāliā|muha|saṃsagga|vaḍḍhia|rasaṃ Seharaādo aṇṇeṇa keṇa vi aṇ|āssādia|puvvaṃ. tā piba edaṃ. kiṃ de ado varaṃ sammāṇaṃ karemi?⌟

VIDŪṢAKAḤ: *(sa|vilakṣa|smitaṃ kṛtvā)* ⌜Seharaa, baṃhaṇo khu ahaṃ.⌟

3.45 VIṬAḤ: ⌜jaï tumaṃ baṃhaṇo, kahiṃ de baṃha|suttaṃ?⌟

VIDŪṢAKAḤ: ⌜taṃ khu imiṇā ceḍeṇa āaḍḍhiamāṇaṃ chiṇ-ṇaṃ!⌟

CEṬĪ: *(vihasya)* ⌜jaï evvaṃ, ved'|akkharāṇiṃ pi kadi i udāhara.⌟

VIDŪṢAKAḤ: ⌜bhodi, sīhu|gandheṇa me ved'|akkharāṇi ṇaṭṭhāṇi. aha va, kiṃ mama bhodīe samaṃ vivādeṇa? eso baṃhaṇo pādesu de paḍaï.⌟ *(pādayoḥ patitum icchati.)*

ROGUE: Manservant, fill this cup right up with fresh liquor.

The MANSERVANT *holding up the cup, mimes filling it.* 3.40

ROGUE: *(taking some flowers from the crest on his head and putting them in the cup, he falls to his knees, offering it to* NAVA·MÁLIKA*)* Nava·málika, have a drink, rinse it round and give it back!*

MAIDSERVANT: *(with a smile)* As Shékharaka instructs! *(She does so.)*

ROGUE: *(offering the cup to the* COMPANION*)* This has never been tasted by anyone, except for Shékharaka, and its flavor has been enhanced by the touch of Nava·málika's mouth. So drink it! How could I honor you more than this?

COMPANION: *(having smiled with embarrassment)* Shékharaka, I'm actually a brahmin.*

ROGUE: But if you're a brahmin, where's your sacred thread? 3.45

COMPANION: Actually, it was broken while I was being dragged around by this servant!

MAIDSERVANT: *(laughing aloud)* If that's the case, then just recite a few words from the Veda.

COMPANION: Madam, for me the words of the Veda are destroyed by the smell of spirits. Oh, I can see there's no point in arguing this with you. This brahmin bows at your feet. *(He goes to bow at her feet.)*

CEṬĪ: *(vihasya, hastābhyāṃ nivārya)* ⌜ayya, mā mā evvaṃ karehi! Seharaa, saccaṃ baṃhaṇo khu eso.⌟ *(*VIDŪṢAKASYA *pādayoḥ patati.)* ⌜ayya, tue ṇa kuvidavvaṃ. sambandhi'|âṇurūvo parihāso kido. Seharaa, tumaṃ pi imaṃ pasādehi.⌟

3.50 VIṬAḤ: ⌜ahaṃ pi imaṃ pasādemi.⌟ *(*VIDŪṢAKASYA *pādayor nipatya)* ⌜marisedu, marisedu ayyo, jaṃ mae mada|para-vaseṇa avaraddhaṃ. jeṇa ahaṃ Ṇomāliāe saha āpāṇaaṃ gamissaṃ.⌟

VIDŪṢAKAḤ: ⌜marisidaṃ mae. gaccha. jāva ahaṃ pi vaassaṃ pekkhāmi.⌟

VIṬAḤ: ⌜ayya, taha.⌟

niṣkrānto NAVAMĀLIKAYĀ VIṬAŚ CEṬAŚ *ca.*

VIDŪṢAKAḤ: ⌜adikkando khu baṃhaṇassa aāla|miccū. tā ahaṃ pi matta|bālaa|jaṇa|saṃsagga|dūsido iha digghiāaṃ ṇhāissaṃ.⌟ *(tathā karoti. puro 'valokya)* ⌜eso khu pia|vaasso rūviṇīṃ via *vara/lacchiṃ* Malaavadiṃ olambia ido evva āacchadi. tā iha evva ciṭṭhissaṃ.⌟ *(sthitaḥ.)*

3.55 *tataḥ praviśati* NĀYAKO MALAYAVATYĀ, *vibhavataś ca parivāraḥ.*

MAIDSERVANT: *(laughing aloud, pushing him away with her hands)* Sir, don't do that! Shékharaka, it's true, he's actually a brahmin. *(She bows to the feet of the* COMPANION.*)* Sir, please don't get angry. I was joking, like I would with a relative. Shékharaka, you make up with him too.

ROGUE: Of course I'll make up with him. *(bowing down at* 3.50
the feet of the COMPANION*)* Forgive me, sir, please forgive me, for the insult made while under the influence of drink. Then I can go to the drinks party with Nava·málika.

COMPANION: I forgive you. Go. Meanwhile, I too will see my friend.

ROGUE: Yes, sir.

With NAVA·MÁLIKA, *the* ROGUE *and his* MANSERVANT *leave.*

COMPANION: The brahmin has escaped a premature death! Even so I'm polluted by my contact with those drunken fools, so I'll bathe in this long pool here. *(He does so. Looking off)* Here comes my dear friend, hanging on to Málayavati as if she were the beautiful *good fortune: Lakshmi* of her husband. I'll wait right here then. *(He waits.)*

At that point there enters the HERO *with* MÁLAYAVATI *and, in* 3.55
order of rank, their entourage.

NĀYAKAḤ:

drṣṭā dṛṣṭim adho dadāti. kurute
n' ālāpam ābhāṣitā.
śayyāyāṃ parivṛtya tiṣṭhati. balād
āliṅgitā vepate.
niryāntīṣu sakhīṣu vāsa|bhavanān
nirgantum ev' ēhate.
jātā vāmatay" âiva me 'dya sutarāṃ
prītyai navoḍhā priyā. [4]

(MALAYAVATĪM *avalokya)* priye Malayavati!

huṅ|kāraṃ dadatā mayā prativaco
yan maunam āsevitaṃ,
yad dāv'|ânala|dīptibhis tanur iyaṃ
candr'|ātapais tāpitā,
dhyātaṃ yac ca bahūny an|anya|
manasā naktaṃ|dināni, priye,
tasy' âitat tapasaḥ phalaṃ, mukham idaṃ
paśyāmi yat te 'dhunā. [5]

NĀYIKĀ: *(apavārya)* ⌜hañje, ṇa kevalaṃ daṃsaṇīo, piaṃ pi bhaṇiduṃ jāṇādi.⌟

3.60 CEṬĪ: *(vihasya)* ⌜aï paḍipakkha|vādiṇi! saccaṃ eva edaṃ. kiṃ ettha «pia|vaaṇaṃ?»⌟

NĀYAKAḤ: Caturike, ādeśaya Kusum'|ākar'|ôdyānasya mārgam.

CEṬĪ: ⌜edu, edu bhaṭṭi|dārao.⌟

HERO:

When I look at her she looks down.
When I speak to her she makes no conversation.
In bed she stays with her back turned.
When I insist on embracing her she trembles.
When her lady friends are leaving our room
  she actually tries to leave with them.
By her coyness my newly wedded wife now becomes
  ever more dear to me.

(looking at MÁLAYAVATI*)* Darling Málayavati!

I observed silence, giving "hmm" as an answer.*
I heated this body by the heat of the moon,
  blazing like a forest fire,
And I meditated, my dear, with a mind on
  nothing else for many days and nights.
Now I behold the fruit of that penance,
  this face of yours.

HEROINE: *(aside)* He's not just handsome, maid, he also knows how to make a pretty speech.

MAIDSERVANT: *(laughing aloud)* Oh, you contrary creature! 3.60
It's only the truth. What's "pretty speaking" in that?

HERO: Cháturika, show us the way to the Flower riot gardens.

MAIDSERVANT: Come, let the prince come this way.

NĀYAKAḤ: *(parikraman,* NĀYIKĀṂ *nirdiśya)* svairaṃ, svairam āgacchatu bhavatī.

khedāya stana|bhāra eva. kim u te
madhyasya hāro 'paras?
tāmyaty ūru|yugaṃ nitamba|bharataḥ.
kāñcy" âmayā kiṃ punaḥ?
śaktiḥ pāda|yugasya n' ōru|yugalaṃ
voḍhuṃ. kuto nūpure?
sv'|âṅgair eva vibhūṣit" âsi. vahasi
kleśāya kiṃ maṇḍanam? [6]

3.65 CEṬĪ: ⌜edaṃ Kusum'|āar'|uyyāṇaṃ. pavisadu bhaṭṭi|dārao.⌟

sarve praviśanti.

NĀYAKAḤ: *(praviśya)* aho Kusum'|ākar'|ôdyānasya śrīḥ! iha hi,

niḥṣyandaś candanānāṃ
śiśirayati latā|maṇḍape kuṭṭim'|ântān.
ārād dhārā|gṛhāṇāṃ
dhvanim anu kurute tāṇḍavaṃ nīla|kaṇṭhaḥ.
yantr'|ônmuktaś ca vegāc
calati viṭapināṃ pūrayann ālavālān
āpāt'|ôtpīḍa|helā|
hṛta|kusuma|rajaḥ|piñjaro 'yaṃ jal'|âughaḥ. [7]

api ca,

HERO: *(walking about, addressing the* HEROINE*)* Gently, come along gently, my lady.

The very weight of your breasts fatigues you.
Why another pearl necklace for your waist?
Your thighs are tired by the weight of your hips.
Why then this tinkling waistband?
Your feet cannot carry your thighs.
Why these anklets?
You are graced by your limbs on their own.
Why wear ornaments just to be fatigued?

MAIDSERVANT: Here are the Flower riot gardens. May my lord enter. 3.65

They all enter.

HERO: *(entering)* Gosh, the Flower riot gardens are lovely! For in here,

The sandalwood sap cools the edges of the tiled floors
in the vine arbors.
Nearby a peacock excitedly dances to the sound
of the waterfalls,
And quickly flows this flood of water forced from
the fountains and filling the basins of trees,
That's yellow from the flower pollen playfully snatched
by the gushing stream.

Moreover,

3.70 amī gīt'|ārambhair
mukharita|latā|maṇḍapa|bhuvaḥ,
parāgaiḥ puṣpāṇāṃ
prakaṭa|paṭavāsa|vyatikarāḥ.
pibantaḥ paryāptaṃ
saha saha|carībhir madhu|rasaṃ
samantād āpān'|ôt-
savam anubhavant' îha *madhu|pāḥ*. [8]

VIDŪṢAKAḤ: *(upasṛtya)* ⌜jedu bhavaṃ. sotthi bhodīe.⌟

NĀYAKAḤ: vayasya, cirād āgato 'si.

VIDŪṢAKAḤ: ⌜bho vaassa, lahuṃ eva āado, kin du iantaṃ kālaṃ vivāha | maṅgal' | ûsava | milida | siddha | vijjāhar' | āpāṇa|daṃsaṇa|kodūhaleṇa paribbhamanto ṇa lakkhido. tā pia|vaasso vi dāva edaṃ pekkhadu.⌟

NĀYAKAḤ: yath" âha bhavān. *(sa|harṣam paritaḥ paśyan)*

3.75 digdh'|âṅgā hari|candanena, dadhataḥ
santānakānāṃ srajo,
māṇiky'|ābharaṇa|prabhā|vyatikaraiś
citrīkṛt'|âcch'|âṃśukāḥ,
sārdhaṃ siddha|gaṇair madhūni dayitā|
pīt'|âvaśiṣṭāny amī
miśrī|bhūya pibanti candana|latā|
cchāyāsu vidyādharāḥ. [9]

The air of the vine arbors is made noisy 3.70
as they start their songs,
Their mixing of the perfumed powders evident
through the pollen of the flowers.
Drinking their fill of mead alongside their
lady companions,
Here these *honey-footed bees : drunkards* enjoy
the drinking party all around.

COMPANION: *(approaching)* Victory to you, your honor. May you be well, my lady.

HERO: You are late, my friend!

COMPANION: I say old man, I came really quickly, but didn't notice the time while I was wandering around in curiosity looking at the drinks party for the Adepts and Magicians. They've met here for the celebration of your marriage ceremony. It's such fun, my dear friend, you should take a look too.

HERO: As you say. *(looking all around with pleasure)*

Carrying garlands of *santánaka* flowers, their limbs 3.75
smeared with yellow sandal,
Their diaphanous clothing colored through
proximity to the radiance of their ruby jewels,
Mingling with the group of Adepts, these Magician
folk down the drinks
Left from being tasted by their women, in the shade
of the sandal vines.

tad ehi, vayam api tamāla|vīthikāṃ gacchāmaḥ.

sarve parikrāmanti.

VIDŪṢAKAḤ: ⌜esā khu tamāla | vīhiā. edaṃ candaṇa | ladā | maṇḍavaṃ, edaṃ ca sarad'|ādava|parikhediaṃ via tatta| hodīe vadaṇaṃ lakkhīadi, tā iha phalia|silā|dale uvavisadu.⌟

NĀYAKAḤ: vayasya, samyag upalakṣitam.

etan mukhaṃ priyāyāḥ
  śaśinaṃ jitvā kapolayoḥ kāntyā
tāp'|ābhitāmram adhunā
  kamalaṃ dhruvam īhate jetum. [10]

(MALAYAVATĪṂ *haste gṛhītvā)* priye, ih' ôpaviśāmaḥ.

sarve upaviśanti.

NĀYAKAḤ: *(*NĀYIKĀ*|mukham unnamayya paśyan)* priye, vṛth" âiva tvam asmābhiḥ Kusum'|ākar'|ôdyāna|darśana|kutūhalibhiḥ parikheditā. kutaḥ,

etat te bhrū|lat"|ôllāsi
  pāṭal'|âdhara|pallavam
mukham nandanam udyānam.
  ato 'nyat kevalaṃ vanam. [11]

CEṬĪ: *(sa|smitaṃ* VIDŪṢAKAṂ *nirdiśya)* ⌜sudaṃ tue, kahaṃ vaṇṇid" êtti?⌟

VIDŪṢAKAḤ: *(sa|smitam)* ⌜Caürie, mā evvaṃ gavvaṃ uvvaha. amhāṇaṃ pi majjhe daṃsaṇīo jaṇo atthi evva, kevalaṃ macchareṇa ko vi ṇa vaṇṇedi.⌟

Come along then, we'll go to the *tamála* avenue as well.

They all move about.

COMPANION: It's the *tamála* avenue here. This is the arbor of sandal vines, and as the good lady's face seems troubled as if by the heat of fall, may she take a seat here on this crystal bench.

HERO: Well noticed, my friend.

> This face of my beloved that has outshone the moon 3.80
> with the beauty of her cheeks,
> Now blushing deeply with the heat,
> surely tries to outdo the lotus.

(taking MÁLAYAVATI *by the hand)* My dear, let's sit down here.

They all take a seat.

HERO: *(raising the* HEROINE*'s face and looking into it)* Darling, we have fatigued you quite needlessly with our curiosity to see the Flower riot gardens. Because,

> This rosy lower lip of yours the seedling,
> the trembling vine your brow,
> Your face is a delightful garden.
> Any other is just a wilderness.

MAIDSERVANT: *(smiling and addressing the* COMPANION*)* Did you hear how she's described? 3.85

COMPANION: *(smiling)* Cháturika, don't get too cocky! There is actually a handsome chap among us too, but solely out of jealousy no one paints a picture of him.

CEṬĪ: *(sa|smitam)* ⌜ayya, ahaṃ de vaṇṇemi.⌟

VIDŪṢAKAḤ: *(sa|harṣam)* ⌜jīvida mhi! karedu hodī pasādaṃ, jeṇa eso vuṇa ṇa bhaṇādi īdiso tādiso makkaḍ'|āāra tti.⌟

CEṬĪ: ⌜ajja tuvaṃ mae vivāha|jāgareṇa ṇijjāamāṇo ṇimīli'|accho sohanto diṭṭho. tā evaṃ evva ciṭṭha.⌟

3.90 VIDŪṢAKAS *tathā karoti.*

CEṬĪ: *(ātma|gatam)* ⌜jāva ṇīlī|ras'|âṇuāriṇā tamāla|pallava|raseṇa muhaṃ se kālī|karissaṃ.⌟

utthāya pallava|grahaṇaṃ kṛtvā niṣpīḍanaṃ ca nāṭayati.

NĀYAKO NĀYIKĀ *ca* VIDŪṢAKASYA *mukhaṃ paśyataḥ.*

NĀYAKAḤ: vayasya, dhanyaḥ khalv asi, yad asmāsu tiṣṭhatsu tvam evaṃ varṇyase.

3.95 CEṬĪ *tamāla|pallavasya rasena* VIDŪṢAKASYA *mukhaṃ nāṭyena kālī|karoti.*

NĀYIKĀ *sa|smitaṃ* VIDŪṢAKAṂ *dṛṣṭvā* NĀYAKAṂ *paśyati.*

NĀYAKAḤ:

smita|puṣp'|ôdgamo 'yaṃ te
  dṛśyate 'dhara|pallave;
phalaṃ tu jātaṃ, mugdh'|âkṣi,
  paśyataś cakṣuṣor mama. [12]

MAIDSERVANT: *(smiling)* Sir, let me paint you.

COMPANION: *(with delight)* I feel revived! Do me a favor and stop that man calling me a this or that kind of monkey any more.

MAIDSERVANT: I saw you today snoozing after staying up for the wedding. You looked handsome with your eyes closed. So you just wait like that.

The COMPANION *does so.*

MAIDSERVANT: *(to herself)* I'll blacken his face with the juice from some *tamála* shoots. It's like liquid indigo.

She gets up and acts taking hold of the shoots and squeezing them.

The HERO AND HEROINE *look at the face of the* COMPANION.

HERO: My friend, you're really lucky being painted like this while we're here.

The MAIDSERVANT, *miming, blackens the face of the* COMPANION *with the juice of the tamála shoots.*

The HEROINE *smiling, sees the* COMPANION *and looks at the* HERO.

HERO:

> Here the blossoming of the flower that is your smile
> can be seen in the bud of your lower lip,
> But the fruit, you sweet-eyed girl, is born in my eyes
> as I look.

VIDŪṢAKAḤ: ⌜bhodi, kiṃ de kidaṃ?⌟

CEṬĪ: ⌜ṇaṃ vaṇṇido si!⌟

3.100 VIDŪṢAKAḤ: *(hastena mukhaṃ parāmṛjya, hastaṃ dṛṣṭvā, sa|roṣaṃ daṇḍa|kāṣṭham udyamya, sa|saṃrambham)* ⌜dāsīe dhīde! rāa|ulaṃ khu edaṃ! kiṃ de karissaṃ?⌟ *(*NĀYAKAM *uddiśya)* ⌜bho, tumhāṇaṃ purado evva ahaṃ dāsīe dhīdāe khalī|kido mhi. kiṃ mama iha ṭṭhideṇa? aṇṇado gamissaṃ.⌟

niṣkrāntaḥ.

CEṬĪ: ⌜kuvido khu mama ayyo Atteo. jāva gadua pasādemi.⌟

NĀYIKĀ: ⌜hañje Caürie, kahaṃ maṃ eāiṇiṃ ujjhia gacchasi?⌟

CEṬĪ: *(*NĀYAKAM *uddiśya sa|smitam)* ⌜evaṃ eva ciraṃ eāiṇī hohi!⌟ *(niṣkrāntā.)*

NĀYAKAḤ:

3.105 dinakara|kar'|āmṛṣṭaṃ bibhrad
dyutiṃ paripāṭalāṃ,
daśana|kiraṇair utsarpadbhiḥ
sphuṭī|kṛta|kesaram,
ayi, mukham idaṃ, mugdhe, satyaṃ
samaṃ kamalena te;
madhu madhu|karaḥ kin tv etasmin
piban na vibhāvyate. [13]

NĀYIKĀ *vihasya mukham unnamayati.*

COMPANION: Madam, what have you done?

MAIDSERVANT: I've painted you, have I not!

COMPANION: *(rubbing his face with his hand, looking at his hand, angrily raising his wooden staff, in agitation)* You little bitch! This is the royal party! What shall I do with you? *(addressing the* HERO*)* Hey, I've been insulted by this little bitch right in front of you. There's no point in my staying here. I'm going somewhere else. 3.100

He leaves.

MAIDSERVANT: Mr Atréya is really angry with me. I'll go to him and make up.

HEROINE: Maid Cháturika, how can you go off and leave me all alone?

MAIDSERVANT: *(indicating the* HERO, *smiling)* May you be alone just like this for a long time! *(She leaves.)*

HERO:

Brushed by the beams of the sun, glowing pink all over, 3.105
Hair revealed by the rising gleam of your teeth,
Ah, this face of yours, you sweet girl, is truly like a lotus,
Though there appears to be no honey bee drinking the honey therein.

The HEROINE *laughs and turns away her face.*

NĀYAKO *«dinakar'» êti tad eva paṭhati.*

praviśya

CEṬĪ: *(sahas" ôpasṛtya)* ⌜eso khu siddha|juarāo Mittāvasū keṇa vi kajj'|antareṇa kumāraṃ pekkhiduṃ āado.⌟

3.110 NĀYAKAḤ: priye, gaccha tvam ātmano gṛham, aham api Mitrāvasuṃ dṛṣṭvā tvaritataram āgata eva.

CEṬĪ/*sahitā niṣkrāntā* NĀYIKĀ.

tataḥ praviśati MITRĀVASUḤ.

MITRĀVASUḤ:

> anihatya taṃ samarthaḥ
> katham iva Jīmūtavāhanasy' âham
> kathayiṣyāmi, «tava hṛtaṃ
> rājyaṃ ripuṇ"» êti nirlajjaḥ? [14]

tath" âpy a|nivedy' â|yukta|rūpaṃ gamanam, iti nivedya gacchāmi. *(upasarpati.)*

3.115 NĀYAKAḤ: Mitrāvaso, iha āsyatām.

MITRĀVASUR *upaviśati.*

NĀYAKAḤ: sa|saṃrambha iva lakṣyase.

The HERO *repeats the verse.*

entering

MAIDSERVANT: *(approaching quickly)* It's the crown prince of the Adepts, Mitra·vasu, come to see the prince on some other business.

HERO: Go take yourself home, my dear, and I'll see Mitra·vasu and return really quickly. 3.110

The HEROINE *leaves with her* MAIDSERVANT.

At that point MITRA·VASU *enters.*

MITRA·VASU:

> I have not destroyed him though I could have.
> How exactly to Jimúta·váhana
> Will I say without embarrassment,
> "The enemy has seized your kingdom"?*

I'll tell him before I go, since it would be wrong to leave without telling him. *(He approaches.)*

HERO: Mitra·vasu, sit here. 3.115

MITRA·VASU *takes a seat.*

HERO: You seem to be excited.

MITRĀVASUḤ: kaḥ khalu Mataṅga|hatake saṃrambhaḥ?

NĀYAKAḤ: kiṃ kṛtaṃ Mataṅgena?

3.120 MITRĀVASUḤ: sva|nāśāya yuṣmadīyaṃ kila rājyam ākrāntam.

NĀYAKAḤ: *(sa|harṣam ātma|gatam)* api nāma satyam etat syāt.

MITRĀVASUḤ: tad | ucchittaye mām ājñāpayatu kumāraḥ. kiṃ bahunā,

saṃsarpadbhiḥ samantāt
kṛta|sakala|viyan|mārga|yānair vimānaiḥ
kurvāṇāḥ prāvṛṣ' îva
sthagita|ravi|rucaḥ śyāmatāṃ vāsarasya
ete yātāś ca sadyas
tava vacanam itaḥ prāpya yuddhāya siddhāḥ,
siddhaṃ c' ôdvṛtta|śatru|
kṣaya|bhaya|vinamad|rājakaṃ te sva|rājyam.
[15]

atha vā kiṃ bal'|âughaiḥ,

3.125 ekākin" âpi hi mayā *rabhas'|âvakṛṣṭa|*
nistriṃśa|dīdhiti|saṭā|bhara|bhāsureṇa
ārān nipatya hariṇ" êva *mataṅgaj'|êndram*
ājau *Mataṅga|hatakaṃ* hatam eva viddhi. [16]

MITRA·VASU: What's exciting about that cursed Matánga?

HERO: What has Matánga done?

MITRA·VASU: They are saying that he has overrun your kingdom, to his own destruction. 3.120

HERO: *(happily to himself)* If only this were true.

MITRA·VASU: Let the prince instruct me to have him destroyed. In short,

As soon as they receive your order, these Adepts
will be gone from here for the battle-field,
Making the day as dark as the rainy season,
blocking the light from the sun
As they glide all around in their sky-chariots making
their way through every passage in the air,
And your kingdom will be secured, your tributary
princes bowing in awe at the destruction
wrought on your insubordinate enemy.

Mind you, there's no need for an overwhelming force:

Know that I will totally crush that *cursed Matánga*⁝ *stunned elephant* 3.125
As if a *bull elephant*⁝ *Lord Matánga* was ambushed
by a lion close at hand,
Just me alone, on the battle-field, radiant,
*Bearing my braided hair in devotion and my sword
drawn in fury*⁝ *With my massive mane,
majestic, merciless, clawing him down in fury.*

NĀYAKAḤ: *(karṇau pidhāya, ātma|gatam)* hahaha, dāruṇam abhihitam! atha vā, evaṃ tāvat. *(prakāśaṃ, sa|smitam)* Mitrāvaso, kiyad etat? bahutaram ato 'pi bahu|śālini tvayi sambhāvyate. kin tu,

sva|śarīram api par'|ârthe
yaḥ khalu dadyām a|yācitaḥ kṛpayā,
rājyasya kṛte sa kathaṃ
prāṇi|vadha|krauryam anumanye? [17]

api ca kleśān vihāya śatru|buddhir eva me n' ânyatra. yadi te 'smat|priyaṃ kartum īhā, tad anukampyatām asau kleśa|dāsī|kṛtas tapasvī.

MITRĀVASUḤ: *(s'|āmarṣaṃ sa|hāsaṃ ca)* kathaṃ n' ânukampyate, yādṛśo 'sāv asmākam upakārī kṛpaṇaś ca?

3.130 NĀYAKAḤ: *(ātma|gatam)* pratyagra|kop'|ākṣipta|cetās tāvad asau na śakyate nivartayitum. tad evaṃ tāvat. *(prakāśaṃ)* Mitrāvaso, uttiṣṭha. abhyantaram eva praviśāvaḥ, tatra ca tvāṃ bodhayiṣyāmi. samprati pariṇatam ahaḥ. tathā hi,

HERO: *(covering his ears, to himself)* Oh dear, cruelly spoken! Never mind, I know what to do for now. *(aloud, smiling)* Mitra·vasu, how important is this? With your abundant prowess much worse than this is possible, but,

When I would actually give even my own body
  for the sake of another person
Out of pity and without being asked,
How could I agree to the savagery of killing
  living beings
On account of the kingdom?

In fact, I don't feel that anything is my enemy other than mental defilements.* If you want to be dear to me, then feel sympathy for the person who is tortured by being enslaved to the defilements.

MITRA·VASU: *(smiling angrily)* How can one not have sympathy for such a person, who is both our benefactor and pitiful?

HERO: *(to himself)* It's not possible to change his mind while 3.130
it is dominated by fresh anger. So I shall say this. *(aloud)* Mitra·vasu, get up. Let's go indoors, and I shall enlighten you there.* The day has drawn in now. For,

nidrā|mudr"|âvabandha|vyatikaram a|niśaṃ
padma|kośād apāsyann,
āśā|pūr'|âika|karma|pravaṇa|nija|kara|
prīṇit'|âśeṣa|viśvaḥ,
dṛṣṭaḥ siddhaiḥ prasakta|stuti|mukhara|mukhair
astam apy eṣa gacchann
ekaḥ ślāghyo vivasvān, para|hita|karaṇāy'
âiva yasya prayāsaḥ [18]

niṣkrāntau.

tṛtīyo 'ṅkaḥ.

Removing from the lotus bud day after day
  the closing touch made by the seal of sleep,*
Gratifying the entire universe with his own rays
  inclined for the sole function of *fulfilling hope:*
  filling the four quarters,
Seen here by the Adepts even as he sets, their mouths
  ceaselessly eloquent with hymns,
The shining sun, whose efforts effect the benefit of
  others, is the one to be praised.

The two leave.

End of the third act.

INTRODUCTORY SCENE

4.1 *tataḥ praviśati gṛhīta|vastra|yugalaḥ* KĀÑCUKĪYAḤ, PRATĪHĀRAŚ *ca.*

KĀÑCUKĪYAḤ:

antaḥ|purāṇāṃ vihita|vyavasthaḥ,
pade pade 'haṃ *skhalitāni* rakṣan,
jar"|āturaḥ samprati daṇḍa|nītyā
sarvaṃ nṛpasy' ânukaromi vṛttam [1]

PRATĪHĀRAḤ: ārya, kva nu khalu bhavān prasthitaḥ?

KĀÑCUKĪYAḤ: ādiṣṭo 'smi devyā Mitrāvasor jananyā, yathā, «kañcukin, tvayā daśa|rātraṃ yāvan Malayavatyā jāmātuś ca rakta|vāsāṃsi netavyān' îti.» kutra prathamaṃ gacchāmi? rāja|sutā ca śvaśura|kule vartate, Jīmūtavāhano 'pi yuva|rājena Mitrāvasunā saha samudra|velāṃ draṣṭum adya gata iti mayā śrutam. tan na jāne kiṃ Malayavatyāḥ samīpaṃ gacchāmy ut' āho jāmātur iti.

4.5 PRATĪHĀRAḤ: ārya, varaṃ rāja|putryāḥ samīpa|gamanaṃ, tatra hi kadā cid iyatyā velayā jāmātā pratyāgato bhaviṣyati.

KĀÑCUKĪYAḤ: Sunanda, sādh' ûktam. bhavatā punaḥ kva gamyate?

Thereupon enters a BUTLER, *holding a pair of garments, and a* DOORMAN. 4.1

BUTLER:

> *Running the women of the household*, guarding
> *against stumbles step by step with the help of*
> *my stick*,
> *Decrepit from old age nowadays*, I imitate the entire
> business of the king
> Who, *ordaining the laws inside the cities*,
> guarding *at every stage against wrongs*,
> *By means of the policy of punishment at the right*
> *moment*, is *fond of being praised*.

DOORMAN: Now where are you off to, sir?

BUTLER: I've been asked by the queen, the mother of Mitra·vasu, as follows: "Butler, you must deliver these red garments to Málayavati and our son-in-law over the next ten days."* Where shall I go first? The king's daughter is staying at her father-in-law's, but I've heard that Jimúta·váhana, along with the crown prince Mitra·vasu, has gone today to see the sea tides. So I don't know whether to go to Málayavati or to the son-in-law.

DOORMAN: It's better to go to the king's daughter, sir, because the son-in-law may be returning soon. 4.5

BUTLER: Good point, Sunánda. And where are you going?

PRATĪHĀRAḤ: aham api mahārāja|Viśvāvasunā samādiṣṭaḥ, yathā, «Sunanda, gaccha. Mitrāvasuṃ brūhi, ‹asmin divase pratipad|utsave Malayavatyā jāmātuś c' âitad utsav'|ânurūpaṃ kiñ cid āgatya nirūpay' êti.› » tad gacchatu rāja|putryāḥ sakāśam āryaḥ, aham api Mitrāvasor āhvānāya gacchāmi.

niṣkrāntau.

viṣkambhakaḥ.

DOORMAN: I too have been requested, by the Great King Vishva·vasu, as follows: "Go, Sunánda. Tell Mitra·vasu, 'On this first day of the festival* come and look for something festive for Málayavati and our son-in-law.'" So, you sir, go to the king's daughter, and I myself will go to summon Mitra·vasu.

They both leave.

End of the introductory scene.

ACT FOUR

4.10 *tataḥ praviśati* NĀYAKO MITRĀVASUŚ *ca.*

NĀYAKAḤ:

śayyā śādvalam; āsanaṃ śuci|śilā;
sadma drumāṇām adhaḥ;
śītaṃ nirjhara|vāri pānam; aśanaṃ
kandāḥ; sahāyā mṛgāḥ.
ity a|prārthita|labhya|sarva|vibhave
doṣo 'yam eko vane:
duṣ|prāp'|ârthini yat par'|ârtha|ghaṭanā|
vandhyair vṛthā sthīyate. [2]

MITRĀVASUḤ: *(ūrdhvam avalokya)* kumāra, tvaryatāṃ, tvaryatām! samayo 'yaṃ calitum ambu|rāśeḥ.

NĀYAKAḤ: *(ākarṇya)* samyag upalakṣitam.

udgarjaj|jala|kuñjar'|êndra|rabhas'|ā-
sphāl'|ânubaddh'|ôddhataḥ,
sarvāḥ parvata|kandar'|ôdara|bhuvaḥ
kurvan pratidhvāninīḥ,
uccair uccarati dhvaniḥ śruti|path'|ôn-
māthī yath" âyaṃ, tathā
prāyaḥ preṅkhad|asaṅkhya|śaṅkha|valayā
vel" êyam āgacchati. [3]

4.15 MITRĀVASUḤ: kumāra, nanv āgat" âiva. paśya!

kavalita|lavaṅga|pallava|
kari|makar'|ôdgāra|surabhiṇā payasā
eṣā samudra|velā
ratna|dyuti|rañjitā bhāti. [4]

At that point there enters the HERO *and* MITRA·VASU. 4.10

HERO:

A verdant lot as my bed; a clean stone for a seat;
my home beneath a tree;
The cool water of the cascade to drink; roots for food;
the deer for friends.
So it is, that in the wilderness, where everything
can be obtained unsought, there is one fault:
When beggars are difficult to find, one stays there
in vain, useless at the job of helping others.

MITRA·VASU: *(looking up)* Hurry, prince, please hurry. It's time for the tide to come in.

HERO: *(listening)* Well spotted.

Enhanced in harmony with the vigorous ear flapping
of bull elephants as they trumpet in the water,
Making every piece of ground, every hollow and
valley on the mountain reverberate,
This noise resounds powerfully, beating on the ears.
So it seems it is the tide
That's coming in, with countless breakers in which
shells whoosh back and forth.

MITRA·VASU: It's already come in, prince. Look! 4.15

Its waters fragrant from the spouts of the elephants
and *mákaras* that have chewed on
clove tree shoots,
The sea-tide appears to be tinged with the luster
of jewels.

NĀYAKAḤ: Mitrāvaso, paśya! śarat|samaya|pāṇḍubhiḥ payoda|paṭalaiḥ prāvṛtāḥ Prāley'|âcala|śikhara|śriyam udvahanty acala|sānavaḥ.

MITRĀVASUḤ: kumāra, n' âiv' âmī Malaya|sānavaḥ. nāgānām asthi|saṅghātāḥ khalv ete.

NĀYAKAḤ: *(s'|ôdvegam)* kaṣṭaṃ. kin nimittaṃ punar amī saṅghāta|mṛtyavo jātāḥ?

4.20 MITRĀVASUḤ: kumāra, kumāra, n' âiv' âmī saṅghāta|mṛtyavaḥ.

NĀYAKAḤ: Mitrāvaso, kim anyat?

MITRĀVASUḤ: śrūyatāṃ. purā kila sva|pakṣa|pavan'|âpāsta|sāgara|jalas tarasā rasātalād uddhṛtya bhujaṅ|gamān anudinam āhārayati sma Vainateyaḥ.

NĀYAKAḤ: *(s'|ôdvegam)* kaṣṭam. ati|duṣkaraṃ karoti. tatas tataḥ?

MITRĀVASUḤ: tataḥ sakala|nāga|loka|vināśa|śaṅkinā nāga|rājena Garutmān abhihitaḥ.

4.25 NĀYAKAḤ: *(s'|ādaram)* kiṃ «māṃ bhakṣay"» êti?

MITRĀVASUḤ: na hi, na hi.

NĀYAKAḤ: kim anyat?

MITRĀVASUḤ: idam uktaṃ: «tvad|abhisampāta|trāsāt sahasraśaḥ sravanti bhujaṅg'|âṅganānāṃ garbhāḥ, śiśavaś ca pañcatvam upayānti. evañ ca santati|samucchedād asmākaṃ tav' âiva sv'|ârtha|hānir bhaved, yad|artham

HERO: Look Mitra·vasu! The mountain tops, covered with a veil of cloud as white as in autumn, are as lovely as the peaks of the icy mountains.

MITRA·VASU: Prince, these are not the tops of the Málaya mountain. These are in fact masses of Naga bones.

HERO: *(upset)* This is terrible. What was the cause of these mass deaths?

MITRA·VASU: Prince, prince, these deaths were not really en 4.20
masse.

HERO: How else, Mitra·vasu?

MITRA·VASU: Listen. Apparently, in the past Gáruda, the son of Vínata, violently scattered the seawater with the draft from his wings, dragged out the serpents from the nether regions and ate them day after day.

HERO: *(upset)* This is terrible. What he did was really dreadful. What then?

MITRA·VASU: Then, fearing the destruction of the entire Naga people, the king of the Nagas spoke to Gáruda.

HERO: *(in awe)* Did he say, "Eat me"? 4.25

MITRA·VASU: No, no.

HERO: What else?

MITRA·VASU: This is what he said: "Because of the terror of your attacks the fetuses of female serpents abort in their thousands and the youngsters pass away. If you continue like this, our and your best interests will be harmed because our race will be destroyed by your attack on the

abhipatati bhavān pātālam. tad ek' | âikaṃ bhujaṅgamānām anudivasaṃ samudra | taṭa | sthitasy' âham eva preṣayiṣyām'» îti. pratipannaṃ ca tat pakṣi | rājena.

ity ekaśaḥ pratidinaṃ vihita|vyavastho
yān bhakṣayaty ahi|patīn patag'|âdhirājaḥ,
yāsyanti, yānti ca, gatāś ca dinair vivṛddhiṃ
teṣām amī tuhina|śaila|ruco 'sthi|kūṭāḥ. [5]

4.30 NĀYAKAḤ: kaṣṭaṃ. rakṣitāḥ kil' âivaṃ nāga|rājena pannagāḥ?

jihvā|sahasra|dvitayasya madhye
n' âik" âpi sā tasya kim asti jihvā,
«ek'|âhi|rakṣ'|ârtham ahi|dviṣo 'dya
datto may" ātm"» êti yayā bravīti? [6]

āścaryam, āścaryam!

sarv'|âśuci|nidhānasya kṛta|ghnasya vināśinaḥ
śarīrakasy' âpi kṛte mūḍhāḥ pāpāni kurvate. [7]

kaṣṭam. an | avasān" êyaṃ vipattir nāgānām. *(ātma|gatam)* api nāma śaknuyām ahaṃ sva | śarīra | dānād ekasy' âpi phaṇa|bhṛtaḥ parirakṣāṃ kartum?

4.35 *tataḥ praviśati* PRATĪHĀRAḤ

nether region. So every day I myself will ensure a single serpent is sent to you as you wait on the seashore." And the Bird king agreed to this.

> Thus, one by one, each day, the overlord of flying creatures
> Will eat the masterly snakes, having made this agreement.
> These are the heaps of their bones shining like the frosted sierra
> Since they have, do and will increase day on day.

HERO: This is terrible. This is the so-called protection the Naga king offers his snakes? 4.30

> Does he not have even a single tongue among his thousand double tongues
> With which he can say, "I give myself today to the snakes' enemy in order to save just a single snake"?

It's astonishing, truly astonishing!

> Even for the sake of their body, decaying and ungrateful,
> The locus for everything impure, deluded people commit evil deeds.

This is dreadful. There is no end to this disaster for the Nagas. *(to himself)* Surely it must be possible for me to save just one serpent by the gift of my own body?

At that point there enters the DOORMAN. 4.35

PRATĪHĀRAḤ: ārūḍho 'smi giri|śikharam. *(vilokya)* aye Mitrāvasur jāmātuḥ samīpe vartate. yāvad upasarpāmi. *(upasṛtya praṇamya)* vijayetāṃ kumārau.

MITRĀVASUḤ: Sunanda, kin|nimittam ih' āgamanam?

PRATĪHĀRAḤ: *(karṇe)* evam.

MITRĀVASUḤ: kumāra, tāto mām āhvayate.

4.40 NĀYAKAḤ: gamyatām.

MITRĀVASUḤ: kumāreṇ' âpi bahu|pratyavāye 'smin pradeśe kutūhalān na ciraṃ sthātavyam.

niṣkrānto MITRĀVASUḤ PRATĪHĀRAŚ *ca.*

NĀYAKAḤ: yāvad aham api giri|śikharād avatīrya samudra|taṭam avalokayāmi. *(parikrāmati.)*

NEPATHYE: ⌈hā puttaa Śaṅkhacūla! kahaṃ vāvādiamāṇo kila ajja tuvaṃ mae pekkhidavvo?⌋

4.45 NĀYAKAḤ: *(ākarṇya)* aye, yoṣita iv' ārta|pralāpaḥ. tad yāvad upetya k" êyaṃ kuto 'syā bhaya|kāraṇam iti sphuṭī|karomi. *(parikrāmati.)*

tataḥ praviśati krandantyā VṚDDHAY" *ânugamyamānaḥ* ŚAṄKHACŪḌO, *gopāyita|vastra|yugalaḥ* KIṄKARAŚ *ca.*

VṚDDHĀ: *(s'|âsram)* ⌈hā puttaa Śaṅkhacūla! kahaṃ vāvādiamāṇo kila ajja tuvaṃ mae pekkhidavvo?⌋ *(cibuke gṛhītvā)* ⌈imiṇā mukha|candeṇa virahidaṃ andhaārī|bhavissadi pāālaṃ.⌋

DOORMAN: I've climbed to the top of the mountain. *(looking around)* Ah, Mitra·vasu is in the company of the son-in-law. I'll go to him. *(approaching him and bowing)* May the young gentlemen be victorious!

MITRA·VASU: Sunánda, what's the reason for coming here?

DOORMAN: *(in his ear)* This is why.

MITRA·VASU: Prince, I am called away.

HERO: By all means, go. 4.40

MITRA·VASU: The prince himself shouldn't linger in this rather dangerous place out of curiosity.

MITRA·VASU *and the* DOORMAN *leave.*

HERO: I'll just come down from the mountain top too and have a look at the shoreline. *(He moves about.)*

OFF STAGE: Oh, my child, Shankha·chuda! How can I watch today when you are due to be slaughtered?

HERO: *(listening)* Hmm, sounds like a woman's cry of dis- 4.45
tress. I shall approach and clarify who she is and what is the cause of her fear. *(He moves about.)*

At that point there enters SHANKHA·CHUDA *followed by an* OLD WOMAN *who is weeping and a* RETAINER *looking after a pair of garments.*

OLD WOMAN: *(in tears)* Oh, my little boy! Shankha·chuda! How can I look at you today when you are due to be slaughtered? *(holding his chin)* The nether region deprived of this moon face will be darkened.

ŚAṄKHACŪḌAḤ: amba, kim evam ati|viklavā sutarām ātmānaṃ pīḍayasi?

VṚDDHĀ: *(nirvarṇya, putrasy' âṅgāny āmṛśantī)* ⌜hā puttaa! kahaṃ de a|diṭṭha|sūra|suumāraṃ sarīraṃ ṇigghiṇa|hiao Galulo āhārayissadi?⌟

4.50 *kaṇṭhe gṛhītvā roditi.*

ŚAṄKHACŪḌAḤ: amba, alam! alaṃ paridevitena. paśya,

krodī|karoti prathamaṃ jātaṃ nityam a|nityatā,
dhātr" îva jananī paścāt! tadā śokasya kaḥ kramaḥ? [8]

VṚDDHĀ: ⌜hā puttaa! ciṭṭha. muhuttaaṃ pi dāva vadanaṃ de pekkhissaṃ.⌟

KIṄKARAḤ: ⌜ehi, kumāla! kiṃ tava etāe bhaṇantīe? putta|śiṇeha|mohidā kkhu eśā ṇa lāa|kajjaṃ jāṇādi.⌟

4.55 ŚAṄKHACŪḌAḤ: bhadra, ayam aham āgacchāmi.

KIṄKARAḤ: *(ātma/gatam)* ⌜āṇīdo kkhu mae vajjha|śilā|śamīvaṃ Śaṅkhacūlo. jāva edaṃ vajjha|ciṇhaṃ latt'|aṃsua|jualaṃ daïa vajjha|śilaṃ daṃśemi.⌟

NĀYAKAḤ: aye, iyam asau yoṣit. *(ŚAṄKHACŪḌAṂ dṛṣṭvā)* nūnam anen' âpy asyāḥ sutena bhavitavyaṃ, yad|artham ākrandati. *(samantād avalokya)* na khalu punaḥ kiñ cid bhaya|kāraṇaṃ paśyāmi. tat kuto 'sya bhayaṃ bhaviṣyat'

SHANKHA·CHUDA: Mom, you are already really distressed, so why are you winding yourself up like this even more?

OLD WOMAN: *(looking closely and stroking her son's limbs)* Oh, my little boy! How will hard-hearted Gáruda eat your so tender body that has never seen the sun?

She takes him by the neck and weeps. 4.50

SHANKHA·CHUDA: Mom, enough! There's no point in grieving. Look,

> Impermanence is always the first to cuddle
> the new-born,
> The mother comes after, like the nurse!
> What then is the reason for grief?

OLD WOMAN: Oh, my little boy! Stay. I want to look at your face for just a moment.

RETAINER: Come, young man! There's nothing for you in her talking. She's deluded by her affection for her child. She doesn't understand duty to the king.

SHANKHA·CHUDA: Good man, here, I am coming. 4.55

RETAINER: *(to himself)* I've actually brought Shankha·chuda close to the slaughter stone. So I'll give him this pair of red garments that are the victim's sign and then show him the slaughter stone.

HERO: Ah, here is the woman. *(seeing* SHANKHA·CHUDA*)* Surely this must be her son, for whom she is keening. *(looking all around)* But I cannot see any cause for fear. So shall I go and ask her what it is she fears? But now a

îti kim upetya pṛcchāmi? atha vā prasakta ev' âyam ālāpaḥ. kadā cid ita eva vyaktir bhaviṣyati. tad viṭap'|ântaritas tāvac chṛṇomi.

KIṄKARAḤ: *(s'|âsram, kṛt'|âñjaliḥ)* ⌜kumāla Śaṅkhacūla, eśo śāmiṇo ādeśo ti kalia īdiśaṃ pi ṇiṭṭhulaṃ mantīadi.⌟

ŚAṄKHACŪḌAḤ: bhadra, kathaya.

4.60 KIṄKARAḤ: ⌜ṇāa|lāo Vāśuī āṇavedi!⌟

ŚAṄKHACŪḌAḤ: *(śirasy añjaliṃ kṛtvā, s'|ādaram)* kiṃ mām ājñāpayati svāmī?

KIṄKARAḤ: ⌜«edaṃ latt'|aṃsua|jualaṃ palihia āloha vajjha|śilaṃ, jeṇa latt'|aṃśua|ciṇh'|ôvalakkhidaṃ Galulo gaṇhia āhāla|kalaṇāa ṇaïśśadi.»⌟

NĀYAKAḤ: *(s'|âsram)* kaṣṭam! asau Vāsukinā parityaktas tapasvī.

KIṄKARAḤ: ⌜Śaṅkhacūla, gaṇha edaṃ.⌟ *(vastra|yugalam arpayati.)*

4.65 ŚAṄKHACŪḌAḤ: *(s'|ādaram)* upanaya. *(iti gṛhītvā śirasi svāmy|ādeśam arpayati.)*

VṚDDHĀ: *(putra|haste vāsasī dṛṣṭvā, s'|ôrastāḍanam)* ⌜hā vaccha! edaṃ kkhu taṃ vajjha|ciṇhaṃ vasaṇaṃ, jeṇa bhāedi me hiaaṃ.⌟ *(moham upagatā.)*

KIṄKARAḤ: ⌜āśaṇṇā kkhu Galulassa āgamaṇa|velā. tā lahu avakkamāmi.⌟ *(niṣkrāntaḥ.)*

conversation has just started. This might clarify things. So I'll just listen hidden among the branches.

RETAINER: *(tearfully, with hands held together in respect)* Young man, it's because it's by our master's command that this hard speech is addressed to you.

SHANKHA·CHUDA: Speak, good man.

RETAINER: Vásuki, the chief of the Nagas, commands! 4.60

SHANKHA·CHUDA: *(placing his hands together in respect on his head, attentively)* What does our master command me?

RETAINER: "Put on this pair of red garments and mount the slaughter stone, where, identified by the sign of the red garments, Gáruda will seize you and take you off to eat."

HERO: *(tearfully)* This is terrible! Here is the poor wretch offered up by Vásuki.

RETAINER: Shankha·chuda, take this. *(He offers the pair of garments.)*

SHANKHA·CHUDA: *(in awe)* Bring it here. *(Thus, taking them,* 4.65
he places the command of his master on his head.)*

OLD WOMAN: *(seeing the clothes in the hand of her son, beating her chest)* Oh, my boy! These are the clothes, the sign of the victim. They terrify my heart. *(She swoons.)*

RETAINER: The time for Gáruda to come has arrived. So I'm leaving quickly. *(He leaves.)*

ŚAṄKHACŪḌAḤ: amba, samāśvasihi, samāśvasihi!

VṚDDHĀ: *(samāśvasya, s'|âsram)* ⌜hā jāda! hā puttaa! hā maṇoraha|sada|laddha! kahiṃ tumaṃ puṇo pekkhissaṃ?⌟ *(kaṇṭhe gṛhītvā roditi.)*

4.70 NĀYAKAḤ: *(s'|âsram)* aho nairghṛṇyaṃ Garutmataḥ! api ca,

mūḍhāyā muhur aśru|santati|mucaḥ
kṛtvā pralāpān bahūn,
«kas trātā mama putrak'?» êti kṛpaṇaṃ
dikṣu kṣipantyā dṛśam
aṅke mātur apāśritaṃ śiśum imaṃ
tyaktvā ghṛṇām aśnataś
cañcur n' âiva, khag'|âdhipasya hṛdayaṃ
vajreṇa, manye, kṛtam. [9]

ŚAṄKHACŪḌAḤ: *(ambāyā aśrūṇi parimārjayan)* amba, alam alaṃ vaiklavyena! nanu samāśvasihi. samāśvasihi!

VṚDDHĀ: *(s'|âsram)* ⌜puttaa, kahaṃ samassasimi? kiṃ eka|putto tti kid'|âṇukampeṇa ṇivattāvido si ṇāa|lāeṇa? hā kadanta|hadaa, kahaṃ dāṇi tue ṇigghiṇa|hiaeṇa evvaṃ vitthiṇṇe jīva|loe mama puttao evva sumarido? savvahā hada mhi manda|bhāiṇī.⌟ *(mūrchāṃ nāṭayati.)*

SHANKHA·CHUDA: Be brave, mom, please be brave!

OLD WOMAN: *(coming round, tearfully)* Oh, my boy! Oh, my little boy! Oh, you, won from a hundred wishes! Where shall I see you again? *(Taking him by the neck, she weeps.)*

HERO: *(tearfully)* Aah, the heartlessness of Gáruda! And what is more, 4.70

I think the Lord of Birds' heart is made of diamond,
not just his beak,
Abandoning pity and eating this child resting on
the lap of his mother
Who's shedding streams of tears all the while,
wailing and wailing,
Demanding, "Who will save my son?" casting
pitiful looks in all directions.

SHANKHA·CHUDA: *(wiping away his mother's tears)* Mom, enough, don't be so agitated. Surely you can bear up. Be brave!*

OLD WOMAN: My little boy, how can I bear up? Why didn't the Naga king put you aside out of compassion, knowing that you are an only son? Oh death, you vile thing, how come it is my little boy that you, with your pitiless heart, have remembered like this in the wide world of beings? I am stricken in every way, with my miserable lot. *(She acts a swoon.)*

NĀYAKAḤ:

> ārtaṃ, kaṇṭha|gata|prāṇaṃ,
> parityaktaṃ sva|bāndhavaiḥ
> trāye n' âinaṃ yadi, tataḥ
> kaḥ śarīreṇa me guṇaḥ? [10]

4.75 tad yāvad upasarpāmi.

ŚAṄKHACŪḌAḤ: amba, saṃstambhay' ātmānam.

VṚDDHĀ: ⌜hā puttaa! Saṃkhacūla, dul|laho satthaṃbho. jadā evva ṇāa|loa|parirakkhaeṇa Vāsuiṇā saaṃ pariccatto si, tadā ko de parittāṇaṃ karissadi?⌟

NĀYAKAḤ: *(upasṛtya)* nanv ayam aham!

VṚDDHĀ: *(sa|sambhramam uttarīyeṇa putram ācchādya,* NĀYAKAM *upasṛtya)* ⌜Galula! Viṇadā|ṇandaṇa, vāvādehi maṃ! ahaṃ de āhāra|ṇimittaṃ parikappidā.⌟

4.80 NĀYAKAḤ: *(s'|âsram)* aho putra|vātsalyam!

> asyā vilokya, manye,
> putra|snehena viklavatvam idam
> a|karuṇa|hṛdayaḥ karuṇāṃ
> kurvīta bhujaṅga|śatrur api. [11]

ŚAṄKHACŪḌAḤ: amba, alam alaṃ trāsena! na khalv ayaṃ nāga|śatruḥ. paśya,

HERO:

> What virtue is there in this body of mine if I
> do not save him,
> Abandoned by his own relatives, pained, his life
> in his throat!

That's why I must go to them right now. 4.75

SHANKHA·CHUDA: Mom, compose yourself.

OLD WOMAN: Oh my little boy! Shankha·chuda, it's hard to be composed. When you've been abandoned by Vásuki himself, the protector of the Naga people, who is it will save you?

HERO: *(approaching)* For sure, I am he!

OLD WOMAN: *(confusedly covering her son with her shawl, approaching the* HERO*)* Gáruda! You who pleased Vínata,* kill me! I have been chosen as the food lure for you.

HERO: *(in tears)* Oh, the tenderness for her son! 4.80

> Seeing this distress of hers on account of her son,
> I think
> Even the enemy of snakes, who has no compassion
> in his heart, will be compassionate.

SHANKHA·CHUDA: Mom, enough! There's no point in being afraid. This isn't the enemy of the snakes. See,

mah"|âhi|mastiṣka|vibheda|mukta|
  rakta|cchaṭā|carcita|caṇḍa|cañcuḥ
kv' âsau Garutmān, kva ca nāma soma|
  saumya|svabhāv'|ākṛtir eṣa sādhuḥ? [12]

VṚDDHĀ: ⌜hā puttaa! ahaṃ puṇa tujjha maraṇa | bhīdā savvaṃ eva Galula|maaṃ pekkhāmi.⌟

4.85 NĀYAKAḤ: amba, mā bhaiṣīḥ. nanv ayam ahaṃ vidyā | dharaḥ, tvat|suta|saṃrakṣaṇ'|ârtham ev' āyātaḥ.

VṚDDHĀ: *(sa|harṣam)* ⌜puttaa, puṇo puṇo evvaṃ bhaṇa!⌟

NĀYAKAḤ: amba, kim anena punaḥ punar abhihitena? karmaṇ" âiva sampādayāmi.

VṚDDHĀ: *(śirasy añjaliṃ kṛtvā)* ⌜puttaa, ciraṃ jīva!⌟

NĀYAKAḤ:

mam' âitad, amb', ârpaya vadhya|cihnaṃ.
  prāvṛtya yāvad Vinat"|ātmajāya
putrasya te jīvita|rakṣaṇ'|ârthaṃ
  svaṃ deham āhārayituṃ dadāmi. [13]

4.90 VṚDDHĀ: *(karṇau pidhāya)* ⌜paḍihadaṃ khu edaṃ! tumaṃ pi me Saṃkhacūla|ṇivviseso puttao evva. aha va Saṃkhacūlādo ahiadaro, jo evvaṃ bandhu|jaṇa|pariccattaṃ me puttaaṃ sarīra|ppadāṇeṇa rakkhiduṃ icchasi.⌟

The difference between that Gáruda, whose
fierce beak is streaked with clots of blood loosed
from tearing out the brains of big serpents,
And this good man, whose nature and appearance
is gentle like the moon's.

OLD WOMAN: Oh, my little boy! I am terrified about you dying and see Gáruda in everything.

HERO: Mother, do not be afraid. For sure, see, I am a Magician. I have come here in order to help protect your son. 4.85

OLD WOMAN: *(delighted)* Son, say it again and again!

HERO: Mother, there's no point saying it again and again. I'll make it happen by actually doing it.

OLD WOMAN: *(placing her hands together in respect on her head)* Son, may you live long!

HERO:

Mother, give me this victim's mark. I will put it on
and offer my own body
To the son of Vínata to eat in order to protect the life
of your son.

OLD WOMAN: *(blocking her ears)* Perish the thought! And you are no different from my own little boy, Shankha·chuda. In fact, you are better than Shankha·chuda, because you want to protect my little boy with the gift of your body when he has been abandoned by his own kind. 4.90

ŚAṄKHACŪḌAḤ: *(sa|smitam)* aho, jagad|viparītam asya mahā|sattvasya caritam. kutaḥ,

Viśvāmitraḥ śva|māṃsaṃ
śva|paca iva pur" |âbhakṣayad yan|nimittaṃ,
Nāḍījaṅgho vijaghne
kṛta|tad|upakṛtir yat|kṛte Gautamena,
putro 'yaṃ Kāśyapasya
pratidinam uragān atti Tārkṣyo yad|arthaṃ,
prāṇāṃs tān eva, citraṃ,
tṛṇam iva kṛpayā yaḥ par'|ârthe jahāti. [14]

(NĀYAKAM *uddiśya)* bho mahātman, darśitā tvay" êyam ātma|pradān'|âdhyavasāyān nirvyājā mayi dayālutā. tad alam anena nirbandhena. kutaḥ,

jāyante ca mriyante ca
mādṛśāḥ kṣudra|jantavaḥ.
par'|ârthe baddha|kakṣāṇāṃ
tvādṛśām udbhavaḥ kutaḥ? [15]

4.95 tat kim anena? mucyatām ayam adhyavasāyaḥ.

NĀYAKAḤ: (ŚAṄKHACŪḌAṂ *haste gṛhītvā)* kumāra Śaṃkhacūḍa, na me cirāl labdh'|âvasarasya par'|ârtha|sampādana|manorathasy' ântarāyaṃ kartum arhati bhavān. *(pādayoḥ patitvā)* tad alaṃ vikalpena. dīyatāṃ vadhya|cihnam.

ŚAṄKHACŪḌAḤ: bho mahā|sattva, kim anena vṛthā prayāsena? na khalu Śaṅkhacūḍaḥ śaṅkha|dhavalaṃ Śaṅkhapāla|kulaṃ malinī|kariṣyati. atha te vayam anukampanīyāḥ, tad iyam asmad|vipatti|viklavā yathā na parityajati jīvitam ambā, tath" âbhyupāyaś cintyatām.

SHANKHA·CHUDA: *(smiling)* Well, the behavior of this great person goes against the norm. Because,

It was the cause of Vishva·mitra once eating dog flesh
like a dog-cooker;
It was the reason that Gáutama killed the crane
Nadi·jangha to whom he was obliged;
It is the point of Tarkshya, the son of Káshyapa,
eating snakes every day;
That very life breath he splendidly gives up,
like a straw, in pity for another's sake.*

(addressing the HERO*)* Oh, noble-souled man, you have shown this sincere compassion for me through your resolve to give your self, but do not persist. For,

Inferior creatures like me are born and they die.
Where do people like you come from,
Who are ready to do anything to help others?

So enough of this. Abandon this resolve. 4.95

HERO: *(taking* SHANKHA·CHUDA *by his hand)* Shankha·chuda, young man, it's not appropriate for you to obstruct my desire to help others, a long awaited opportunity. *(bowing at his feet)* That's why you needn't hesitate. Give me the victim's mark.

SHANKHA·CHUDA: Oh, noble-souled man, there's no point in troubling yourself pointlessly. Shankha·chuda will never stain the clan of Shankha·pala that is as white as the conch. So, if we deserve your sympathy, think of a plan to prevent my mother here from giving up her life tortured by my disaster.

NĀYAKAḤ: kim atra cintyate? cintita ev' âbhyupāyaḥ. sa tu tvad|āyattaḥ.

ŚAṄKHACŪḌAḤ: katham iva?

NĀYAKAḤ:

4.100 mriyate mriyamāṇe yā
tvayi, jīvati jīvati,
tāṃ yad' îcchasi jīvantīṃ,
rakṣ' ātmānaṃ mam' âsubhiḥ. [16]

ayam abhyupāyaḥ. tad arpaya tvaritaṃ vadhya|cihnam. yāvad anen' ātmānam ācchādya vadhya|śilām ārohāmi. tvam api jananīṃ puras|kṛty' âsmād deśān nivartasva. kadā cid iyam āloky' âiva sannikṛṣṭam āghāta|sthānaṃ strī|sahabhuvā kātaratven' âmbā prāṇān jahyāt. kiṃ ca na paśyati bhavān idaṃ vipanna|pannag'|âneka|kaṅkāla|saṅkulaṃ mahā|śmaśānam? tathā hi,

cañcac|cañc"|ûddhṛt'|ârdha|cyuta|piśita|lava|
grāsa|saṃvṛddha|gardhair
gṛdhrair ārabdha|pakṣa|dvitaya|vidhutibhir
baddha|sāndr'|ândhakāre
vaktr'|ôdvāntāḥ patantyaś chim iti śikhi|śikhā|
śreṇayo 'smiñ śivānām
āsra|srotasy ajasra|sruta|bahala|vasā|
vāsa|visre svananti. [17]

ŚAṄKHACŪḌAḤ: kathaṃ na paśyāmi?

HERO: What needs planning here? The plan is already conceived. But it depends on you.

SHANKHA·CHUDA: How so?

HERO:

> If you want her living, when you dying she'd die 4.100
> And you living she'd live, then save your life
> with my life.

I am the plan. Just give me the victim's mark quickly, so that I can put it on and get up on the slaughter stone. And you should leave this place with your mother ahead of you. It's possible your mother might lose her life out of feminine faint-heartedness, just looking around this slaughter place hereabout. Don't you see this vast charnel ground crowded with the skeletons of many dead serpents? For,

> The jets of burning fire, vomited from the mouths
> of jackals, make a noise like "chim"
> As they fall in the stream of blood that stinks with
> the smell of thick marrow that runs on and on,
> Here in this place made densely dark by vultures
> who have begun to shake their paired wings,
> Their greed leaping at mouths of flesh chunks
> half dropped as they're yanked out by their
> quivering beaks.

SHANKHA·CHUDA: How can I not see it?

pratidinam a|śūnyam *ahin" ā-*
hāreṇa Vināyak'|āhita|prīti
śaśi|dhaval'|âsthika|pālaṃ
vapur iva raudraṃ śmaśānam idam. [18]

4.105 tad gaccha. kim ebhis trāsan'|ôpāyaiḥ? āsannaḥ khalu Garuḍasy' āgamana|samayaḥ. *(mātur agrato jānubhyāṃ sthitvā, śiro|nihit'|âñjaliḥ)* amba, tvam api nivartasv' êdānīm.

samutpatsyāmahe, mātar,
yasyāṃ yasyāṃ gatau vayam,
tasyāṃ tasyāṃ, priya|sute,
mātā bhūyās tvam eva naḥ. [19]

pādayoḥ patati.

VṚDDHĀ: *(s'|âsram ātma|gatam)* ⌜kahaṃ? paccimaṃ se vaaṇaṃ?⌟ *(prakāśam)* ⌜puttaa, tumaṃ ujjhia aṇṇado me pāā ṇa pasaranti. tā tue saha *gamissaṃ.*⌟

ŚAṄKHACŪḌAḤ: *(utthāya)* yāvad aham api n' âtidūre bhagavantaṃ dakṣiṇa|Gokarṇaṃ pradakṣiṇī|kṛtya svāmy|ādeśam anutiṣṭhāmi.

4.110 *ubhau niṣkrāntau.*

NĀYAKAḤ: kaṣṭam. na sampannam abhilaṣitam. tat ko 'tr' âbhyupāyaḥ?

Everyday this charnel ground
has a frightful appearance, preserving bones as white
as the moon and delights Gáruda as it is never
empty of snakes for food :
delights Ganésha with its embodiment as Shiva,
adorned with a moon, and pale bones and
*skulls and never without its snake garland.**

So, go. What's the point of these alarming plans? The time 4.105
for Gáruda's arrival is quite near. *(kneeling in front of his mother, placing his hands together on his head in respect)* Mother, you too must now turn back.

In whatever realm we may be reborn, mother,
May it be you who are my mother,
you who loves your son!

He bows at her feet.

OLD WOMAN: *(tearfully to herself)* What's this? His last words? *(aloud)* My little boy, leaving you behind, my feet could not move away. So I will *go : die* with you.

SHANKHA·CHUDA: *(getting up)* I myself shall next circumambulate the holy one at the nearby southern Gokárna* and then carry out my master's order.

The two leave. 4.110

HERO: This is terrible. My wish is not fulfilled. So what's the plan now?

sahasā praviśya

KĀÑCUKĪYAḤ: idaṃ vāso|yugalam…

NĀYAKAḤ: *(dṛṣṭvā sa|harṣam, ātma|gatam)* diṣṭyā! siddham abhivāñchitam anen' â|tarkit'|ôpanatena rakt'|âṃśuka|yugalena.

4.115 KĀÑCUKĪYAḤ: idaṃ vāso|yugalaṃ devyā Mitrāvasor jananyā kumārāya preṣitam. paridhattāṃ kumāraḥ.

NĀYAKAḤ: upanaya.

KĀÑCUKĪYA *upanayati.*

NĀYAKAḤ: *(gṛhītv" ātma|gatam)* saphalī|bhūto me Malayavatyāḥ pāṇi|grahaṇa|vidhiḥ. *(paridhāya, prakāśam)* kañcukin, gamyatām. mad|vacanād abhivādanīyā devī.

KĀÑCUKĪYAḤ: yad ājñāpayati kumāraḥ. *(niṣkrāntaḥ.)*

NĀYAKAḤ:

4.120 vāso|yugam idaṃ raktaṃ
prāpta|kāle mam' āgatam
karoti mahatīṃ prītiṃ
par'|ârthaṃ deham ujjhataḥ. [20]

(diśo vilokya) yath" âyaṃ calita|Malay'|âcala|śikhara|śilā|sañcayaḥ pracaṇḍo nabhasvāṃs, tathā tarkayāmy, āsannī|bhūtaḥ pakṣi|rāja iti. api ca,

entering hastily

DOORMAN: This pair of garments...

HERO: *(seeing him, delighted, to himself)* Thank goodness! What I've wanted is made possible by this pair of red garments brought out of the blue.

DOORMAN: This pair of garments has been sent to the prince by the queen, the mother of Mitra·vasu. May the prince put them on. 4.115

HERO: Bring them here.

The DOORMAN *brings them.*

HERO: *(taking them, to himself)* My taking the hand of Málayavati in marriage has borne fruit. *(putting them on, aloud)* Doorman, you can go. Respectfully salute the queen in my name.

DOORMAN: As the prince requests. *(He leaves.)*

HERO:

> The pair of red garments that has come to me 4.120
> at the right time
> Makes me greatly happy as I surrender my body
> to help another.

(looking all around) I guess that the King of Birds is arriving since this furious wind rattles the heaps of rocks on top of Málaya mountain. In fact,

tulyāḥ saṃvartak'|âbhraiḥ
pidadhati gaganaṃ paṅktayaḥ pakṣatīnāṃ,
tīraṃ vegān nirastaṃ
kṣipati bhuva iva plāvanāy' âmbu sindhoḥ,
kurvan kalp'|ânta|śaṅkāṃ
sapadi ca sa|bhayaṃ vīkṣito dig|dvip'|êndrair,
deh'|ôddyoto daś' āśāḥ
kapiśayati śiśu|dvādaś'|āditya|dīptiḥ. [21]

tad yāvad asau n' āgacchaty eva Śaṅkhacūḍaḥ, tāvad tvaritataram imāṃ vadhya|śilām ārohāmi. *(tathā kṛtv", ôpaviśya, sparśaṃ nāṭayan)* aho sparśo 'syāḥ!

na tathā sukhayati manye
Malayavatī Malaya|candana|ras'|ārdrā,
abhivāñchit'|ârtha|siddhyai
vadhya|śil" êyaṃ yathā spṛṣṭā. [22]

4.125 atha vā, kiṃ Malayavatyā?

śayitena mātur aṅke
visrabdhaṃ śaiśave na tat prāptam,
labdhaṃ sukhaṃ may" âsyā
vadhya|śilāyā yad utsaṅge. [23]

tad ayam āgata eva Garutmān. yāvad ātmānam ācchādya tiṣṭhāmi. *(tathā karoti.)*

tataḥ praviśati GARUḌAḤ.

GARUḌAḤ: eṣa bhoḥ!

The rows of his plumage overcast the sky like clouds
 at the end of the world,
With his speed he hurls the seawater scattered
 on the shore as if to flood the earth,
And instantly creating fear of universal destruction,
 as he's beheld in terror by the elephants
 of the four quarters,
His body shining, alight like the twelve newly risen
 suns, he makes the ten quarters brown.*

So, before Shankha·chuda himself comes back, I'll quickly climb onto this slaughter stone. *(doing so, sitting and acting its touch)* Ah, how it feels!

I don't think Málayavati when she is wet
 with the juice of sandal from Málaya,
Has given me such pleasure as the touch of this
 slaughter stone that wins me what I crave

In fact, who needs Málayavati? 4.125

The happiness I find here in the lap of this
 slaughter stone
I never had lying at ease as a child in the lap
 of my mother.

Here's Gáruda coming. I'll dress and wait. *(He does so.)*

At that point GÁRUDA *enters.*

GÁRUDA: Aha! Here he is.

4.130 kṣiptvā bimbaṃ him'|âṃśor,
bhaya|kṛta|valayāṃ saṃharan Śeṣa|mūrtiṃ,
s'|ānandaṃ syandan'|âśva|
trasana|vicalite pūṣṇi dṛṣṭo 'grajena,
eṣa prānt'|âvasajjaj|
jala|dhara|paṭal'|âtyāyatī|bhūta|pakṣaḥ
prāpto velā|mahīdhraṃ
Malayam aham ahi|grāsa|gṛdhnuḥ kṣaṇena. [24]

NĀYAKAḤ:

saṃrakṣatā pannagam adya puṇyaṃ
may" ârjitaṃ yat sva|śarīra|dānāt,
bhave bhave tena mam' âivam evaṃ
bhūyāt par'|ârthaḥ khalu deha|lābhaḥ. [25]

GARUḌAḤ: *(nāyakaṃ nirvarṇya)*

asmin vadhya|śilā|tale nipatitaṃ
śeṣān ahīn rakṣituṃ
nirbhidy' âśani|daṇḍa|caṇḍatarayā
cañcv" âdhunā vakṣasi
bhoktuṃ bhoginam uddharāmi tarasā
rakt'|âmbara|prāvṛtaṃ,
digdhaṃ mad|bhaya|dīryamāṇa|hṛdaya|
prasyandin" êv' âsṛjā. [26]

(abhipatya NĀYAKAṂ *gṛhṇāti. nepathyāt puṣpāṇi patanti, dundubhi|dhvaniś ca. ūrdhvaṃ dṛṣṭv" ākarṇya ca)* aye, puṣpa|vṛṣṭir dundubhi|dhvaniś ca.

Glancing at the disc of the cool-rayed moon, 4.130
curling Shesha up into a circle* in terror,
Seen with joy by my elder brother when
the nourishing sun was shaken by the fear
of its chariot horses,
My wings extended by the cloud layer
streaming from the tips,
See, greedy for a mouthful of snake, in a moment
I have reached Málaya, the mountain
on the shore.

HERO:

By the merit I have accrued today by protecting
a snake through the gift of my own body,
In every birth may I in this very way acquire
a body in order to help others.*

GÁRUDA: *(examining the hero)*

His lot is this slaughter stone, so as to save
the remaining snakes.
I shall split open his chest now with my beak
more terrible than a thunderbolt
Then lift him up directly to eat, this snake
covered in red clothing
As if smeared with the blood oozing from its heart
bursting open in fear of me.

(Swooping down, he grabs the HERO. *From behind the curtain flowers rain down, and there is the sound of drums. Looking up and listening)* Ah, there is a rain of flowers and the sound of drums.

4.135 āmod'|ānandit'|âlir nipatati kim iyaṃ
puṣpa|vṛṣṭir nabhastaḥ?
svarge kiṃ v" âiṣa cakraṃ mukharayati diśāṃ
dundubhīnāṃ ninādaḥ?
(vihasya) ā! jñātaṃ! so 'pi, manye, mama java|marutā
kampitaḥ pārijātaḥ
sārdhaṃ Saṃvartak'|âbhrair idam api rasitaṃ
jāta|saṃhāra|śaṅkaiḥ. [27]

NĀYAKAḤ: *(ātma|gatam)* diṣṭyā kṛt'|ârtho 'smi!

GARUḌAḤ: *(kalayan)*

nāgānāṃ *rakṣitā* bhāti
gurur eṣa yathā mama,
tathā sarp'|âśan'|āśaṅkāṃ
vyaktam ady' *âpanesyati*. [28]

tad yāvad ahaṃ Malaya|śikharam āruhya yath"|êṣṭam ahārayāmi.

4.140 NĀYAKAṂ *gṛhītvā niṣkrāntaḥ.*

caturtho 'ṅkaḥ.

Why does there fall from the sky a rain of flowers* 4.135
that delights the bees with its fragrance?
Why too this roar of drums in heaven that makes
the whole compass sound?
(laughing aloud) Aah! I understand! I think
the *parijáta* tree is shaken by the draft of wind
from my speed
And this is the thunder that accompanies
the Samvártaka clouds presuming the destruction
of the universe is at hand.

HERO: *(to himself)* Thank heavens! My mission is accomplished.

GÁRUDA: *(hefting him)*

As this *guardian* of the Nagas seems *heavy* to me,
Clearly he'll *take away* my hunger for eating
snakes today!
This *savior* of the Nagas looks like my *teacher*
Since today he will clearly *put paid to* my desire
to eat snakes!

Now I'll perch on the top of Málaya and eat him at my leisure.

Clutching the HERO, *he leaves.* 4.140

End of Act Four.

ACT FIVE

5.1 *tataḥ praviśati* PRATĪHĀRAḤ.

PRATĪHĀRAḤ:

sva|gṛh'|ôdyāna|gate 'pi
snigdhe pāpaṃ viśaṅkyate snehāt.
kim u dṛṣṭa|bahv|apāya|
pratibhaya|kāntāra|madhya|sthe? [1]

tathā hi, jala | nidhi | vel" | âvalokana | kutūhalī niṣkrāntaḥ kumāro Jīmūtavāhanaś cirayat' îti duḥkham āste mahā|rājo Viśvāvasuḥ, samādiṣṭaś c' âsmi tena, yathā, «Sunanda! śrutaṃ mayā sannihita|Garuḍa|pratibhayam uddeśaṃ gato jāmātā Jīmūtavāhanas tatra cirayat' îti. śaṅkita iv' âsmy anena vṛttāntena. tvaritataraṃ viditv" āgaccha, kim asau sva|gṛhaṃ gato vā na v"» êti. tad yāvat tatr' âiva gacchāmi. *(parikrāmann, agrato dṛṣṭvā)* aye, ayam asau Jīmūtavāhanasya pitā Jīmūtaketur uṭaj' | âṅgaṇe saha | dharma | cāriṇyā vadhvā Malayavatyā paryupāsyamānas tiṣṭhati. tathā hi,

kṣaume bhaṅgavatī taraṅgita|daśe
phen'|âmbu|tulye vahan,
Jāhnavy" êva *virājitaḥ sa/vayasā*
devyā mahā|puṇyayā,
dhatte toya|nidher ayaṃ su|sadṛśīṃ
Jīmūtaketuḥ śriyaṃ,
yasy' âiṣ" ântika|vartinī *Malayavaty*
ābhāti velā yathā. [2]

Thereupon there enters the DOORMAN. 5.1

DOORMAN:

Out of affection one is apprehensive of danger
even when a loved one steps into one's
own garden.
How much more when they are in the midst
of a fearsome wilderness where the perils are
many and apparent?

For example, the great king Vishva·vasu is uneasy because Prince Jimúta·váhana has been a long time gone, curious to watch the sea tides, and I've been instructed by him as follows: "Sunánda, I have heard that our son-in-law Jimúta·váhana has been a long time at that dangerous place where Gáruda is about. I am unsettled by this news. Go quickly and check whether or not he has returned to his own home." That's why I am off there now. *(moving about, looking off stage)* Ah, here's Jimúta·ketu, the father of Jimúta·váhana, in the courtyard of his hermitage, being waited upon by his wedded wife and his daughter-in-law, Málayavati. For sure,

Jimúta·ketu here imparts a glory much like
that of the ocean,
Clothed in a pair of waving silken garments,
hems billowing like foaming water,
Shimmering : *In state* with his Ganges-like queen,
in her vigor : *with its birds*, rich in virtue,
While *Málayavati* : *Málaya mountain* appears here
close by as the shore.

5.5 tad upasarpāmi.

tataḥ praviśaty āsana|sthaḥ patnī|vadhū|sameto JĪMŪTA-KETUḤ.

JĪMŪTAKETUḤ:

> bhuktāni yauvana|sukhāni; yaśo vikīrṇaṃ;
> rājye sthitaṃ sthira|dhiyā, caritaṃ tapo 'pi;
> ślāghyaḥ sutaḥ su|sadṛś'|ânvaya|jā snuṣ" êyaṃ.
> cintyo mayā nanu kṛt'|ârthatay" âdya mṛtyuḥ. [3]

PRATĪHĀRAḤ: *(sahas" ôpasṛtya)* Jīmūtavāhanasya...

JĪMŪTAKETUḤ: *(karṇau pidhāya)* śāntaṃ, śāntaṃ pāpam!

5.10 DEVĪ: ⌜paḍihadaṃ khu a|maṃgala|vaaṇaṃ!⌟

MALAYAVATĪ: ⌜imiṇā duṇ|ṇimitteṇa vevadī via me hiaaṃ.⌟

JĪMŪTAKETUḤ: bhadra, kiṃ Jīmūtavāhanasya?

PRATĪHĀRAḤ: Jīmūtavāhanasya vārtām anveṣṭuṃ mahārāja|Viśvāvasunā yuṣmad|antikaṃ preṣito 'smi. tad ājñāpayatu mahā|rājaḥ, kiṃ mayā svāmino vijñāpanīyam iti.

JĪMŪTAKETUḤ: kim a|sannihitas tatr' âpi me vatsaḥ?

5.15 DEVĪ: *(sa|viṣādam)* ⌜mahā|rāa, jaï tahiṃ pi ṇ' atthi, tā kahiṃ dāṇiṃ gao me puttao, jeṇa evvaṃ ciraädi?⌟

I'll go to them. 5.5

Thereupon appears JIMÚTA·KETU, *seated, accompanied by his wife and daughter-in-law.*

JIMÚTA·KETU:

I enjoyed my pleasures in youth; my fame is
spread abroad;
I've ruled with a firm will, and performed
penance too;
My son is a laudable man and his wife here
of appropriate family.
Surely now, my aims fulfilled, I should be
thinking about my own death.

DOORMAN: *(rushing up)* Jimúta·váhana's...

JIMÚTA·KETU: *(covering his ears)* May evil be allayed!

QUEEN: Perish unlucky words! 5.10

MÁLAYAVATI: My heart's throbbing at this bad omen.

JIMÚTA·KETU: Good man, "Jimúta·váhana's" what?

DOORMAN: Jimúta·váhana's news, I've been sent to you by the great king Vishva·vasu to find it out. May the great king please instruct me as to what I should inform my master.

JIMÚTA·KETU: Is my dear boy absent there as well?

QUEEN: *(with dismay)* If he's not there either, then where has my little boy gone to be away for so long? 5.15

JĪMŪTAKETUḤ: niyatam asmat|prāṇa|yātr"|ârthaṃ dūraṃ gato bhaviṣyati.

MALAYAVATĪ: *(sa|viṣādam, ātma|gatam)* ⌜ahaṃ puṇa muhuttaaṃ pi ayya|uttaṃ a|pekkhantī aṇṇaṃ evva kiṃ vi āsaṃkāmi.⌟

PRATĪHĀRAḤ: ājñāpayatu, kiṃ mayā svāmino vijñāpanīyam.

JĪMŪTAKETUḤ: *(vām'|âkṣi|spandanaṃ sūcayan)* Jīmūtavāhanaś cirayat' îti mayy ākule vicintayati,

5.20 sphurasi kim, *a|dakṣiṇ*'|ēkṣaṇa,
muhur muhuḥ kathayituṃ mam' ân|iṣṭam?
hata|cakṣur! apahataṃ te
sphuritaṃ! mama putrakaḥ kuśalī! [4]

(ūrdhvaṃ paśyan) ayam eva me bhuvan'|âika|cakṣur bhagavān sahasra|dīdhitiḥ sphuran Jīmūtavāhanasya śreyaḥ kariṣyati. *(sa|vismayam)*

ālokyamānam ati|locana|duḥkha|dāyi,
rakta|cchaṭā nija|marīci|ruco vimuñcat,
utpāta|kāla|taralī|kṛta|tārak'|ābham
etat puraḥ patati kiṃ sahasā nabhastaḥ? [5]

kathaṃ? caraṇayor eva patitam.

sarve nirūpayanti.

JIMÚTA·KETU: Doubtless he will have gone a long way to find the provisions for us.

MÁLAYAVATI: *(with dismay, to herself)* For my part, not seeing my husband even for a moment makes me worried that it's something else.

DOORMAN: Please instruct me as to what I should inform my master.

JIMÚTA·KETU: *(indicating the throbbing of his left eye)* When I'm pre-occupied worrying about Jimúta·váhana being away so long,

Why, you *unlucky : left* eye, do you keep throbbing, 5.20
telling me something undesirable?
Damn my eye! Be gone your throbbing!
May my boy be safe!

(looking up) The lordly sun himself, the sole eye of the world, shining with a thousand rays, will restore Jimúta·váhana. *(surprised)*

What is this falling above me suddenly from the sky
Appearing, giving extreme pain to the eyes,
Scintillating red with its internal color,
Resembling a star tossed about at the time of
some disaster?

What's this? It has fallen right at my feet.

Everyone looks at it.

5.25 JĪMŪTAKETUḤ: aye, lagna|sarasa|māṃsa|keśaś cūḍā|maṇiḥ. kasya punar ayaṃ bhaviṣyati?

DEVĪ: *(sa|viṣādam)* ⌜puttaassa via me edaṃ cūḍā|raaṇaṃ.⌟

MALAYAVATĪ: ⌜mā evaṃ bhaṇa!⌟

PRATĪHĀRAḤ: mahā|rāja, mā a|vijñāy' âivaṃ viklavo bhūḥ. atra hi,

> Tārkṣyeṇa bhakṣyamāṇānāṃ pannagānām an|ekaśaḥ
> ulkā|rūpāḥ patanty ete śiro|maṇaya īdṛśāḥ. [6]

5.30 JĪMŪTAKETUḤ: devi, s'|ôpapattikam abhihitam anena. kadā cid evam api syāt.

DEVĪ: ⌜Suṇanda, avi ṇāma kadā i ettiāe velāe sosura|ulaṃ evva gado me puttao bhavissadi. tā gaccha, jāṇia lahuṃ evva amhāṇaṃ ṇivedehi.⌟

PRATĪHĀRAḤ: yad ājñāpayati devī. *(niṣkrāntaḥ.)*

JĪMŪTAKETUḤ: devi, api nāma nāga | cūḍā | maṇir ayaṃ bhavet...

tataḥ praviśati rakta|vastra|saṃvītaḥ ŚAṄKHACŪḌAḤ.

5.35 ŚAṄKHACŪḌAḤ: *(s'|âsram)* kaṣṭaṃ. bhoḥ kaṣṭaṃ.

JIMÚTA·KETU: Ay, this is a crest gem with wet flesh and hair adhering to it. Whose could it be?

QUEEN: *(with dismay)* This crest jewel is just like my little boy's.

MÁLAYAVATI: Don't speak like that!

DOORMAN: Great king, don't get distressed like this without checking. For here,

> Head gems of this sort frequently fall, like meteors,
> As snakes are being eaten by Tarkshya.

JIMÚTA·KETU: Queen, he's made a good point. It's quite possible it's that.

QUEEN: Sunánda, maybe my little boy will have reached his father-in-law's residence in the meantime. So go, find out and let us know quickly.

DOORMAN: As the Queen instructs. *(He leaves.)*

JIMÚTA·KETU: Queen, if only this were a Naga's crest gem...

At this point there enters SHANKHA·CHUDA, *dressed in the red garments.*

SHANKHA·CHUDA: *(in tears)* This is horrible, really horrible.

Gokarṇam arṇava|taṭe
tvaritaṃ praṇamya
prāpto 'smi tāṃ khalu bhujaṅ-
gama|vadhya|bhūmim,
ādāya taṃ nakha|mukha|
kṣata|vakṣasaṃ ca
vidyā|dharaṃ gaganam ut-
patito Garutmān. [7]

hā niṣkāraṇ'|âika|bāndhava! hā parama|kāruṇika! hā para|duḥkha|duḥkhita! kva nu khalu gato 'si? prayaccha me prativacanam. hā Śaṅkhacūḍa! hataka! kiṃ tvayā kṛtam?

n' âhi|trāṇāt kīrtir ekā may" āptā,
n' âpi ślāghyā svāmino 'nuṣṭhit" ājñā.
dattv" ātmānaṃ rakṣito 'nyena, śocyo,
hā dhik kaṣṭaṃ, vañcito, vañcito 'smi! [8]

tan n' âham evaṃ|vidhaḥ kṣaṇam api jīvann apahāsyam ātmānaṃ karomi! yāvad enam anugantuṃ prayatiṣye. *(parikrāman, bhūmau datta|dṛṣṭiḥ)*

5.40 ādāv utpīḍa|pṛthvīṃ pravirala|patitāṃ,
sthūla|binduṃ tato 'gre,
grāvasv āpāta|śīrṇa|prasṛta|tanu|kaṇāṃ,
kīṭa|kīrṇāṃ sthalīṣu,
dur|lakṣāṃ dhātu|bhittau, ghana|taru|śikhare

I had hurriedly worshipped at Gokárna
on the ocean shore,
Then returned to the place where serpents are
slaughtered,
And Gáruda had taken the Magician, wounded
in the chest by claws and beak,
And flown up into the sky!

Ah, you, who, without motive, are like my closest relative! Oh, supremely compassionate! Oh, you, pained by the pain of others! Where have you gone? Give me an answer! Oh, Shankha·chuda! Ruined! What have you done?

In the first place, I have failed to acquire the glory
of saving the serpents.
Neither have I carried out the laudable command
of my master,
Since I, miserable me, was saved by another
giving up his own life.
Good grief! This is horrible! Deceived.
I've been deceived.

I'll not make myself a laughing stock staying alive in this way for even a moment! First, I'll follow him. *(moving about, looking at the ground)*

Desperate to see Tarkshya I'll go on, following 5.40
this trail of blood with care;
At first broad from the gush, then thick drops
fallen at wide intervals further on;
On stones, its tiny drops scattered as they splash from
the fall; on the soil it's crawling with insects;

gahvare styāna|rūpām
etāṃ Tārkṣyaṃ didṛkṣur nipuṇam anusaran
rakta|dhārāṃ vrajāmi. [9]

parikrāmati.

DEVĪ: *(sa|sādhvasam)* ⌜mahā|rāa, eso ko vi paruṇṇa|vadaṇo ido evva turia|turiaṃ āacchanto hiaaṃ me āulī|karedi. tā jāṇīadu dāva, ko eso tti.⌟

JĪMŪTAKETUḤ: yath" āha devī.

ŚAṄKHACŪḌAḤ: *(s'|ākrandam)* hā tri|bhuvan'|âika|cūḍā|maṇe! kv' âsi prasthito? may" â|draṣṭavyaḥ. muṣito 'smi! bho, muṣito 'smi!

5.45 JĪMŪTAKETUḤ: *(ākarṇya sa|harṣam)* muñca, devi, viṣādam. asy' âyaṃ cūḍā|maṇiḥ. nūnaṃ māṃsa|lobhāt ken' âpi pakṣiṇā mastakād utkhāya nīyamāno 'smin patitaḥ.

DEVĪ: *(sa|harṣaṃ* MALAYAVATĪM *āliṅgya)* ⌜a|vihave, dhīrā hohi! ṇa khu de īdisī āidī vehavva|dukkhaṃ aṇuhodi.⌟

MALAYAVATĪ: *(sa|harṣaṃ)* ⌜amba, tuha esā āsī.⌟ *(pādayoḥ patati.)*

JĪMŪTAKETUḤ: *(*ŚAṄKHACŪḌAM *upasṛtya)* vatsa, kiṃ tava cūḍā|maṇir apahṛtaḥ?

ŚAṄKHACŪḌAḤ: ārya, na mam' âikasya. tribhuvanasy' âpi!

5.50 JĪMŪTAKETUḤ: katham iva?

Hard to spot on veins of mineral; on the tops of
tree clumps in the valleys it's congealed.

He moves about.

QUEEN: *(nervously)* Great king, whoever this person is, coming this way so quickly with a shattered face,* he's alarming me. Find out who he is.

JIMÚTA·KETU: As the queen suggests.

SHANKHA·CHUDA: *(wailing)* Ah, you, the unique crest gem of the three worlds. Where have you gone? I can't see you. I've been robbed! Oh, I've been robbed!

JIMÚTA·KETU: *(listening, with delight)* Leave off your dis- 5.45
may, my queen. It's his, this crest gem! Surely some bird, greedy for flesh, has snatched it from his head and while being carried off it has dropped down here.

QUEEN: *(delighted, and hugging* MÁLAYAVATI*)* You're a married woman yet! Be strong. Someone who looks like you should never experience the pain of being a widow.

MÁLAYAVATI: *(delighted)* Mother, this is your blessing! *(She bows at her feet.)*

JIMÚTA·KETU: *(approaching* SHANKHA·CHUDA*)* My boy, has your crest gem been carried off?

SHANKHA·CHUDA: Sir, not mine. But of the three worlds!

JIMÚTA·KETU: What do you mean? 5.50

ŚAṄKHACŪḌAḤ: duḥkh'|âtiśayād bāṣp'|ôparudhyamāna|kaṇṭho na śaknomi kathayitum.

JĪMŪTAKETUḤ: *(ātma|gatam)* hanta hato 'smi! *(prakāśam)*

āvedaya mam' ātmīyaṃ,
putra, duḥkhaṃ su|dussaham.
mayi saṅkrāntam etat te
yena sahyaṃ bhaviṣyati. [10]

ŚAṄKHACŪḌAḤ: śrūyatām. Śaṅkhacūḍo nāma nāgaḥ khalv aham, āhār'|ârtham avasara|prāpto Vāsukinā Vainateyasya preṣitaḥ. kiṃ vā vistareṇa? kadā cid iyaṃ rudhira|dhārā|paddhatiḥ pāṃsubhir avakīryamāṇā durlakṣatām upayāti. tat saṃkṣepataḥ kathayāmi.

5.55 vidyādhareṇa ken' âpi
karuṇ"|āviṣṭa|cetasā
mama saṃrakṣitāḥ prāṇā
dattv" ātmānaṃ Garutmate. [11]

JĪMŪTAKETUḤ: *(sa|viṣādam)* ko 'nya evaṃ para|hita|vyasanī? nanu spaṣṭam ev' ôcyatāṃ, putreṇa Jīmūtavāhanen' êti. hā hato 'smi manda|bhāgyaḥ.

DEVĪ: ⌜hā puttaa! kiṃ tue kidam?⌟

MALAYAVATĪ: ⌜hā, kahaṃ saccī|bhūdaṃ evva me duc|cindidam.⌟

sarve mohaṃ gatāḥ.

5.60 ŚAṄKHACŪḌAḤ: *(s'|âsram)* aye, nūnam etau pitarau tasya mahā|sattvasya! a|priya|nivedanān may" âitām avasthāṃ gamitau. atha vā viṣād ṛte kim anyad viṣa|dharasya

SHANKHA·CHUDA: I cannot say as my throat is choked with tears of extreme sorrow.

JIMÚTA·KETU: *(to himself)* No! I am destroyed. *(aloud)*

> Child, tell me about your own suffering that is
> so hard to bear,
> So that, passed to me, it will become bearable
> for you.

SHANKHA·CHUDA: Listen. I am a Naga, called Shankha·chuda. It was me who was sent by Vásuki to Vínata's son as food, when my turn came up. But such detail is a waste of time. This path of the blood trail may get hard to follow, if it gets covered with dust. So I'll tell it in brief.

> My life was saved by some Magician 5.55
> Whose heart was filled with compassion
> And gave himself to Gáruda.

JIMÚTA·KETU: *(with dismay)* Who else is as addicted as this to helping others? Why not say plainly that it was my son Jimúta·váhana? Ah, I am ruined. My lot is miserable.

QUEEN: Oh, my little boy! What have you done?

MÁLAYAVATI: Ah, how that evil thought has come to be true.

They all swoon.

SHANKHA·CHUDA: *(in tears)* These must be the parents of 5.60
that great being!* They've been reduced to this state by me announcing the unwelcome news. But then, does anything other than poison come from the mouth of

mukhān niṣkrāmati? aho prāṇa|pradasya sadṛśaṃ pratyupakṛtaṃ Jīmūtavāhanasya Śaṅkhacūḍena. tat kim adhun" âiv' ātmānaṃ vyāpādayāmi? atha vā samāśvāsayāmi tāvad etau. tāta, samāśvasihi, samāśvasihi! amba, samāśvasihi, samāśvasihi.

ubhau samāśvasitaḥ.

DEVĪ: ⌜vacche, uṭṭhehi, uṭṭhehi. mā roa. amhe vi kiṃ Jīmūdavāhaṇeṇa viṇā jīvamha? tā samassasa dāva.⌟

MALAYAVATĪ: *(samāśvasya)* ⌜hā ayya|utta! kahiṃ tuvaṃ mae pekkhidavvo?⌟

JĪMŪTAKETUḤ: hā vatsa guru|caraṇa|śuśrūṣ"|âbhijña!

5.65 cūḍā|maṇiṃ caraṇayor mama pātayatā tvayā
lok'|ântara|gaten' âpi n' ôjjhito vinaya|kramaḥ. [12]

(cūḍā|maṇiṃ gṛhītvā) hā vatsa, katham etāvan|mātra|darśano 'si me saṃvṛttaḥ? *(hṛdaye dattvā)* hahaha,

bhaktyā vidūra|vinat'|ānana|namra|mauleḥ
śaśvat tava praṇamataś caraṇau madīyau
cūḍā|maṇir nikaṣaṇair masṛṇo 'py ayaṃ hi
gāḍhaṃ vidārayati me hṛdayaṃ kathaṃ nu? [13]

a poison snake? Ha, this is how Shankha·chuda has repaid Jimúta·váhana who gave him his life. So why don't I kill myself right now? Perhaps I should first help those two recover. Bear up, father, please bear up! Mother, be brave. Please be brave!

The two come round.

QUEEN: Get up, my girl. Please get up. Don't cry. We cannot live without Jimúta·váhana either. So be brave now.

MÁLAYAVATI: *(coming round)* Oh, husband! Where can I get to see you?

JIMÚTA·KETU: Oh, my child, you well know how to serve your parents!

> Making your crest gem fall at my feet, 5.65
> You fail not in due humility,
> Even as you go to another world.

(taking the crest gem) Oh, my child, how is it you have changed so I can only see you like this? *(placing it on his heart)* Oh, oh, oh,

> How is it this crest gem of yours deeply lacerates my heart,
> Even though worn smooth from rubbing,
> As you constantly saluted my two feet
> Your head in devotion bowed down with your modest face far away?

DEVĪ: ⌜hā puttaa Jīmūdavāhaṇa! jassa de guru|jaṇa|sussūsaṃ vajjia aṇṇaṃ suhaṃ ṇa roadi, so kahaṃ dāṇiṃ pidaraṃ ujjhia sagga|sokkhaṃ aṇubhaviduṃ patthido si?⌟

JĪMŪTAKETUḤ: *(s'|âsram)* devi, kiṃ vayaṃ Jīmūtavāhanena vinā jīvāmaḥ, yen' âivaṃ vilapasi?

5.70 MALAYAVATĪ: *(pādayor nipatya kṛt'|âñjaliḥ)* ⌜tāda, dehi me ayya|uttassa cūḍā|raaṇaṃ, jeṇa imaṃ hiae karia jolaṇa| ppaveseṇa attaṇo sandāvaṃ avaṇemi.⌟

JĪMŪTAKETUḤ: *(s'|âsram)* pativrate, kiṃ mām ākulayasi? nanu sarveṣām ev' âsmākam ayaṃ niścayaḥ.

DEVĪ: ⌜mahā|rāa, tā kiṃ paḍivālīadi?⌟

JĪMŪTAKETUḤ: devi, na khalu kiñ cit. kin tv āhit'|âgner n' ânyen' âgninā saṃskāro vihitaḥ. tad agni|hotra|śaraṇād agnīn ādāy' ātmānam ādīpayāmaḥ.

ŚAṄKHACŪḌAḤ: *(ātma|gatam)* hā kaṣṭam! mam' âikasya pāpasy' ârthe sakalam ev' êdaṃ vidyādhara|kulam utsannaṃ bhaviṣyati. tad evaṃ tāvat. *(prakāśam)* tāta, na khalv a|niścity' âiva yuktam īdṛśaṃ sāhasam anuṣṭhātum. vicitrāṇi hi vidher vilasitāni. kadā cid «n' âyaṃ nāga» iti jñātvā jīvantam eva Jīmūtavāhanaṃ parityajen nāga| śatruḥ. tad anay" âiva tāvad rudhira|dhārayā Vainateyam anusarāmaḥ.

QUEEN: Oh, my little boy Jimúta·váhana! You took no pleasure in anything other than serving your parents. How come you've left your father now and gone off to experience the pleasure of heaven?

JIMÚTA·KETU: *(in tears)* My Queen, can we carry on living without Jimúta·váhana, for whom you mourn like this?

MÁLAYAVATI: *(bowing at his feet with her hands held together* 5.70
in respect) Father, give me the crest jewel of my husband, so that I can place it on my heart and take away my burning when I enter the funeral fire.

JIMÚTA·KETU: *(in tears)* You, devoted to your husband, why are you so distressed? Surely every one of us has the same resolve.

QUEEN: Great king, what are we waiting for?

JIMÚTA·KETU: Nothing really, my queen. Only that for a brahmin who maintains the sacred fire, cremation by any other flame is not allowed. For this reason we shall fetch the flame from the abode of the sacred fire and then set fire to ourselves.

SHANKHA·CHUDA: *(to himself)* Ah, this is appalling! For the sake of a single evil person like me, this entire family of Magicians will be destroyed. This is what I shall say. *(aloud)* Father, surely it's not right to carry out this rash act without even checking? For the sports of fate are manifold. Maybe the Enemy of Nagas, finding out that he's not a Naga, will leave Jimúta·váhana alone still alive. That's why we must follow the son of Vínata for now via this trail of blood.

5.75 DEVĪ: ⌜savvahā devadāṇaṃ pasādeṇa jīvantaṃ evva me puttaaṃ pekkhissaṃ.⌟

MALAYAVATĪ: *(ātma|gatam)* ⌜dul | lahaṃ khu edaṃ mama manda|bhāāe.⌟

JĪMŪTAKETUḤ: vatsa, a|vitath" âiṣā bhāratī te bhavatu. tath" âpi s' | âgnīnām ev' âsmākaṃ yuktam anusartum. tad anusaratu bhavān, vayam apy agni|hotra|śaraṇād agnīn ādāya tvaritataram anugacchāmaḥ. *(patnī|vadhū|sameto niṣkrāntaḥ.)*

ŚAṄKHACŪḌAḤ: tad yāvad Garuḍam anusarāmi. *(calann, agrato nirvarṇya)*

kurvāṇo rudhir'|ārdra|cañcu|kaṣaṇair
droṇīr iv' âdres taṭīḥ,
pluṣṭ'|ôpānta|van'|ântaraḥ sva|nayana|
jyotiś|śikhā|sañcayaiḥ,
majjad|vajra|kaṭhora|ghora|nakhara|
prānt'|âvagāḍh'|âvaniḥ
śṛṅg'|âgre Malayasya pannaga|ripur
dūrād ayaṃ lakṣyate. [14]

5.80 *tataḥ praviśaty āsana|sthaḥ, puraḥ|pātita|*NĀYAKO GARUḌAḤ.

GARUḌAḤ: *(ātma|gatam)* ā, janmanaḥ prabhṛti bhujaṅga| patīn aśnatā mayā na c' ēdṛśam āścaryaṃ dṛṣṭa|pūrvaṃ. yad ayaṃ *mahā|sattvo* na kevalaṃ vyathate, prahṛṣṭa eva dṛśyate. tathā hi,

QUEEN: There's no way I will get to see my little boy alive again other than through the grace of the gods. 5.75

MÁLAYAVATI: *(to herself)* For me, with my luck, that will be impossible.

JIMÚTA·KETU: My boy, may this proposition of yours not be false. Nevertheless, for us it would only be proper to follow with the fire. So you please follow the trail, and we will quickly come after you bringing the flame from the abode of the sacred fire. *(He leaves with his wife and daughter-in-law.)*

SHANKHA·CHUDA: I'll get on and follow after Gáruda then. *(moving, looking ahead)**

> Here on top of Málaya the Enemy of Snakes
> can be seen from afar,
> Making the slopes of the mountain like valleys
> by scraping his blood wet beak,
> Burning the contents of nearby forests with
> frequent fiery glances from his eyes,
> The earth pierced by the plunging tips of his
> terrible claws, sharp and hard.

At that point there enters GÁRUDA *seated with the* HERO *dropped to the ground before him.* 5.80

GÁRUDA: *(to himself)* Well, I've been feeding on serpents since I was born, but never before have I seen a wonder such as this. For this *large creature : Great being* is not only in pain, but actually seems delighted. For example,

glānir n' âdhika|pīyamāna|rudhirasy'
âpy asti dhairy'|ôdadher.
māṃs'|ôtkartana|jā rujo 'pi vahataḥ
prītyā *prasannaṃ* mukham.
gātraṃ yan na viluptam, eṣa pulakas
tatra sphuṭo lakṣyate!
dṛṣṭir mayy upakāriṇ' îva nipataty
asy' âpakāriṇy api. [15]

tat kautūhalam eva me janitam asy' ânayā dhairya|vṛttyā. bhavatu, na bhakṣayāmy enam. jānāmi tāvat ko 'yam iti. *(apasarpati.)*

NĀYAKAḤ: *(māṃs'|ôtkartana|vimukham upalakṣya)*

5.85 sirā|mukhaiḥ syandata eva raktam.
ady' âpi dehe mama māṃsam asti.
tṛptiṃ na paśyāmi tav' êha tāvat.
kiṃ bhakṣaṇāt tvaṃ virato, Garutman? [16]

GARUḌAḤ: *(ātma|gatam)* aho, āścaryam! katham ayam asyām apy avasthāyām evam atyūrjitam abhidhatte? *(prakāśam)*

āvarjitam mayā cañcvā hṛdayāt tava śoṇitam.
anena dhairyeṇa punas tvayā hṛdayam eva naḥ [17]

ataḥ kas tvam iti śrotum icchāmi.

NĀYAKAḤ: evaṃ kṣud|upatapto na śravaṇa|yogyaḥ, tat kuruṣva tāvad asman|māṃsa|śoṇitena tṛptim.

He is not wearied, this ocean of courage, even though
his blood is being drunk up more and more.
His face is *bright : calm* with delight as he bears
the pains caused by tearing off his flesh.
On the limb that hasn't been plucked off,
one can clearly see the thrill of pleasure!
His gaze falls on me as if I am a benefactor,
even as I am harming him!

This courageous behavior has roused my curiosity about him. So be it, I shall not eat him. I'll just ask who he is. *(He stands back from him.)*

HERO: *(observing that he has given up tearing his flesh)*

The blood still flows from my open veins. 5.85
Even now there is flesh on my body.
I can see that you are not yet satisfied.
Gáruda, why have you left off eating?

GÁRUDA: *(to himself)* Ah, it's amazing! How is it that even in this plight, he speaks with extraordinary valor like this! *(aloud)*

With my beak I have made the blood pour
from your heart.
With this courage, however, you have in turn
humbled my heart.

Therefore I want to hear who you are.

HERO: While you are pained by hunger you are not ready to hear, so for the moment satisfy yourself with my flesh and blood.

5.90 ŚAṄKHACŪḌAḤ: *(sahas" ôpasṛtya)* na khalu! na khalu sāhasam anuṣṭheyam! n' âyaṃ nāgaḥ. parityaj' âinam. māṃ bhakṣaya. aham asau tav' āhār' | ârthaṃ Vāsukinā preṣitaḥ. *(uro dadāti.)*

NĀYAKAḤ: *(*ŚAṄKHACŪḌAṂ *paśyan, sa|viṣādam, ātma|gatam)* kaṣṭaṃ! viphalī|bhūto me mano|rathaḥ Śaṃkhacūḍen' āgacchatā.

GARUḌAḤ: *(ubhau nirūpayan)* ubhayor api bhavator vadhya|cihnam asty eva. kaḥ khalu nāga iti n' âvagacchāmi.

ŚAṄKHACŪḌAḤ: a|sthāna eva te bhrāntiḥ.

āstāṃ svastika|lakṣma vakṣasi; tanau
n' ālokyate kañcukaṃ.
jihve jalpata eva me na gaṇite
nāma tvayā dve api?
tisras tīvra|viṣ'|âgni|dhūma|paṭala|
vyājihma|ratna|tviṣo
n' âitā dus|saha|śoka|śūtkṛta|marut|
sphītāḥ phaṇāḥ paśyasi? [18]

5.95 GARUḌAḤ: *(*ŚAṄKHACŪḌASYA *phaṇāḥ paśyan,* NĀYAKAṂ *ca vīkṣamāṇaḥ)* kaḥ khalv ayaṃ mayā vyāpāditaḥ?

ŚAṄKHACŪḌAḤ: bho vidyādhara|rāja|vaṃśa|tilaka! kathaṃ kāruṇiken' âpi tvay" âitad ati|niṣṭhuram anuṣṭhitam?

GARUḌAḤ: aye, ayam asau vidyādhara|kumāro Jīmūtavāhanaḥ,

Merau, Mandara|kandarāsu, Himavat|
sānau, Mahendr'|âcale,
Kailāsasya śilā|taleṣu, Malaya|

SHANKHA·CHUDA: *(rushing up)* No! No, don't do this rash deed! He is not a Naga. Leave him alone. Eat me! I am the one sent by Vásuki as your food. *(He offers his chest.)* 5.90

HERO: *(seeing* SHANKHA·CHUDA, *disappointed, to himself)* Impossible! My heart's desire is scotched because Shankha·chuda has arrived.

GÁRUDA: *(looking at the two)* Both of you have the victim's mark. I don't understand who is the Naga.

SHANKHA·CHUDA: Your confusion is so misplaced.

> Leave aside the *svástika** on his chest, no snakeskin
> can be seen on his body.
> Can't you count the two tongues too just as
> I am speaking?
> Can't you see these three hoods, swollen by the air
> from hissing my grief so hard to bear,
> The glint of their jewels dulled by the cloud of fumes
> from the fire of my harsh poison?

GÁRUDA: *(seeing* SHANKHA·CHUDA*'s hoods, and inspecting the* HERO*)* Who is this whom I have killed? 5.95

SHANKHA·CHUDA: O you, the ornament of the Magician king's lineage! How could you, despite being compassionate, do such an extremely cruel thing?

GÁRUDA: Ah no, this is the Magician prince, Jimúta·váhana,

> Of whose fame I have heard as it was being sung by
> groups of bards roaming the ends of the world,*
> On Meru, in the glens of Mándara, on the peak
> of Hímavat, on the Mount of Indra,

prāg|bhāra|deśeṣv api,
uddeśeṣv api teṣu teṣu bahuśo
yasya śrutaṃ tan mayā
Lokāloka|vicāri|cāraṇa|gaṇair
udgīyamānaṃ yaśaḥ. [19]

sarvath" âham a|yaśaḥ|paṅke nimagno 'smi.

5.100 NĀYAKAḤ: bhoḥ phaṇi|pate, kim evam āvigno 'si?

ŚAṄKHACŪḌAḤ: kim idam a|sthānam āvegasya? paśya,

sva|śarīreṇa śarīraṃ
Tārkṣyāt parirakṣatā madīyam idam
yuktaṃ netuṃ bhavatā
pātāla|talād api talaṃ mām? [20]

GARUḌAḤ: aye, karuṇ'|ārdra|cetas" ânena mah"|ātmanā mam' āsya|gocaraṃ prāptasy' âsya phaṇinaḥ prāṇān parirakṣituṃ svayam ev' ātmā mam' āhār'|ârtham upanītaḥ? tan mahad a|kṛtyam idaṃ mayā kṛtam. kiṃ bahunā, bodhi|sattva ev' âyaṃ mayā vyāpāditaḥ. tad asya mahataḥ pāpasy' âgni|praveśād ṛte n' ânyat prāyaś|cittaṃ paśyāmi. kva nu khalu vahnim āsādayāmi? *(diśaḥ paśyan)* aye, amī ke cid gṛhīt'|âgnaya ita ev' āgacchanti. yāvad etān pratipālayāmi.

ŚAṄKHACŪḌAḤ: kumāra, pitarau te prāptau.

5.105 NĀYAKAḤ: *(sa|sambhramam)* Śaṅkhacūḍa, ehi. samupaviśy' ânen' ôttarīyeṇ' ācchādita|śarīraṃ kṛtvā samupasthito dhāraya mām. anyathā kadā cid īdṛg|avasthaṃ māṃ sahas" âiv' ālokya ambā jīvitaṃ jahyāt.

On the stone slabs of Kailása, even in places
on the summit of Málaya,
And in the higher regions, here and there,
all the time.

In every possible way, I am sunk in the mire of disgrace.

HERO: Ho, master snake, why are you upset about this? 5.100

SHANKHA·CHUDA: Is upset out of place? Look,

Saving this body of mine from Tarkshya
with your own body,
Is it right for you to lead me to a region
even lower than the dank nether region?*

GÁRUDA: This noble-souled man, his heart tender with compassion, actually offered himself as my food so as to protect the life-breath of this serpent even as it reached my mouth? Then I have committed a great misdeed. In short, this is a bodhisattva I have murdered.* I can see no atonement for this great evil other than entering the funeral fire. How can I get hold of fire? *(looking all around)* Uh, here come some people clutching a flame. I shall wait for them.

SHANKHA·CHUDA: Prince, your parents have arrived.

HERO: *(flurried)* Shankha·chuda, come here. Sit me up, 5.105
cover my body with this shawl and stand next to me to hold me up. Otherwise, if she suddenly sees me in such a state, mother may drop dead.

ŚAṄKHACŪḌAḤ *pārśva|patitam uttarīyaṃ gṛhītvā tathā karoti.*

tataḥ praviśati patnī|vadhū|sameto JĪMŪTAKETUḤ.

JĪMŪTAKETUḤ: *(s'|âsram)* hā putra! Jīmūtavāhana!

«ātmīyaḥ, para» ity ayaṃ khalu kutaḥ
satyaṃ kṛpāyāḥ kramaḥ?
«kiṃ rakṣāmi bahūn, kim ekam?» iti te
cintā na jātā katham?
Tārkṣyāt trātum ahiṃ sva|jīvita|pari-
tyāgaṃ tvayā kurvatā
yen' ātmā, pitarau, vadhūr—iti hataṃ
niś|śeṣam etat kulam. [21]

5.110 DEVĪ: (MALAYAVATĪM *uddiśya)* ⌜jāde, muhuttaaṃ pi dāva virama. imehiṃ a|virada|paḍantehiṃ assu|bindūhiṃ de ṇivvāpīadi aaṃ aggī.⌟

sarve parikrāmanti.

GARUḌAḤ: «hā putra! Jīmūtavāhan'!» êti bravīti. vyaktam ayam asya pitā. ataḥ kṛtam etadīyen' âgninā. api ca na śaknomy asya putra|ghāti|lajjayā mukhaṃ darśayitum. atha vā kim agni|hetoḥ paryākulo 'ham. taṭa|stha ev' âsmi jala|nidheḥ. tad yāvad idānīṃ,

jvālā|bhaṅgais trilokī|
grasana|rasa|calat|*kāla*|jihv'|âgra|kalpaiḥ
sarpadbhiḥ sapta sarpiṣ|
kaṇam iva kabalī|kartum īśe samudrān,

SHANKHA·CHUDA *takes up the shawl fallen at his side and does so.*

Thereupon there enters JIMÚTA·KETU *accompanied by his wife and daughter-in-law.*

JIMÚTA·KETU: *(in tears)* Oh, my son! Jimúta·váhana!

Knowing, "this one's mine, this a stranger," in truth
  isn't there actually a proper order for compassion?
How come you did not think, "Shall I save one
  or many?"
Giving your own life to save a snake from Tarkshya,
You have destroyed this entire family—yourself,
  your parents and your wife!

QUEEN: *(addressing* MÁLAYAVATI*)* My darling, just stop for 5.110
a while. The flame is being quenched by this ceaseless flood of your tears.

They all move about.

GÁRUDA: He said, "Oh, my son! Jimúta·váhana!" Clearly, this is his father. I cannot use the fire he brought. I cannot even show my face out of shame at being his son's killer. In fact, why am I bothered about a flame? Here I am, stood on the shore of the ocean. Right now,

I shall plunge into the "mare's fire" beneath the sea,*
  dreadful like the holocaust at eon's end,
Kindled by the draft of my very own wings that's
  keener than the blast of some calamitous wind,
Able to swallow up the seven seas like a drop of ghee
  with spreading waves of fire

svair ev' ôtpāta|vāta|
prasara|paṭutarair dhukṣite pakṣa|vātair
asmin kalp'|âvasāna|
jvalana|bhaya|kare vāḍab'|âgnau patāmi. [22]

(utthātum icchati.) NĀYAKAḤ: bhoḥ patag'|âdhirāja, alam anena vyavasāyena. n' âyaṃ pratīkāro 'sya pāpmanaḥ.

5.115 GARUḌAḤ: *(jānubhyāṃ sthitvā kṛt'|âñjaliḥ)* mahātman, kas tarhi? kathyatām.

NĀYAKAḤ: pratipālaya kṣaṇam. pitarau me prāptau. yāvad etau praṇamāmi.

GARUḌAḤ: evam.

JĪMŪTAKETUḤ: *(dṛṣṭvā sa|harṣam)* devi, diṣṭyā vardhase. ayam asau vatso Jīmūtavāhano na kevalaṃ dhriyate, pratyuta puraḥ kṛt'|âñjalinā śiṣyeṇ' êva Garuḍena paryupāsyamānas tiṣṭhati!

DEVĪ: ⌈mahā|rāa, kid'|attha mhi. a|kkhada|sarīrassa evva puttaassa muhaṃ diṭṭhaṃ.⌋

5.120 MALAYAVATĪ: ⌈jaṃ saccaṃ evva ayya|uttaṃ pekkhantī vi a|saṃbhāvaṇīaṃ tti karia ṇa pattiāmi.⌋

JĪMŪTAKETUḤ: *(upasṛtya)* vatsa, ehy, ehi. pariṣvajasva mām.

NĀYAKA *utthātum icchan patit'|ôttarīyo mūrchitaḥ.*

ŚAṄKHACŪḌAḤ: kumāra, samāśvasihi, samāśvasihi.

JĪMŪTAKETUḤ: hā vatsa! kathaṃ? dṛṣṭv" âpi māṃ parityajya gato 'si?

Like the tongue tips of *Time : Death* flickering with a taste for swallowing the three worlds.

HERO: *(He tries to stand up.)* Hey, you, King of the Birds, give up this resolve. It's not the remedy for this evil deed.

GÁRUDA: *(kneeling, with hands held together in respect)* Tell 5.115
me what is, then, noble soul.

HERO: Wait for a moment. My parents have arrived. I shall just bow to them.

GÁRUDA: Please do so.

JIMÚTA·KETU: *(seeing his son with delight)* My queen, you are lucky! Here's your dear child Jimúta·váhana—he not only survives, but is being waited upon by Gáruda who has his hands held in respect like a pupil!

QUEEN: I've got what I wanted. I have seen the face of my son with his body unhurt.

MÁLAYAVATI: In truth, though I am looking at my husband, 5.120
I think it's impossible and don't believe it.

JIMÚTA·KETU: *(approaching him)* Come here, my child, come. Embrace me.

Trying to stand, the HERO *faints, his shawl dropping.*

SHANKHA·CHUDA: Bear up, prince, please bear up.

JIMÚTA·KETU: Oh, my boy! What's this? You only look at me, and then abandon me and go?

5.125 DEVĪ: ⌜hā puttaa! kahaṃ vāā|mattaeṇa vi tue ṇa saṃbhāvida mhi.⌟

MALAYAVATĪ: ⌜hā ayya|utta! kahaṃ guru|jaṇo vi tue uvekkhidavvo?⌟

mohaṃ gacchanti.

ŚAṄKHACŪḌAḤ: hā Śaṅkhacūḍa|hataka! garbha eva kiṃ na vipanno 'si, yen' âivaṃ kṣaṇe kṣaṇe maraṇ'|âdhikaṃ duḥkham anubhavasi.

GARUḌAḤ: sarvam etan mama nṛśaṃsasy' â|samīkṣya|kāritāyā vijṛmbhitam. tad etad api tāvat karomi. *(pakṣābhyāṃ vījayan)* samāśvasihi, mahātman, samāśvasihi.

5.130 NĀYAKAḤ: *(samāśvasya)* Śaṅkhacūḍa, samāśvasaya gurūn.

ŚAṄKHACŪḌAḤ: *(upasṛtya)* tāta, samāśvasihi. amba, samāśvasihi. samāśvasito Jīmūtavāhanaḥ. kiṃ na paśyatha, pratyuta yuṣmān eva samāśvāsayitum upaviṣṭas tiṣṭhati.

ubhau samāśvasitaḥ.

DEVĪ: ⌜hā puttaa, pekkhantāṇaṃ evva amhāṇaṃ kadanta|hadaeṇa avahārīasi.⌟

JĪMŪTAKETUḤ: devi, m" âivam a|maṅgalaṃ vādīḥ. dhriyata ev' āyuṣmān. tad vadhūs tāvad āśvāsyatām.

QUEEN: Oh, my little boy! How come you don't greet me with even a word? 5.125

MÁLAYAVATI: Oh, husband, how can you ignore your parents?

They all faint.

SHANKHA·CHUDA: Oh wretched Shankha·chuda, why didn't you perish already in the womb? Instead every moment now you suffer a pain worse than death.

GÁRUDA: All this is the consequence of my wicked thoughtless action. I know what I should do for the time being. *(fanning him with his wings)* Bear up, noble soul, please bear up.

HERO: *(coming round)* Shankha·chuda, please console my 5.130
parents.

SHANKHA·CHUDA: *(approaching them)* Father, bear up. Be brave, mother. Jimúta·váhana has come round. Don't you see that he's actually sitting up in order to console you?

The two come round.

QUEEN: Oh my little boy, even as we look at you, you are snatched by death, the vile thing.

JIMÚTA·KETU: My queen, don't say such an unlucky thing. Our long-lived boy is still alive. Come on, comfort our daughter-in-law.

5.135 DEVĪ: *(vastreṇa mukham āvṛṇvatī, rudaty eva)* ⌜paḍihadaṃ khu a|maṅgalaṃ. ṇa rodissaṃ. jāde, samassasa dāva. varaṃ ettiaṃ velaṃ bhattuṇo de muhaṃ diṭṭhaṃ.⌟

MALAYAVATĪ: *(samāśvasya)* ⌜hā ayya|utta! kiṃ karomi manda| bhāiṇī?⌟

DEVĪ: *(*MALAYAVATYĀ *mukhaṃ pāṇinā parāmṛjya)* ⌜vacche, mā evvaṃ karehi. paḍihadaṃ khu edaṃ!⌟

JĪMŪTAKETUḤ: *(s'|âsram)*

viluptaļśeṣ'|âṅgatayā prayātān
  nirāśrayatvād iva kaṇṭha|deśam
prāṇān vahantaṃ tanayaṃ nirīkṣya
  kathaṃ na pāpaḥ śatadhā vrajāmi? [23]

5.140 MALAYAVATĪ: ⌜adi|dukkhara|kāriṇī hu ahaṃ. jā īdisaṃ pi ayya|uttaṃ pekkhantī ajja vi jīviaṃ ṇa pariccaāmi.⌟

DEVĪ: *(*NĀYAKASY' *âṅgāni parāmṛśantī,* GARUḌAM *uddiśya)* ⌜ṇisaṃsa! kahaṃ dāṇi tue edaṃ āpūriamāṇa|ṇava|rūva| jovvaṇa|sohaṃ evva edad|avatthaṃ puttaassa me sarīraṃ kidaṃ?⌟

NĀYAKAḤ: amba, mā, m" âivam. kim anena kṛtam? nanu pūrvam apy etad īdṛśam eva param'|ârthataḥ? paśya,

medo|'sthi|majjā|māṃs'|âsṛk|
  saṅghāte 'smin tvag|āvṛte
śarīra|nāmni kā śobhā
  sadā bībhatsa|darśane? [24]

QUEEN: *(covering her face with her garment, weeping)* Perish the bad luck! I shall not weep. My dear child, be brave for now. Its best to look on your husband's face at this hour. 5.135

MÁLAYAVATI: *(bearing up)* Oh, what shall I do, noble soul? I'm so unlucky.

QUEEN: *(wiping* MÁLAYAVATI*'s face with her hand)* My dear girl, don't do this. Perish the thought!

JIMÚTA·KETU: *(in tears)*

How come I, an evil person, do not shatter into
a hundred pieces,
Having watched my son bearing his life's breaths
Climbing to his throat as if with nowhere to shelter,
His other limbs plucked off?

MÁLAYAVATI: I'm a really bad person. I don't even give up my life now when I am watching my husband in such a state. 5.140

QUEEN: *(stroking the* HERO*'s limbs and addressing* GÁRUDA*)* You are cruel! How can you have reduced to this state my little boy's body, that was bursting with the loveliness of blossoming youth?

HERO: Mother, no, don't speak like this. What has he done? Surely even before, in reality, it was just the same? Look,

What beauty is there in this thing called a body,
that is always dreadful to look at,
Concealed by a skin, a cluster of fat, bone, meat,
marrow and blood?*

GARUḌAḤ: bho mahātman! narak'|ânala|jvāl"|âvalīḍham ātmānaṃ manyamāno duḥkhaṃ tiṣṭhāmi. tad upadiśyatāṃ yena mucye 'ham asmād enasaḥ.

5.145 NĀYAKAḤ: anujānātu māṃ tātaḥ, yāvad asya pāpasya pratipakṣam upadiśāmi.

JĪMŪTAKETUḤ: vatsa, evaṃ kriyatām.

NĀYAKAḤ: Vainateya, śrūyatām.

GARUḌAḤ: *(jānubhyāṃ sthitvā, kṛt'|âñjaliḥ)* ājñāpaya.

NĀYAKAḤ:

nityaṃ prāṇ'|âtipātāt
prativirama, kuru prāk|kṛte c' ânutāpaṃ.
yatnāt puṇya|pravāhaṃ
samupacinu diśan sarva|sattveṣv a|bhītim,
magnaṃ yen' âtra n' âinaḥ
phalati parimita|prāṇi|hiṃs"|āttam etad,
dur|gādh'|âpāra|vārer
lavaṇa|palam iva kṣiptam antar hradasya. [25]

GARUḌAḤ:

5.150 ajñāna|nidrā|śayito
bhavatā pratibodhitaḥ
sarva|prāṇi|vadhād eṣa
virato 'dya prabhṛty aham. [26]

GÁRUDA: Oh, noble soul. I'm still in pain. I feel like I am enveloped in the fire and flames of hell. Explain to me how I can be freed from this misfortune.

HERO: May father instruct me to explain the antidote to 5.145
this evil.

JIMÚTA·KETU: My dear boy, please do so.

HERO: Vínata's son, listen.

GÁRUDA: *(kneeling, his hands placed together in respect)* Instruct me.

HERO:

Always refrain from taking life, and feel remorse for
what you have done in the past.
Promoting fearlessness among all beings,
build up with effort a constant flow of merit,
Whereby this misfortune obtained from harming
a measured number* of beings is drowned
and does not fruit,
Like a grain of salt thrown into a lake whose waters
are boundless and unfathomable.

GÁRUDA:

You have awakened me from the sleep of ignorance. 5.150
From today onwards I shall refrain from killing
any beings.

samprati hi,

kva cid dvīp"|ākāraḥ
pulina|vipulair bhoga|nivahaiḥ,
kṛt" āvarta|bhrāntir
valayita|śarīraḥ kva cid api,
vrajan kūlāt kūlaṃ
kva cid api ca setu|pratisamaḥ
samājo nāgānāṃ
viharatu mah"|ôdanvati sukham. [27]

api ca,

srastān pātāla|lagnāṃs
timira|caya|nibhān keśa|hastān vahantyaḥ,
sindūreṇ' êva digdhaiḥ
prathama|ravikara|sparśa|tāmraiḥ kapolaiḥ
āyāsād ālas'|âṅgyo 'py
a|vigaṇita|rujaḥ kānane candanānām
asmin gāyantu rāgād
uraga|yuvatayaḥ kīrtim etāṃ tav' âiva. [28]

5.155 NĀYAKAḤ: sādhu, mahā|sattva, sādhu! anumodāmahe! sarvathā dṛḍha|samādhāno bhava. *(*ŚAṄKHACŪḌAM *uddiśya)* sva|bhavanam eva gamyatām.

ŚAṄKHACŪḌO *niḥśvasy' âdhomukhas tiṣṭhati.*

NĀYAKAḤ: *(niḥśvasya mātaraṃ paśyan)*

utprekṣamāṇā tvāṃ Tārkṣya|
cañcu|koṭi|vipāṭitam
tvad|duḥkha|duḥkhitā duḥkham
āste sā jananī tava. [29]

For now,

May the community of Nagas dwell in the ocean
happily,
In some places looking like islands with their bodies
heaped like broad sandbanks,
In other places their coiled bodies making
the illusion of whirlpools,
In other places yet, resembling bridges as they go
from shore to shore.

Moreover,

Let the serpent girls sing this your fame with passion
in this sandalwood forest,
Not minding their toil, though their limbs are
indolent from fatigue,
With their cheeks ruddy from the touch of
the first sun rays as if made up with red powder,
Wearing ornate hair hanging loose down
to their feet, like a mound of darkness.

HERO: Well done, great being, well done! We applaud you! 5.155
Be firm in every way in your resolve. *(addressing* SHANKHA·CHUDA*)* Please go to your home.

SHANKHA·CHUDA *remains sighing with his face cast down.*

HERO: *(sighing, and looking at his mother)*

Your mother is sunk in pain, pained by your pain,
Fancying that you have been torn open by the tip of
Tarkshya's beak.

DEVĪ: ⌜dhaṇṇā khu sā, jā Garuḍa|muha|paḍidaṃ pi a|kkhada|sarīraṃ evva puttaaṃ pekkhissadi.⌟

5.160 ŚAṄKHACŪḌAḤ: amba, satyam ev' âitad, yadi kumāraḥ svastho bhaviṣyati!

NĀYAKAḤ: *(vedanāṃ nāṭayan)* hahaha, par'|ârtha|sampādan'|âmṛta|ras'|āsvād'|âkṣiptatvād etāvatīṃ velāṃ na viditā, samprati māṃ bādhitum ārabdhā vedanā. *(maraṇ'|âvasthāṃ nāṭayati.)*

JĪMŪTAKETUḤ: *(sa|sambhramam)* hā vatsa, kim evaṃ karoṣi?

DEVĪ: ⌜hā kiṇ ṇu hu edaṃ vattadi?⌟ *(s'|ôras|tāḍanam)* ⌜parittāaha. parittaaha. eso me puttao vivajjadi.⌟

MALAYAVATĪ: ⌜hā ayya|utta, pariccaïdu|kāmo via lakkhīasi.⌟

5.165 NĀYAKAḤ: *(añjaliṃ kartum icchan)* Śaṃkhacūḍa, samānaya me hastau.

ŚAṄKHACŪḌAḤ: *(tathā kurvan, s'|âsram)* kaṣṭam. a|nāthī|bhūtaṃ jagat.

NĀYAKAḤ: *(ardh'|ônmīlit'|âkṣaḥ pitarau paśyan)* ayaṃ paścimaḥ praṇāmaḥ.

gātrāṇy amūni na vahanti vicetanāni.
śrotraṃ sphuṭ'|âkṣara|padān na giraḥ śṛṇoti.
kaṣṭaṃ, nimīlitam idaṃ sahas" âiva cakṣur.
hā tāta! yānti vivaśasya mam' âsavo 'pi. [30]

QUEEN: The mother is really lucky who sees her little boy with an unhurt body even when he has fallen from the mouth of Gáruda.

SHANKHA·CHUDA: Mother, what you say would be true, if 5.160
only the young man will be well!

HERO: *(acting pain)* Aaah, all this time I had not noticed the pain because I was distracted by the ambrosial taste of achieving something good for another, but now it has begun to torment me. *(He acts his throes of death.)*

JIMÚTA·KETU: *(flurried)* Oh, my dear boy, why are you doing this?

QUEEN: Oh, why is this happening? *(beating her breast)* Help. Please help. This is my little boy dying.

MÁLAYAVATI: Oh, husband, you look as if you want to leave us.

HERO: *(trying to place his hands together in respect)* Shankha· 5.165
chuda, put my hands together.

SHANKHA·CHUDA: *(doing so, in tears)* This is dreadful. The world has lost its protector.

HERO: *(looking at his parents with his eyes half closed)* This is my final salutation.

These senseless limbs do not move.
My ear cannot hear speech in distinct words
and syllables.
It's terrifying. Suddenly this eye has closed.
Oh, father! I'm helpless, even my life breath is leaving!

atha vā kim anena? *(«saṃrakṣatā pannagam adya puṇyam» iti pūrva|ślokam eva paṭhitvā patati.)*

5.170 DEVĪ: ⌜hā vaccha! hā guru|jaṇa|vacchala. hā Jīmūdavāhaṇa! kahiṃ si mae puṇo pekkhidavvo?⌟

JĪMŪTAKETUḤ: *(s'|âsram)* hā putra Jīmūtavāhana. hā praṇayi|jana|vatsala. hā sarva|guṇa|nidhe. kv' âsi? prayaccha me prativacanam. *(hastāv utkṣipya)* kaṣṭaṃ. bhoḥ kaṣṭam.

nir|ādhāraṃ dhairyaṃ.
kam iva śaraṇaṃ yātu vinayaḥ?
kṣamaḥ kṣāntiṃ voḍhuṃ
ka iha? viratā dāna|paratā.
hataṃ satyaṃ satyaṃ.
vrajatu kṛpaṇā kv' âdya karuṇā?
jagat kṛtsnaṃ śūnyaṃ
tvayi, tanaya, lok'|ântara|gate. [31]

MALAYAVATĪ: *(s'|âsram)* ⌜hā ayya|utta, kahiṃ maṃ pariccaïa gado si? ṇigghiṇe Malaavadi, kiṃ edaṃ pekkhidavvaṃ tti ettiaṃ velaṃ jīvidā si?⌟

ŚAṄKHACŪḌAḤ: kumāra, kva prāṇebhyo 'pi vallabhataraṃ parijanaṃ parityajya gato 'si? tad avaśyam anveti tvāṃ Śaṃkhacūḍaḥ.

5.175 GARUḌAḤ: *(s'|ôdvegam)* hā kaṣṭam. uparato 'yaṃ mahātmā. kim idānīṃ mayā kartavyam?

But what's the point of this? *(He recites the verse beginning, "By the merit I have accrued today by protecting a snake,"* and collapses.)*

QUEEN: Oh, my dear boy! So fond of your parents. O 5.170
Jimúta·váhana! Where shall I see you again?

JIMÚTA·KETU: *(in tears)* Oh, my son, Jimúta·váhana. You, so fond of your friends. Oh, hoard of all virtues. Where are you? Answer me. *(throwing up his hands)* This is dreadful, just dreadful.

> Fortitude has no support. Who might good conduct
> go to as refuge?
> Who in the world can bear forbearance?
> Commitment to giving is lost.
> The truth is truly destroyed. Where now might
> grieving compassion go?
> Son, when you have gone to another world,
> this world is wholly empty.*

MÁLAYAVATI: *(in tears)* Oh husband, where have you gone, leaving me behind? Shameless Málayavati, have you lived this long in order to watch a sight like this?

SHANKHA·CHUDA: Prince, where have you gone, leaving your people who are more dear than life? Without question Shankha·chuda must follow you.

GÁRUDA: *(agitated)* Oh this is terrible. This noble soul is 5.175
dead. What shall I do now?

DEVĪ: *(s'|âsram ūrdhvaṃ dṛṣṭvā)* ⌈bhaavanto loa|pālā! amideṇa siñcia puttaaṃ me jīvāveha.⌋

GARUḌAḤ: *(sa|harṣam, ātma|gatam)* amṛta|saṅkīrtanāt sādhu smṛtam! manye pramṛṣṭam a|yaśaḥ. tad yāvat tridaśa|patim abhyarthya tad|visṛṣṭen' âmṛta|varṣeṇa na kevalaṃ Jīmūtavāhanam, etān api pūrva|bhakṣitān asthi|śeṣān āśī|viṣān pratyujjīvayāmi. atha vā na dadāty asau, tato 'haṃ,

paks'|ôtkṣipt'|âmbu|nāthaḥ paṭu|java|pavana|
preryamāṇe samīre
netr'|ârciḥ|ploṣa|mūrchā|vidhura|vinipatat|
s'|ânala|dvādaś'|ârkaḥ
cañcvā sañcūrṇya Śakr'|âśani|Dhanada|gadā|
preta|lok'|ēśa|daṇḍān
antaḥ|saṃmagna|pakṣaḥ kṣaṇam amṛta|mayīṃ
vṛṣṭim abhyutsṛjāmi. [32]

tad ayaṃ gato 'smi. *(niṣkrāntaḥ.)*

5.180 JĪMŪTAKETUḤ: Śaṅkhacūḍa! kim ady' âpi sthīyate? samāhṛtya dārūṇi putrasya me viracaya citām, yena vayam apy anena saha gacchāmaḥ.

DEVĪ: ⌈puttaa Saṃkhacūḍa, lahu sajjehi. dukkhaṃ khu amhehi viṇā bhāduo de vaṭṭaï.⌋

QUEEN: *(in tears, looking upwards)* My lords, Guardians of the World! Sprinkle some ambrosia and make my little boy live.

GÁRUDA: *(delighted, to himself)* The mention of ambrosia well reminds me! I think my infamy will be wiped away. I shall make a request of Indra, Lord of the Thirty Gods, and with the rain of ambrosia he emits, I will bring back to life not just Jimúta·váhana but also the serpents I ate before and left as bones. But if he does not give it, then I,

The ocean, lord of the waters, whipped up by
my wings, when the breeze is driven away
by the harsh, swift air,
Making the twelve fiery suns fall down helpless
in a faint, frazzled by the fire from my eyes,
Pulverizing with my beak Shakra's thunderbolt,
Dhánada's mace and the Lord of the
hungry ghosts' staff,*
In a second, my wings plunged into it, I shall
produce a shower made of ambrosia.

I am going for ambrosia. *(He leaves.)*

JIMÚTA·KETU: Shankha·chuda, what are we waiting for now? 5.180
Gather firewood for my son, and build the funeral pyre, so that we too can follow after him.

QUEEN: My little boy, Shankha·chuda, prepare it quickly. Your brother is really unhappy without us.

ŚAṄKHACŪḌAḤ: *(s'|âsram)* yad ājñāpayanti guravaḥ. nanu puras|sara ev' âham atra yuṣmākam. *(utthāya, citā|racanāṃ nāṭayitvā)* tāta, sajjī|kṛt" êyaṃ citā.

JĪMŪTAKETUḤ: kaṣṭaṃ. bhoḥ kaṣṭam.

uṣṇīṣaḥ sphuṭa eva mūrdhani, vibhāty
ūrṇeyam antar bhruvoś,
cakṣus tāmaras'|ânukāri, hariṇā
vakṣaḥ|sthalaṃ spardhate.
cakr'|âṅkau caraṇau, tath" âpi hi kathaṃ,
hā vatsa, mad|duṣ|kṛtais
tvaṃ vidyādhara|cakravarti|padavīm
a|prāpya viśrāmyasi? [33]

5.185 devi, kim iva rudyate? tad uttiṣṭha. citām ārohāmaḥ.

sarve parikrāmanti.

MALAYAVATĪ: *(baddh'|âñjalir ūrdhvaṃ paśyantī)* ⌜bhaavadi Gauri, tue āṇattaṃ, «vijjāhara|cakkavaṭṭī de bhattā bhavissidi» tti. tā kahaṃ mama manda|bhāāe tumaṃ pi alia|vādiṇī saṃvuttā?⌟

tataḥ praviśati sa|saṃbhramā GAURĪ.

GAURĪ: mahā|rāja Jīmūtaketo! na khalu, na khalu sāhasam anuṣṭheyam!

5.190 JĪMŪTAKETUḤ: katham? a|mogha|darśanā bhagavatī Gaurī.

SHANKHA·CHUDA: *(in tears)* As my elders instruct. Surely, I shall be the first among you here to follow him! *(getting up, acting building the pyre)* Father, the pyre is prepared.

JIMÚTA·KETU: This is terrible, so terrible.

> The crown of his head is distinct. The hair between
> his eyebrows catches the eye.
> His eyes resemble a red lotus. His chest rivals a lion's,
> And though this pair of feet have the mark
> of the circle, how is it, my dear boy, that
> through my evil deeds
> You are at rest without achieving the status of
> emperor of the Magicians?*

My queen, why are you weeping? Please rise. We shall climb on the funeral pyre together. 5.185

They all move about.

MÁLAYAVATI: *(placing her hands together in respect and looking upwards)* My Lady Gauri, you instructed me, "The emperor of the Magicians will be your husband." So how is it that your words have turned out to be untrue for me, unlucky that I am?

Thereupon enters GAURI *in a flurry.*

GAURI: Great King, Jimúta·ketu, no! Don't be rash.

JIMÚTA·KETU: How's this? It's my lady Gauri, whose appearance is never pointless. 5.190

GAURĪ: (MALAYAVATĪM *uddiśya)* vatse Malayavati, katham aham alīka|vādinī? dṛśyatām! (NĀYAKAM *upasṛtya kamaṇḍalu|vāriṇ" âbhyukṣantī)*

nijena jīviten' âpi jagatām upakāriṇaḥ
parituṣṭ" âsmi te, vatsa. jīva, Jīmūtavāhana! [34]

NĀYAKA *uttiṣṭhati.*

JĪMŪTAKETUḤ: *(sa|harṣam)* devi, diṣṭyā vardhase! yad ayam a|kṣata|śarīro Jīmūtavāhanaḥ samutthitaḥ.

5.195 DEVĪ: *(sa|harṣam)* ⌜bhaavadīe pasādeṇa.⌟

ubhau GAURYĀḤ *pādayoḥ patitvā* NĀYAKAM *āliṅgataḥ.*

MALAYAVATĪ: *(sa|harṣam)* ⌜diṭṭhiā paccujjīvido ayya|utto.⌟ (GAURYĀḤ *pādayoḥ patati.)*

NĀYAKAḤ: (GAURĪṂ *dṛṣṭvā baddh'|âñjaliḥ)* bhagavati!

abhilaṣit'|âdhika|vara|de!
  praṇipatita|jan'|ārti|hāriṇi! śaraṇye!
caraṇau namāmy ahaṃ te,
  vidyādhara|devate, Gauri! [35]

5.200 *pādayoḥ patati.*

sarva ūrdhvaṃ paśyanti.

JĪMŪTAKETUḤ: katham? *an|abhrā vṛṣṭiḥ*! bhagavati, kim etat?

GAURI: *(addressing* MÁLAYAVATI*)* My dear girl Málayavati, how can I speak what is not true? Watch this! *(going to the* HERO*, and sprinkling him with water from her water jar)*

You are benefactor to the world
  by means of your very own life.
I am very pleased with you, my dear boy.
  Live, Jimúta·váhana!

The HERO *gets up.*

JIMÚTA·KETU: *(delighted)* My queen, you are fortunate! See, Jimúta·váhana has got up, his body unhurt.

QUEEN: *(delighted)* By the grace of my lady. 5.195

Both bow at the feet of GAURI*, then embrace the* HERO.

MÁLAYAVATI: *(delighted)* How wonderful, my husband has returned to life. *(She bows at the feet of* GAURI.*)*

HERO: *(looking at* GAURI*, his hands held together in respect)* My lady!

Lady who gives more than is asked! Who takes away
  the distress of those who worship you! Refuge!
I bow to your feet, Goddess of the Magicians, Gauri!

He bows to her feet. 5.200

All look upwards.

JIMÚTA·KETU: What's this? There is a *shower without clouds : an unexpected blessing*! My lady, what is this?

GAURĪ: mahā|rāja, Jīmūtavāhanam ujjīvayitum etāṃś ca pūrva|bhakṣitān asthi|śeṣān uraga|patīn samupajāta|paścāt|tāpena pakṣi|patinā deva|lokād iyam amṛta|vṛṣṭir nipātitā. *(aṅguly|agreṇa nirdiśantī)* kiñ ca na paśyati mahā|rājaḥ,

samprāpt'|âkhaṇḍa|dehāḥ
sphuṭa|phaṇa|maṇibhir, bhāsurair uttam'|âṅgair,
jihvā|koṭi|dvayena
kṣitim amṛta|ras'|āsvāda|lobhāl lihantaḥ
sampraty ābaddha|vegā
Malaya|giri|sarid|vāri|pūrā iv' âmī
vakraiḥ prasthāna|mārgair
viṣa|dhara|patayas toya|rāśiṃ viśanti. [36]

5.205 (NĀYAKAM *uddiśya)* vatsa Jīmūtavāhana, tvaṃ jīvita|mātra|dānakasy' âiva na yogyaḥ. tad ayam aparas te prasādaḥ,

haṃs'|âṃs'|āhata|hema|paṅkaja|rajaḥ|
samparka|paṅk'|ôjjhitair,
utpannair mama *mānasād* api paraṃ
toyair mahā|pāvanaiḥ,
sv'|êcchā|nirmita|ratna|kumbha|nihitair
eṣ" âbhiṣicya svayaṃ
tvāṃ vidyādhara|cakravartinam ahaṃ
prītyā karomi kṣaṇāt. [37]

GAURI: Great king, this shower of ambrosia is made to fall from the world of the gods by the Lord of Birds, Gáruda, his remorse roused, in order to revive Jimúta·váhana and those serpents he ate before and left as bones. *(pointing with her finger)* And do you not see, great king,

Their bodies made whole again, with their heads
radiant, the gems in their hoods plain,
Licking the ground with the double tip of their
tongues greedy for the taste of ambrosial juice,*
These masterly serpents enter into the water-filled
sea, right now, with some speed,
In sinuous paths like the flood waters of the rivers
on Málaya mountain.

(addressing the HERO*)* My dear boy Jimúta·váhana, you de- 5.205
serve to be granted more than just your life. So here is a further favor for you.

I shall gladly make you the emperor of the Magicians
in an instant,
Sprinkling you myself with waters held in
jeweled jugs magically manifest at my will,
Drawn from *my own mind: from Lake Mánasa,**
very pure, free from mud,
Mingled with golden lotus pollen knocked down
by the shoulders of geese.

api ca,

agresarī|bhavatu kāñcana|cakram etad,
eṣa dvipaś ca dhavalo daśanaiś caturbhiḥ,
śyāmo harir, Malayavaty api c'—êty amūni
ratnāni te samavalokaya, cakravartin! [38]

ete ca mat|pracoditāś caṭula|cūḍāmaṇi|marīci|racit'|Êndra|cāpa|paṅktayo bhakty" âvanata|pūrva|kāyāḥ praṇamanti tvāṃ Mataṅga|dev'|ādayo vidyādhara|patayaḥ! vatsa, kiṃ te bhūyaḥ priyam upaharāmi?

5.210 NĀYAKAḤ: *(jānubhyāṃ sthitvā)* priya|kāriṇi! kim ataḥ param api priyam asti?

trāto 'yaṃ Śaṃkhacūḍaḥ pataga|pati|mukhād.
Vainateyo vinītas.
tena prāg bhakṣitā ye viṣa|dhara|patayo,
jīvitās te 'pi sarve.
mat|prāṇ'|āptyā vimuktā na gurubhir asavaś.
cakravartitvam āptaṃ
tvattas. tvaṃ, devi, dṛṣṭā. priyam aparam ataḥ
prārthyate kiṃ mayā yat? [39]

What's more,

Let this golden discus be the best,
And this white elephant with four tusks,
The black horse and Málayavati too—
Behold these your treasures, emperor!*

And here, at my urging, King Matánga and other people, as well as the lords of the Magicians, bow to you in devotion, their upper bodies bent down, making a row of rainbows displayed by the scintillation from their unsteady crest gems! My dear boy, what further favor can I provide for you?

HERO: *(on his knees)* You who gives favors! Is there a favor 5.210
beyond this?

Shankha·chuda here has been saved from the mouth
of the Lord of Birds.
The son of Vínata has been disciplined.*
Absolutely every snake formerly eaten by him
has been given life.
Through the return of my own life, my parents
have not given up theirs.
You have made me emperor.
I have seen you, goddess. What favor beyond this
can I ask for?

tath" âpy etāvad astu:

bharata|vākyam

vṛṣṭiṃ hṛṣṭa|śikhaṇḍi|tāṇḍava|bhṛtaḥ
kāle kirantv ambudāḥ,
kurvantaḥ pratirūḍha|santata|harit|
sasy'|ôttarīyāṃ kṣitim.
cinvānāḥ sukṛtāni vīta|vipado
nirmatsarair mānasair
modantāṃ ghana|baddha|bāndhava|suhṛd|
goṣṭhī|pramodāḥ prajāḥ. [40]

5.215 api ca,

śivam astu sarva|jagatāṃ.
para|hita|niratā bhavantu bhūta|gaṇāḥ.
doṣāḥ prayāntu nāśaṃ.
sarvatra sukhī bhavatu lokaḥ. [41]

niṣkrāntāḥ sarve.

pañcamo 'ṅkaḥ.

Nāgānandaṃ samāptam.

Even so, may the following come true:

Concluding Benediction

Let the clouds make rain showers at the due time,
bringing wild dancing to the delighted peacocks,
Clothing the earth with dense sprouted green corn.
Let people rejoice with minds free from jealousy,
heaping up good deeds,
Free from misfortune, delighting in the close-bound
society of relatives and friends.

What's more, 5.215

May all worlds have prosperity. Let the multitude
of beings be determined to help others.
Let wickedness be destroyed. Let the world
become completely happy.*

They all leave.

End of Act Five.

"How the Nagas were Pleased" is finished.

THE SHATTERED THIGHS

INTRODUCTION

Source

"THE SHATTERED THIGHS" (*Ūrubhaṅga*) is a one-act play based on the "Maha·bhárata." One of seven plays by Bhasa that share this source, it explores the duel between Bhima and Duryódhana that is the penultimate action of the great war at the core of the epic. The eighteenth day of the battle between the Pándava and Káurava clans has seen the latter almost entirely destroyed. Its remnants have fled, among them Duryódhana who has hidden in a lake. The triumphant Pándava army, while rooting out survivors, finds him and forces him into the fatal duel with Bhima.

In the first third of the play, three soldiers describe the battle ground and witness for us, at first hand, the duel that ends with the foul blow, below the waist, delivered by Bhima. The remainder of the play has various parties interact with the fatally wounded Kuru chief, Duryódhana, and concludes with his death, the withdrawal of his father, Dhrita·rashtra, to the wilderness and Ashva·tthaman's departure to slaughter the sleeping Pándavas at night.

The significance of the "Shattered Thighs" lies not just in the rehearsal of an infamous and traumatic scene from the epic, but also in its unexpected reworking of the ethos of the dying chief Duryódhana. In the "Maha·bhárata" he is a greedy and overweening character who dies bitterly exhorting those who remain on his side to wipe out the Pándavas in revenge for his unfair death. There the manner of his death reflects his earlier conduct. In this play he is noble, just and reconciled to his death and its manner. He pleads with his family and clan members to be reconciled to the outcome of the war and for his son to honor and obey his vanquishers. He argues with Bala·rama and Ashva·tthaman not to continue the fight, and that his own ugly and dishonorable demise is justified in the light of the bad deeds of his own side against their foes. As he dies he tells us his vision of a celestial elevation appropriate to a hero's death. Against the conventions of Sanskrit drama, he dies on stage.

The keen reader will take pleasure, no doubt, from reading the "Shattered Thighs" in conjunction with the final section of 'Shalya' (*Śalyaparvan*), the section of the "Maha·bhárata" on the mace battle (*Gadāyuddhaparvan*),[1] and the brief account of Duryódhana's dying moments after the night massacre in 'Dead of the Night' (*Sauptikaparvan*), from which its action is drawn, and in doing so may note several other changes made by the playwright (or, less likely in my view but nevertheless suggested by other commentators, taken from a different version of the epic known to him). A brief summary of other major changes includes: Krishna, rather than Árjuna, incites Bhima to strike the foul blow, but after the blow it is not Krishna who pacifies Bala·rama, but Duryódhana himself; Dhrita·rashtra and other members of his family enter the battlefield to find Duryódhana, rather than being informed of his death in Hástina·pura; rather than invest Ashva·tthaman as general in order to conduct the night slaughter of the Pándavas, Duryódhana attempts to dissuade him; and Duryódhana here dies quickly, before the night slaughter takes place, rather than after Ashva·tthaman's return from it.

Bhasa, "Bhasa" or Anon?

No one can discuss the "Shattered Thighs" without addressing the identity of its author. Bhasa is the name of an illustrious predecessor of the great Sanskrit poet Kali·dasa, mentioned by him with great respect. However, except for a few quotations in late collections of belles lettres, his works were apparently lost. The world of Sanskrit literature was therefore electrified by the announcement by GANAPATI SHASTRI (G) of his discovery in 1909–10 of some thirteen plays by Bhasa, found by him in a manuscript in the Manalikkara Matham, near Padmanabhapuram, Travancore. He went on to publish them in the "Trivandrum Sanskrit Series" and they are thus sometimes referred to as "the Trivandrum plays."[2] Here then were thirteen plays, one of which was apparently Bhasa's lost *Svapnavāsavadatta*, and another, called *Cārudatta*, clearly related to Shúdraka's "Little Clay Cart" (*Mṛcchakaṭikā*). The others were interesting compositions taking their themes mainly from the epic literature, utilizing a robust, naturalistic descriptive style free from the elaboration that characterized the later literary ideal; the Prakrit speakers used what appeared to be a form of that language falling neatly between that used by Ashva·ghosha and that of Kali·dasa (i.e. second–fifth century CE). The formal structure of these plays was different from that otherwise universally employed, and was thought to shed light on the development of the drama as a literary form. Everyone should have been happy.

Yet within a decade dissatisfaction with the attribution to Bhasa was appearing in print, both in vernacular journals in India and in Western academic journals. Two brothers, A.K. and K.R. Pisharoti, made it clear that a number of features of these plays, far from being unique were in fact common in plays performed in the theater of Kerala. One by one, as the scholarly discussion of the issues evolved, each of the features thought to confirm the identification of Bhasa was scrutinized and shown to be wanting. Scholarship had found "the Bhasa problem" and it became de rigueur for Indian and Western scholars to take it up and declare their colors for or against the attribution. While it was possible for Warder to write in 1974 of "the[se] plays which perhaps the prevailing, but not the unanimous, opinion of modern readers ascribes to Bhasa," current Western scholarship, if represented by Brückner and Tieken, firmly locates them as more recent anonymous compositions coming out of the Keralan performance tradition and possibly dating from the seventh century CE. (All known manuscripts of Bhasa plays come from Kerala.) In between are a number of positions, which include the possibilities that only two (*Svapna* and *Pratimā*) are by Bhasa, or that the corpus consists of texts based on genuine works of Bhasa but subsequently rewritten or revised, particularly for the needs of performance in the theater of later centuries. Sukthankar also proposed that the five one-act "Maha·bhárata" plays were in fact the separated acts of a lengthy dramatic rendering of the epic, the full version of which might yet emerge from the manuscript records. Estimations of the date of the plays has ranged between sixth–fourth century BCE and eleventh century CE, and direct citations of any, other than *Svapna*, occur only from fifteenth-century Keralan sources! As far as I am aware, all arguments regarding the author's identity or date are circumstantial.

The reader should therefore feel free to read this play as the work of Bhasa, the honored predecessor of Kali·dasa, or perhaps to take a more agnostic stance thinking of it as a revised "Bhasa" work, or even to side with that more skeptical strand of scholarship that looks to Kerala as the source and simply think of the author as "anon." My own opinion is closest to the last position, since my comparison of the text of the play with its "source" in the *Śalyaparvan* of the "Maha·bhárata" suggests that it is possibly modeled on the Southern recension of the epic and is therefore more likely composed in Kerala, but I must confess that at a certain level I do not much care. It is no great concern to me whether one can associate this text with a "great" name, such as Bhasa, although a part of me is illogically happy to continue to do so, and for convenience in present purposes I write of Bhasa as the author. More importantly, is "The Shattered Thighs" itself a great work?

Literary Quality

Ganapati Shastri was convinced of the superior literary merits of these works:

> *[T]he characteristic merits of these Natakas are also in consonance with their extreme antiquity. The manner of expression in them is quite unique; for their language is so clear, lofty and majestic, as well sweet and charming; and it is very seldom, if at all, that we meet with such excellences in works which are less than ten centuries old. ... That these dramas issued forth from the mouth of the poet as freely as breath itself, will be apparent to all learned men on examination. In every way it appears*

> *to me that the elegance of diction as well as exposition in these dramas is only a different but a more pleasing form of Rishisuktis.* (Ganapati Shastri 1925: 53–59)

He goes on to quote as illustration of these merits "The Shattered Thighs" v. 28:

> *'Til here today I raise my plow to Bhima's*
> *broad chest,*
> *Making furrows in that meadow inundated in*
> *sweat and gore, ripe and fresh,*
> *In its mouth the remains of Saubha, the aerial city,*
> *the grappling hook for the battlements on the*
> *ramparts of the great ásura's city;*
> *That diverted the waters of the Kalíndi, and is*
> *honored with gifts that are the lives of the forces*
> *of my foes.* (75 [28])

The Pisharotis assess the virtues of the plays somewhat differently:

> *One who is familiar with the Kerala stage and its mode of acting can easily understand that these dramas would be successful on our stage, and will be forced even to say that all their merit lies in their fitness for the stage. Even the casual reader must be struck by the general simplicity and elegance of their language, the importance assigned to incidents and situations of dramatic character, the prominence given to character-evolution, the numerous gaps left in each drama to be filled up by the actors, the brisk and vigorous dialogues.* (Pisharoti & Pisharoti 1923: 114)

"The Shattered Thighs" is certainly a powerful piece of literature, that shapes in a radically new way the well-known episode of the epic from which it is drawn. That reshaping may have been the result of the powerful imagination of a great literary figure transforming a cad into the model of the *dayāvīra*, the compassionate hero, or of working actors creating a powerful theatrical accompaniment to the rituals of death wherein the need for reconciliation is uppermost (more on these issues shortly).

The Compassionate Hero, Tragedy, and Ritual

How should we understand this rather enigmatic play? Does "The Shattered Thighs" refute colonialist critiques of Sanskrit drama that it lacks tragedy and is therefore, implicitly, inferior to the European drama? How might we understand such a play as an anonymous composition in the context of theater performance in South India?

"The Shattered Thighs" is a *vyāyoga*, a one-act play on a heroic epic subject, that excludes the erotic and comic moods as well as women as major protagonists, and whose action is completed in a single day. Even a superficial reading allows the reader to identify examples of the horrifying, fearful and compassionate moods, *rasa*, but can we say what is the dominant mood? Taking the transformation of Duryódhana's character in "The Shattered Thighs" as a starting point, GEROW develops an interpretation of our play as an exemplification of compassionate heroism, *dayāvīrya*, in which Duryódhana rises above the preoccupations of heroism in battle, *raṇavīrya*, and even of compassion, *karuṇā* (in his interactions with his family), and, as a hero compassionately concerned for his survivors, in the second half of the play attempts to instruct those who survive him in the limitations of grief. In the course of this analysis GEROW also situates the idea of tragedy firmly within the Western tradition derived from Aristotle which revolves around the principle that the tragic protagonist is one who experiences a self-induced downfall usually resulting from a flaw inherent in his character. Duryódhana's downfall here, he suggests, does not result from a personal flaw but from Bhima's trickery. In the light of what GEROW describes as the "uniformly optimistic" outlook of Sanskrit drama, "tragedy" as such has no meaning in the broader Indian outlook in which "the play [is] a celebration of reintegration and wholeness" and even death is "a temporary and resolvable condition."

From a similar starting point, and explicitly at odds with GEROW, TIEKEN develops a rather different interpretation of "The Shattered Thighs." Duryódhana's transformation reflects the needs of a community to understand that a person's anger must be resolved before death, else they will trouble the living from beyond the grave. For TIEKEN "The Shattered Thighs" was composed anonymously within the performance community of South India in order to be integrated with funeral rites proper and so to reassure the living of the peaceful passing over of the deceased and the living's future freedom from supernatural harassment. This context would also explain the several references within the play to funerary practice and the offering of sacrificial food, *piṇḍa*, that must be given to the deceased.

All these concerns are to some extent those of other ages. Readers can enjoy "The Shattered Thighs" now for themselves, and will doubtless illuminate its words with their own experience of life—and death.

The Sanskrit text

I have mentioned that G published "The Shattered Thighs" based on a single manuscript. Subsequently further manuscripts of it and the other Trivandrum plays have been identified, although there is no published text critically utilizing all six manuscripts of the play that have been mentioned in the public record. Indeed, it appears that while as many as five manuscripts of it have surfaced since G's first discovery, three of these six have also sunk once again beneath the horizon of public access. There are therefore three manuscripts that could be used to revise our text, one the source of its original publication and another, that was used by DEVADHAR (D). This suggests that there is left only one manuscript whose evidence has not been represented in print. Sadly the constraints of time have not allowed me to consult it. (Compare BRÜCKNER and UNNI on the manuscripts.) I take some comfort from BRÜCKNER's observations that in general the manuscript tradition for the Bhasa corpus is fairly unitary and records no significant variations—an observation borne out by comparison of G and D. Our materials for this text, then, consist of G's edition, which of course contains his suggestions for emendation where that manuscript is problematic. In addition we have the edition published by D, who had to hand a manuscript now no longer available but that provided a number of variant readings that he incorporated into his text. Sadly D does not record the readings of his manuscript sources in detail, and neither editor explains how they have used their materials. The text I provide here is therefore not a new edition based on new primary sources, but makes choices between these two printed sources while tending to prefer G over D. I have endnoted all variant readings where they involve differences of meaning. All remaining variants, invariably minor, will be noted on the CSL website.

Notes

1 'Shalya,' volume two, translated by MEILAND 2007.

2 GAṆAPATI ŚĀSTRĪ's pioneering edition, long out of print, is now available online and can be downloaded without cost from the Million Book Project at Internet Archive (http://www.archive.org).

Bibliography

There are several printed editions of "The Shattered Thighs" apart from those of GANAPATI SHASTRI and DEVADHAR. Details of these along with a fuller bibliography can be found on the CSL website.

EDITIONS AND TRANSLATIONS

BHATNAGAR, K.N.: *Bhāsa's Ūrubhaṅgam.* Edited with an introduction, Prose Order, Literal Hindi rendering of verses, glossary, English translation, Notes and Appendices of metre, dramaturgical terms, questions, indices of verses and important words, etc., etc. Lahore: Motilal Banarsi Das, 1937.

DEVADHAR, C.R.: *Ūrubhaṅgam (Breaking of thighs). A Sanskrit One-act Play Attributed to Bhasa.* Critically edited with Introduction,

Notes and Translation. Poona Oriental Series no. 72. Poona: Oriental Book Agency, 1940.

GAṆAPATI ŚĀSTRĪ, T.: *The Madhyamavyāyoga, Dūtavākya, Dūtaghaṭotkacha, Karṇabhāra and Ūrubhanga of Bhāsa*. Trivandrum: Government Press, 1912.

MEILAND, J.: *Shalya, Volume Two*. New York: New York University Press & JJC Foundation, 2007.

SECONDARY LITERATURE

BRÜCKNER, H.: "Manuscripts and Performance Traditions of the So-called 'Trivandrum-Plays' Ascribed to Bhāsa—A report on work in progress." *Bulletin d'Études Indiennes* 17–18 (1999–2000), 501–550.

GEROW, E.: "Bhāsa's Ūrubhaṅga and Indian Poetics." *Journal of the American Oriental Society* vol. 105, no. 3. Indological Studies Dedicated to DANIEL H.H. INGALLS (1985), 405–412.

PISHAROTI, A.K. and K.R. PISHAROTI: "'Bhasa's Works'—Are They Genuine?" *Bulletin of the School of Oriental Studies*" vol. 3, no. 1 (1923), 107–117.

TIEKEN, H.: "The So-called Trivandrum Plays Attributed to Bhāsa." *Wiener Zeitschrift für die Kunde Südasiens* 37 (1993), 5–44.

TIEKEN, H.: "The *pūrvaraṅga*, the *prasthāvanā*, and the *sthāpaka*." *Wiener Zeitschrift für die Kunde Südasiens* 45 (2001), 91–124.

UNNI, N.P.: *Bhāsa Afresh: New Problems in Bhāsa Plays*. Delhi: Nag Publishers, 2000.

WARDER, A.K.: *Indian Kāvya Literature. Volume Two: The Origins and Formation of Classical Kāvya*. 2nd revised edition. Delhi: Motilal Banarsidass, 1990 (1st edition, 1974).

Dramatis Personæ

Characters marked with ⌜corner brackets⌟ speak Prakrit.

KURUS

SOLDIERS:	three from DURYÓDHANA's army, on the battlefield of Kuru·kshetra
DURYÓDHANA:	a chief, the eldest and sole surviving son of DHRITA·RASHTRA
DHRITA·RASHTRA:	blind elder, father of a hundred sons of whom DURYÓDHANA is the last
⌜GANDHÁRI⌟:	wife of DHRITA·RASHTRA, mother of those one hundred sons
⌜DÚRJAYA⌟:	DURYÓDHANA's infant son
⌜MÁLAVI⌟ and ⌜PÁURAVI⌟:	the wives of DURYÓDHANA
ASHVA·TTHAMAN:	son of Drona, ally of the Kurus and leader of the night raid that slaughters the Pándava army

OTHERS

BALA·RAMA/BALA·DEVA:	brother of Krishna, tutor in mace fighting to Bhima and DURYÓDHANA
PRODUCER OF THE PLAY	
ASSISTANT:	to the PRODUCER

PROLOGUE

nāndy|ante tataḥ praviśati SŪTRA|DHĀRAḤ.

SŪTRA|DHĀRAḤ:

Bhīṣma|Droṇa|taṭāṃ, Jayadratha|jalāṃ,
Gāndhāra|rāja|hradāṃ,
Karṇa|Drauṇi|Kṛp'|ôrmi|nakra|makarāṃ,
Duryodhana|srotasaṃ
tīrṇaḥ śatru|nadīṃ Śarāsa|sikatāṃ
yena plaven' Ârjunaḥ,
śatrūṇāṃ taraṇeṣu vaḥ sa bhagavān
astu plavaḥ Keśavaḥ. [1]

evam ārya|miśrān vijñāpayāmi... aye, kin nu khalu mayi vijñāpana|vyagre śabda iva śrūyate? aṅga! paśyāmi.

NEPATHYE: ete smo bhoḥ! ete smaḥ!

SŪTRA|DHĀRAḤ: bhavatu! vijñātam.

(praviśya) PĀRIPĀRŚVAKAḤ: bhāva! kuto nu khalv ete

svarg'|ârtham āhava|mukh'|ôdyata|gātra|homā,
nārāca|tomara|śatair viṣamī|kṛt'|âṅgāḥ,
matta|dvipendra|daśan'|ôllikhitaiḥ śarīrair
anyonya|vīrya|nikaṣāḥ puruṣā bhramanti? [2]

After the blessing the* PRODUCER *enters.*

PRODUCER:

> May the illustrious Késhava be a raft for you
> in crossing over your foes,
> The raft by which Árjuna crossed the river of his
> enemies, its gravel Sharása,
> Bhishma and Drona its shores, Jayad·ratha its
> waters, the king of Gandhára its eddies,
> Karna, Drona's son and Kripa its waves, alligators
> and crocodiles, Duryódhana its current.*

So, good people, I announce... Hey! How come there is shouting just as I am getting into my announcement? Hmm! Let me take a look.

OFF STAGE: Ho! It's us! Here we are!

PRODUCER: Well! I see what it is.

ASSISTANT: *(entering)* Sir! Where have these men come from?

> In hope of heaven their bodies are an offering
> readied in the maw of battle's sacrifice,
> Their limbs bristled with hundreds of spears
> and arrow bolts,
> Their bodies carved up by the tusks of furious
> bull elephants,
> These people roam, each the touchstone of
> another's valor.

SŪTRA|DHĀRAḤ: māriṣa, kiṃ n' âvagacchasi? tanaya|śata|naya|śūnye Duryodhan'|âvaśeṣe Dhṛtarāṣṭra|pakṣe, Pāṇḍava|Janārdan'|âvaśiṣṭe Yudhiṣṭhira|pakṣe, rājñāṃ śarīra|samākīrṇe Samantapañcake

etad raṇ'|āhata|gaj'|âśva|narendra|yaudhaṃ
  saṅkīrṇa|lekhyam iva citra|paṭaṃ praviddham.
yuddhe Vṛkodara|Suyodhanayoḥ pravṛtte
  yaudhā narendra|nidhan'|âika|gṛhaṃ praviṣṭāḥ. [3]

niṣkrāntau.

sthāpanā.

PRODUCER: Don't you understand, lad? Now that Duryódhana is the only survivor on Dhrita·rashtra's side, bereft as it is of the wiles of his one hundred sons, and on Yudhi·shthira's side there are only the Pándavas and Janárdana, Samanta·pánchaka is strewn with the bodies of chieftains.

Here soldiers and captains, elephants and horses
killed in battle
Are crammed like a painting with crowded figures.
As Wolf-belly and Suyódhana start to fight
Their troops have already entered death's lonely hall
of lords.

They walk off. 10

End of Prologue.

SUPPORTING SCENE

tataḥ praviśanti BHAṬĀS *trayaḥ.*

SARVE: ete smo bhoḥ! ete smaḥ!

PRATHAMAḤ:

vairasy' ākvathanaṃ, balasya nikaṣaṃ,
māna|pratiṣṭhā|gṛhaṃ,
yuddheṣv apsarasāṃ svayaṃvara|sabhāṃ,
śaurya|pratiṣṭhāṃ nṛṇām,
rājñāṃ paścima|kāla|vīra|śayanaṃ,
prāṇ'|âgni|homa|kratuṃ
samprāptā raṇa|saṃjñam āśrama|padaṃ
rājñāṃ nabhaḥ|saṅkramam. [4]

DVITĪYAḤ: samyag bhavān āha!

upala|viṣamā nāg'|êndrāṇāṃ
śarīra|dharā dharā,
diśi diśi kṛtā gṛdhr'|āvāsā,
hat'|âtirathā rathāḥ,
avani|patayaḥ svargaṃ prāptāḥ
kriyā|maraṇe raṇe,
pratimukham ime tat|tat kṛtvā
ciraṃ nihat'|āhatāḥ. [5]

TṚTĪYAḤ: evam etat.

kari|vara|kara|yūpo,
bāṇa|vinyasta|darbho,
hata|gaja|cayan'|ôcco
vaira|vahni|pradīptaḥ,
dhvaja|vitata|vimānaḥ,

Three SOLDIERS *enter.*

ALL: Ho! It's us! Here we are!

FIRST SOLDIER:

The decoction of enmity,* the touchstone of strength,
  the home of honor and pride
In martial engagements the wedding chapel
  where heavenly nymphs choose husbands,
  the stage for manly heroism,
The hero's crib for chieftains in their last moments,
  a burned sacrifice of life:
We have reached the hermitage called "battle,"
  the royal road to heaven!

SECOND SOLDIER: How right you are!

The ground is hummocked from holding the bodies
  of bull elephants,
On all sides vultures nest, chariots have their
  warriors down,
Lords of the earth have attained heaven in a battle
  where there is death in every action,
Having done this or that deed face to face
  they are long since slain.

THIRD SOLDIER: That's how it is.

The posts are the trunks of these wonderful elephants,
  the sacred grass the arrow shafts spread about;
The teetering woodstack the slaughtered elephants
  blazing with the fire of enmity;
The celestial palaces are the streaming banners,

siṃhanād'|ôcca|mantraḥ,
patita|paśu|manuṣyaḥ
saṃsthito yuddha|yajñaḥ. [6]

PRATHAMAḤ: idam aparaṃ paśyetāṃ bhavantau,

ete paraspara|śarair hṛta|jīvitānāṃ
dehai raṇ'|âjira|mahīṃ samupāśritānām
kurvanti c' âtra piśit'|ārdra|mukhā vihaṅgā
rājñāṃ śarīra|śithilāni vibhūṣaṇāni. [7]

DVITĪYAḤ:

prasakta|nārāca|nipāta|pātitaḥ,
samagra|yuddh'|ôdyata|kalpito gajaḥ
viśīrṇa|varmā, sa|śaraḥ, sa|kārmuko
nṛp'|āyudh'|āgāram iv' âvasīdati. [8]

TṚTĪYAḤ: idam aparaṃ paśyetāṃ bhavantau,

mālyair dhvaj'|âgra|patitaiḥ kṛta|muṇḍa|mālaṃ,
lagn'|âika|sāyaka|varaṃ rathinaṃ vipannam,
jāmātaraṃ pravahaṇād iva bandhu|nāryo
hṛṣṭāḥ śivā ratha|mukhād avatārayanti. [9]

SARVE: aho tu khalu nihata|pātita|gaja|turaga|nara|rudhira|kalila|bhūmi|pradeśasya, vikṣipta|varma|carm'|ātapatra|cāmara|tomara|śara|kunta|kavaca|kabandh'|âdi|pary-ākulasya, śakti|prāsa|paraśu|bhiṇḍipāla|śūla|musala|

the mantras the trembling war cries;
The people are the fallen beasts.
The rite of battle is in place.

FIRST SOLDIER: See over here,

These birds here, their faces wet with gobs of flesh,
Tweak the insignia from the bodies of chieftains
Whose corpses, robbed of life by each other's shafts,
Rest on the soil that forms the arena of battle.

SECOND SOLDIER:

An elephant fully equipped and ready for the fight,
Like a royal armory with his shafts and bows,
Forced down by the deluge of arrow bolts
that rain upon him,
Sinks down, his armor split.

THIRD SOLDIER: See over here,

An unfortunate charioteer, a bridegroom clinging
to a single sword,*
The garland on his shaven head a chaplet
dropped from the banner top.
Like the ladies of the family handing down
a son-in-law from the wedding carriage*
Excited she-jackals pull him down from
the chariot's mouth.

ALL: Aah! Samanta·pánchaka is frightful—a tract of ground awash with the blood of wounded and dead elephants, horses and men; crowded with scattered armor, shields, sun shields, chowries, throwing axes, arrows, lances,

mudgara|varāhakarṇa|kaṇaya|karpaṇa|śaṅku|trāsi|gad”|ādibhir āyudhair ākīrṇasya Samantapañcakasya pratibhayatā!

25 PRATHAMAḤ: iha hi,

rudhira|sarito nistīryante
    hata|dvipa|saṅkramā;
nṛpati|rahitaiḥ srastaiḥ sūtair
    vahanti rathān hayāḥ;
patita|śirasaḥ pūrv'|âbhyāsād
    dravanti kabandhakāḥ;
puruṣa|rahitā mattā nāgā
    bhramanti yatas tataḥ. [10]

DVITĪYAḤ: idam aparaṃ paśyetāṃ bhavantau! ete,

gṛdhrā madhūka|mukul'|ônnata|piṅgal'|âkṣā,
    daity'|êndra|kuñjara|nat'|âṅkuśa|tīkṣṇa|tuṇḍāḥ
bhānty ambare vitata|lamba|vikīrṇa|pakṣā,
    māṃsaiḥ pravāla|racitā iva tāla|vṛntāḥ. [11]

TṚTĪYAḤ:

eṣā nirasta|haya|nāga|narendra|yaudhā,
    vyaktī|kṛtā dinakar'|ôgra|karaiḥ samantāt,
nārāca|kunta|śara|tomara|khaḍga|kīrṇā
    tārā|gaṇaṃ patitam udvahat' îva bhūmiḥ. [12]

mailed torsos and other things; scattered with weapons like pikes, spears, axes,* slingshots, spikes, pestles, battle hammers, arrows, iron bars, lances, darts and terrifying maces.

FIRST SOLDIER: Here,

Dead elephants bridge the streams of blood.
Swift horses draw driverless chariots,
their chieftains lost.
Torsos flail around from habit though their heads
are severed.
Distraught elephants charge hither and thither,
their riders gone.

SECOND SOLDIER: Look over here! See,

The vultures, eyes tawny and bulging like
madhúka buds,*
Beaks as sharp as the goad used on the demon king's
prize elephant,
Gleam in the sky, their huge wings unfurled
and pendant,
Like palm fans studded with corals of meat.

THIRD SOLDIER:

The harsh rays of the sun illumine all around
These fallen steeds and elephants, chiefs and soldiers.
The ground is scattered with arrow bolts, lances,
arrows, swords and throwing axes,
Which it wears like a fallen constellation of stars.

PRATHAMAḤ: īdṛśyām apy avasthāyām a|vimukta|śobhā virājante kṣatriyāḥ. iha hi,

srast'|ôdvartita|netra|ṣaṭpada|gaṇā,
tāmr'|ôṣṭha|patr'|ôtkarā,
bhrū|bhed'|âñcita|kesarā, sva|makuṭa|
vyāviddha|saṃvartikā,
vīry'|āditya|vibodhitā raṇa|mukhe,
nārāca|nāl'|ônnatā,
niṣkampā sthala|padmin" îva racitā
rājñām a|bhītair mukhaiḥ. [13]

DVITĪYAḤ: īdṛśānām api kṣatriyāṇāṃ mṛtyuḥ prabhavati. na śakyaṃ khalu viṣama|sthaiḥ puruṣai rāja|bal'|ādhānaṃ kartum.

TṚTĪYAḤ: kiṃ ca re, prabhavati kṣatriyāṇām iti?

PRATHAMAḤ: kaḥ saṃśayaḥ?

TṚTĪYAḤ: mā, mā bhavān evam!

spṛṣṭvā Khāṇḍava|dhūma|rañjita|guṇaṃ,
saṃśaptak'|ôtsādanaṃ,
svarg'|ākranda|haraṃ, nivāta|kavaca|
prāṇ'|ôpahāraṃ dhanuḥ
Pārthen' âdya balān Maheśvara|raṇa|
kṣep'|âvaśiṣṭaiḥ śarair
darp'|ôtsikta|vaśā nṛpā raṇa|mukhe
mṛtyoḥ pratigrāhitāḥ. [14]

FIRST SOLDIER: Even in such a plight the warriors look regal and do not lose their splendor. For here,

With the bee swarms of their bulging or sunken eyes,
and the leaf drifts of their dark red lips,
With the curved stamen of their frowns,
and the winding leaf shoots of their diadems,
Brought to bloom by the sun of their valor in
the van of battle, lifted up on the lotus stalks
of the arrow bolts,
The fearless faces of these chieftains are arrayed
like a motionless lotus pond on dry land.

SECOND SOLDIER: Death overcomes even warriors such as these. People in dire straits cannot exercise the authority of a chief.*

THIRD SOLDIER: It even overcomes warriors?

FIRST SOLDIER: No doubt!

THIRD SOLDIER: * No, don't say that!

It was Árjuna, the son of Pritha, who forced them
to accept death today in the midst of battle,
Those kings whose authority was overblown
with arrogance, using the arrows from his battle
with the Great Lord Shiva!
He clutched his bow, the annihilator of
the oath-bound confederates, its string stained
with smoke from the Khándava forest,
The bow that made an offering of the lives
of the demons with impervious armor,
that took away the weeping from heaven.*

SARVE: aye, śabdaḥ!

kiṃ meghā ninadanti, vajra|patanaiś
cūrṇī|kṛtāḥ parvatā?
nirghātais tumula|svana|pratibhayaiḥ
kiṃ dāryate vā mahī?
kiṃ muñcaty anil'|âvadhūta|capala|
kṣubdh'|ôrmi|māl"|ākulaṃ
śabdaṃ Mandara|kandar'|ôdara|darīḥ
saṃhatya vā sāgaraḥ? [15]

bhavatu, paśyāmas tāvat.

sarve parikrāmanti.

PRATHAMAḤ: aye! etat khalu Draupadī|keśa|dharṣaṇ'|âvamarṣitasya Pāṇḍava|madhyamasya Bhīmasenasya bhrātṛ|śata|vadha|kruddhasya mahārāja|Duryodhanasya ca Dvaipāyana|Halāyudha|Kṛṣṇa|Vidura|pramukhānāṃ Kuru|Yadu|kula|daivatānāṃ pratyakṣaṃ pravṛttaṃ gadā|yuddham.

DVITĪYAḤ:

Bhīmasy' ôrasi cāru|kāñcana|śilā|
pīne pratisphālite,
bhinne Vāsava|hasti|hasta|kaṭhine
Duryodhan'|âṃsa|sthale,
anyonyasya bhuja|dvay'|ântara|taṭeṣv
āsajyamān'|āyudhe
yasmiṃś caṇḍa|gad"|âbhighāta|janitaḥ
śabdaḥ samuttiṣṭhati. [16]

ALL: What noise!

Is that the clouds thundering or the mountains
being crushed to dust by lightning blows?
Or is the earth being cracked open by earthquakes
that terrify us with tumultuous roaring?
Or is the sea emitting the tumult of a tidal wave,
whipped by the wind, shaking, trembling,
Crashing into the caves deep in the cliffs
of sacred Mount Mándara?

Well, let's look.

They all walk around.

FIRST SOLDIER: So! It's a duel with maces that has begun in front of the divines of the Kuru and Yadu families headed by Island-born Vyasa, plow-bearing Bala·rama,* Krishna and Vídura. Bhima·sena, the middle child of the Pándavas, is enraged over Dráupadi being dragged around by her hair, and the great chief Duryódhana is filled with hate over the death of his hundred brothers.

SECOND SOLDIER:

The noise is coming from the fierce clash of maces
in which Bhima's muscular chest reverberates,
like a beautiful* slab of gold;
Duryódhana's shoulders, as tough as the trunk
of Indra's elephant, are loosened,
The weapons strike home on their flanks
between their arms.

TṚTĪYAḤ: eṣa mahā|rājaḥ,

śīrṣ'|ôtkampana|valgamāna|makuṭaḥ,
krodh'|âdhik'|âkṣ'|ānanaḥ,
sthān'|ākrāmaṇa|vāmanī|kṛta|tanuḥ,
pratyagra|hast'|ôcchrayaḥ,
yasy' âiṣā ripu|śoṇit'|ārdra|kalilā
bhāty agra|haste gadā,
Kailāsasya girer iv' âgra|śikhar'|ôd-
dhūtā Mahendr'|âśaniḥ. [17]

PRATHAMAḤ: eṣa samprahāra|rudhira|sikt'|âṅgas tāvad dṛśyatāṃ Pāṇḍavaḥ.

nirbhinn'|âgra|lalāṭa|vānta|rudhiro,
bhagn'|âṃsa|kūṭa|dvayaḥ,
sāndrair nirgalita|prahāra|rudhirair
ārdrī|kṛt'|ôraḥ|sthalaḥ
Bhīmo bhāti gad"|âbhighāta|rudhira|
klinn'|âvagāḍha|vraṇaḥ,
śailo Merur iv' âiṣa dhātu|salil'|ā-
sār'|ôpadigdh'|ôpalaḥ. [18]

DVITĪYAḤ:

bhīmāṃ gadāṃ kṣipati. garjati valgamānaḥ.
śīghraṃ bhujaṃ harati, tasya kṛtaṃ bhinatti.
cārīṃ gatiṃ pracarati, praharaty abhīkṣṇaṃ.
saṃśikṣito nara|patir, balavāṃs tu Bhīmaḥ. [19]

THIRD SOLDIER: Here is the great chief,

His crest is jumping from the shuddering of his head,
his eyes bulging from his face in fury.*
His body bends low and he shifts his position.
He lifts up his hand repeatedly.
See the mace in his right hand that's covered with
the wet of his enemy's blood;
It looks like great Indra's thunderbolt hurled up
from the topmost peak of Kailása mountain.

FIRST SOLDIER: Look over here at the Pándava. His limbs are spattered with gore from the exchange of blows.

Bhima looks like Mount Meru, its rocks stained
by torrents of water over red ore.
His deep-cut wounds are moist with the gore
from the mace attack.
Gore pours from the tear at the top of his forehead;
the peaks of both shoulders are split.
His chest is wetted by the thick gore
that trickles from the blows.

SECOND SOLDIER:

He strikes with the dreadful mace.
He bellows as he jumps.
Quickly he lifts his arm and blocks the other's blow.
He takes a deft step* and strikes at once.
The lord of men* is well trained, but Bhima is strong.

TṚTĪYAḤ: eṣa Vṛkodaraḥ,

> śirasi guru|nikhāta|srasta|rakt'|ārdra|gātro,
> dharaṇi|dhara|nikāśaḥ, saṃyugeṣv a|prameyaḥ,
> praviśati giri|rājo medinīṃ vajra|dagdhaḥ,
> śithila|visṛta|dhātur Hemakūṭo yath" âdriḥ. [20]

PRATHAMAḤ: eṣa gāḍha | prahāra | śithilī | kṛt' | âṅgaṃ nipatantaṃ Bhīmasenaṃ dṛṣṭvā,

> ek'|âgrāṅguli|dhārit'|ônnata|mukho
> Vyāsaḥ sthito vismitaḥ. [21ab]

DVITĪYAḤ:

> dainyaṃ yāti Yudhiṣṭhiro. 'tra Viduro
> bāṣp'|ākul'|âkṣaḥ sthitaḥ. [21cd]

TṚTĪYAḤ:

> spṛṣṭaṃ Gāṇḍivam Arjunena. gaganaṃ
> Kṛṣṇaḥ samudvīkṣate [21ef]

SARVE:

> śiṣya|prītitayā halaṃ bhramayate
> Rāmo raṇa|prekṣakaḥ. [21gh]

PRATHAMAḤ: eṣa mahā|rājaḥ,

THIRD SOLDIER: Here is Wolf Belly,

Limbs wet with red blood dropping from a deep dug
wound on his head.
He has the look of a mountain. In battles
he is matchless.
The king of mountains, he hugs the earth,
as if he were Golden Peak
Riven by thunderbolts, red ore loosened and scattered.

FIRST SOLDIER: * Seeing Bhima·sena falling as his limbs are loose from a mace blow,

Here Vyasa stands astounded, upraised face propped
on a single fingertip.

SECOND SOLDIER:

Yudhi·shthira is feeling wretched. Here Vídura
stands his eyes dimmed with tears.

THIRD SOLDIER:

Árjuna is fingering his Gándiva bow.
Krishna is staring up at the sky.

ALL:

Watching the fight, Rama brandishes his plow
out of love for his pupil.

FIRST SOLDIER: Here the great chief,

vīry'|ālayo, vividha|ratna|vicitra|maulir,
yukto 'bhimāna|vinaya|dyuti|sāhasaiś ca,
vākyaṃ vadaty upahasan, «na tu, Bhīma, dīnaṃ
vīro nihanti samareṣu. bhayaṃ tyaj'!» êti. [22]

DVITĪYAḤ: eṣa idānīm apahāsyamānaṃ Bhīmasenaṃ dṛṣṭvā svam ūrum abhihatya kām api saṃjñāṃ prayacchati Janārdanaḥ.

TṚTĪYAḤ: eṣa saṃjñayā samāśvāsito Mārutiḥ,

saṃhṛtya bhrukuṭī, lalāṭa|vivare
svedaṃ kareṇ' ākṣipan,
bāhubhyāṃ pratigṛhya bhīma|vadanaś
Citrāṅgadāṃ svāṃ gadām,
putraṃ dīnam udīkṣya Sarvagatinā
labdhv" êva dattaṃ balaṃ,
garjan siṃha|vṛṣ'|ēkṣaṇaḥ kṣiti|talād
bhūyaḥ samuttiṣṭhati. [23]

60 PRATHAMAḤ: hanta, punaḥ pravṛttaṃ gadā | yuddham. anena hi,

bhūmau pāṇi|tale nighṛṣya tarasā,
bāhū pramṛjy' âdhikaṃ,
sandaṣṭ'|ôṣṭha|puṭena *vikrama/balāt*,
krodh'|âdhikaṃ garjatā,
tyaktvā dharma|ghṛṇāṃ, vihāya samayaṃ,
Kṛṣṇasya saṃjñā|samaṃ

A store of valor, his crest brilliant with an array
of gems,
Filled with pride and discipline, threat
and aggression,
Laughing in derision speaks, "But, Bhima,
A hero does not strike someone helpless in action.
Put away your terror!"

SECOND SOLDIER: See now, Janárdana has seen Bhima·sena being mocked. He slaps his thigh to give some kind of sign.

THIRD SOLDIER: The sign has revived him, the son of the Wind.*

Frowning, sweeping the sweat with his hand
from the folds where it has gathered,
Face fearsome as he catches up Chitrángada,
his own mace, with both arms,
He gets up from the ground once more, roaring,
his eyes like a lion king's,
As if the all-pervasive Wind had seen his son
helpless and given him strength.*

FIRST SOLDIER: Look! The mace duel has started again. He

Quickly wipes the palms of his hands on the ground
and vigorously rubs both arms,
Lips bitten *through the force of his gait* : *through the strength of his heroism*, yelling forcefully
out of hate.
Abandoning fellow feeling and duty, discarding
convention, on Krishna's sign

Gāndhārī|tanayasya Pāṇḍu|tanayen'
ōrvor vimuktā gadā. [24]

SARVE: hā dhik! patito mahā|rājaḥ.

TṚTĪYAḤ: eṣa rudhira | patana | dyotit' | âṅgaṃ nipatantaṃ Kuru | rājaṃ dṛṣṭvā kham utpatito bhagavān Dvaipāyanaḥ. ya eṣaḥ,

helā|saṃvṛta|locanena Halinā
netr'|ôparodhaḥ kṛto;
dṛṣṭvā krodha|nimīlitaṃ Haladharaṃ
Duryodhan'|āpekṣayā
sambhrāntaiḥ kara|pañjar'|ântara|gato
Dvaipāyana|jñāpito
Bhīmaḥ Kṛṣṇa|kar'|âvalambita|gatir
nirvāhyate Pāṇḍavaiḥ. [25]

65 PRATHAMAḤ: aye ayam apy amarṣ' | ônmīlita | locano Bhīmasen' | âpakramaṇam udvīkṣamāṇa ita ev' âbhivartate bhagavān Halāyudhaḥ. ya eṣaḥ,

pracala|lalita|mauliḥ, krodha|tāmr'|āyat'|âkṣo,
bhramara|mukha|vidaṣṭāṃ kiñ cid utkṛṣya mālām,
asita|tanu|vilambi|srasta|vastr'|ânukarṣī
kṣiti|talam avatīrṇaḥ, pāriveṣ" îva candraḥ. [26]

That son of Pandu flings the mace against the thighs
of Gandhári's son.

ALL: Oh no! The great chief is down.

THIRD SOLDIER: Blessed Island-born Vyasa has seen the Kuru chief fallen, his legs blanched with loss of blood, and starts up into the sky.*Here,

Eyes filled with contempt,* the Plow Bearer blocks
his own gaze.
Bhima, who sees that the Plow Bearer has closed
his eyes in rage on Duryódhana's behalf,
Is led away by the bewildered Pándavas,
in the net of their hands
As bidden by Island-born Vyasa, while Krishna
steadies Bhima's movements with his hand.

FIRST SOLDIER: Hey, here comes blessed Plow Bearer too. 65
Spotting Bhima·sena's deliverance his eyes stare wide open out of indignation. See,

His lovely crest is shivering.* His eyes are red
and swollen out of rage.
He hitches a little the flower garland crushed
by the mouths of bumblebees.
He draws after him garments slipped and hanging
from his darkened body
Like the enhaloed moon descended to the surface
of the earth.

DVITĪYAḤ: tad āgamyatām, vayam api tāvan mahā|rājasya pratyanantarī|bhavāmaḥ.

UBHAU: bāḍham. prathamaḥ kalpaḥ.

niṣkrāntāḥ.

70 *viṣkambhakaḥ.*

SECOND SOLDIER: Let's go. We should be with him as well.

THE OTHER TWO: Yes. Good idea.

They walk off.

End of the Supporting Scene.

MAIN SCENE

tataḥ praviśati BALADEVAḤ.

BALADEVAḤ: bho bhoḥ pārthivāḥ! na yuktam idam.

mama ripu|bala|kālaṃ lāṅgalaṃ laṅghayitvā,
raṇa|gatam ati|sandhiṃ māṃ ca n' âvekṣya darpāt,
raṇa|śirasi gadāṃ tāṃ tena Duryodhan'|ōrvoḥ
kula|vinaya|samṛddhyā pātitaḥ pātayitvā. [27]

bho Duryodhana! muhūrtaṃ tāvad ātmā dhāryatām,

Saubh'|ôcchiṣṭa|mukhaṃ, mah"|âsura|pura|
prākāra|kūṭ'|âṅkuśaṃ,
Kālindī|jala|deśikaṃ, ripu|bala|
prāṇ'|ôpahār'|ârcitaṃ
hant' ôtkṣipya halaṃ karomi rudhira|
sved'|ārdra|pāk'|ôttare
Bhīmasy' ôrasi yāvad adya vipule
kedāra|mārg'|ākulam. [28]

NEPATHYE: prasīdatu, prasīdatu bhagavān Halāyudhaḥ.

BALADEVAḤ: evaṃ|gato 'py anugacchati māṃ tapasvī Duryodhanaḥ. eṣaḥ

Thereupon enters BALA·DEVA.

BALA·DEVA: Aah, you lords! This is not right.

He has avoided my plow which delivers death
to the forces of my foes.
He has from insolence had no concern for cheating
in combat or for me.
He has brought down that mace on Duryódhana's
thighs in the fore of combat.
He has brought low the fortune and discipline
of his family, and lowered himself thereby.

Oh Duryódhana! Bear up for a moment more,

'Til here today I raise my plow to Bhima's 75
broad chest,
Making furrows in that meadow inundated in
sweat and gore, ripe and fresh,
In its mouth the remains of Saubha, the aerial city,
the grappling hook for the battlements on the
ramparts of the great *ásura*'s city;
That diverted the waters of the Kalíndi, and is
honored with gifts that are the lives of the forces
of my foes.*

OFF STAGE: Be calm. Calm down, Plow Bearer.

BALA·DEVA: Even in this wretched state Duryódhana still follows me. See,

śrīmān, saṃyuga|candanena rudhireṇ'
ārdr'|ânulipta|cchavir,
bhū|saṃsarpaṇa|reṇu|pāṭala|bhujo,
bāla|vrataṃ grāhitaḥ,
nirvṛtte 'mṛta|manthane kṣiti|dharān
muktaḥ suraiḥ s'|âsurair
ākarṣann iva bhogam arṇava|jale
śrānt'|ôjjhito Vāsukiḥ. [29]

tataḥ praviśati bhagn'|ōru|yugalo DURYODHANAḤ.

DURYODHANAḤ: eṣa bhoḥ!

Bhīmena bhittvā samaya|vyavasthāṃ
gadā|nipāta|kṣata|jarjar'|ōruḥ
bhūmau bhujābhyāṃ parikṛṣyamāṇaṃ
svaṃ deham ardh'|ôparataṃ vahāmi. [30]

prasīdatu, prasīdatu bhagavān Halāyudhaḥ.

tvat|pādayor nipatitaṃ patitasya bhūmāv
etac chiraḥ. prathamam adya vimuñca roṣam.
jīvantu te Kuru|kulasya nivāpa|meghā.
vairaṃ ca, vigraha|kathā ca, vayaṃ ca naṣṭāḥ. [31]

BALADEVAḤ: bho Duryodhana, muhūrtaṃ tāvad ātmā dhāryatām.

DURYODHANAḤ: kiṃ bhavān kariṣyati?

He is glorious. His skin is smeared and wet with gore, the sandal paste of conflict.
His arms are dusted pink from crawling on the ground. He has to move like a baby.
He is like Vásuki,* released by the gods and titans from the mountain when the churning of the ambrosia was done,
Hauling his coils through the ocean waters, abandoned and exhausted.

Thereupon enters DURYÓDHANA, *both thighs shattered.*

DURYÓDHANA: It's me!

Bhima has broken the rules of established custom.
My thighs shattered and broken by a mace blow,
I must move my own half dead body
Using both arms to drag it 'cross the ground.

Be calm. Calm down, Plow Bearer.

This, the head of a fallen man, falls to the ground at your feet.
Today, forthwith, let go your fury.
Let the clouds of funeral oblations of the Kuru clan live long.
The enmity is over; the rhetoric of conflict is over; we are over.

BALA·DEVA: O Duryódhana, bear up for a moment more.

DURYÓDHANA: What are you going to do?

BALADEVAḤ: śrūyatām,

āksipta|lāṅgala|mukh'|ôllikhitaiḥ śarīrair,
nirdārit'|âṃsa|hṛdayān musala|prahāraiḥ,
dāsyāmi saṃyuga|hatān sa|rath'|âśva|nāgān
svarg'|ânuyātra|puruṣāṃs tava Pāṇḍu|putrān. [32]

DURYODHANAḤ: mā, mā bhavān evam!

pratijñ"|âvasite Bhīme,
gate bhrātṛ|śate divam,
mayi c' âivaṃ gate, Rāma,
vigrahaḥ kiṃ kariṣyati? [33]

90 BALADEVAḤ: mat|pratyakṣaṃ vañcito bhavān, ity utpanno me roṣaḥ.

DURYODHANAḤ: vañcita iti māṃ bhavān manyate?

BALADEVAḤ: kaḥ saṃśayaḥ?

DURYODHANAḤ: hanta bhoḥ! datta|mūlyā iva me prāṇāḥ. kutaḥ,

ādīpt'|ânala|dāruṇāj jatu|gṛhād
buddhy" ātma|nirvāhiṇā,
yuddhe Vaiśravaṇ'|ālaye 'cala|śilā|
vega|pratisphālinā
Bhīmen' âdya Hiḍimba|rākṣasa|pati|
prāṇa|pratigrāhiṇā

BALA·DEVA: Listen,

I shall offer to you those sons of Pandu as
attendants in heaven,
Along with their chariots and horses and elephants
destroyed in the fight,
Their shoulders and their hearts split open
by pestle blows,
With their bodies sliced open from hurling
my plowshare.

DURYÓDHANA: No, don't be like this!

Now that Bhima has fulfilled his vow,*
Now that my hundred brothers have gone to heaven,
And now that I am in this state, Rama,
What will conflict achieve?

BALA·DEVA: You have been tricked before my eyes. That is why I am furious!

DURYÓDHANA: You think that I was tricked?

BALA·DEVA: Without doubt!

DURYÓDHANA: Surely not! My life-breath is the price paid. Because

Bhima, who by his own wits extricated himself
from the terrible lac house ablaze with fire,
Whose vehemence made reverberate* the mountain
rocks in the battle in Váishravana's abode,
The man who took the life of Hidímba
the demon lord;*

yady evaṃ samavaiṣi māṃ chala|jitaṃ,
bho Rāma, n' âhaṃ jitaḥ. [34]

BALADEVAḤ: Bhīmasena idānīṃ tava yuddha|vañcanām utpādya sthāsyati.

DURYODHANAḤ: kiṃ c' âhaṃ Bhīmasenena vañcitaḥ?

BALADEVAḤ: atha kena bhavān evaṃ|vidhaḥ kṛtaḥ?

RĀJĀ: śrūyatāṃ,

yen' Êndrasya sa Pārijātaka|tarur
mānena tulyaṃ hṛto;
divyaṃ varṣa|sahasram arṇava|jale
suptaś ca yo līlayā;
tīvrāṃ Bhīma|gadāṃ praviśya sahasā
nirvyāja|yuddha|priyas
ten' âhaṃ jagataḥ priyeṇa Hariṇā
mṛtyoḥ pratigrāhitaḥ. [35]

NEPATHYE: ⌜ussaraha, ayyā. ussaraha!⌟

BALADEVAḤ: *(vilokya)* aye! ayam atra|bhavān Dhṛtarāṣṭro Gāndhāryā Durjayen' ādeśita|mārgo 'ntaḥpur'|ânubandhaḥ śok'|âbhibhūta|hṛdayaś cakita|gatir ita ev' âbhivartate. ya eṣaḥ

vīry'|ākaraḥ, suta|śata|pravibhakta|cakṣur,
darp'|ôdyataḥ, kanaka|yūpa|vilamba|bāhuḥ,

Rama, I am not beaten if then you think I have been
beaten by him with a trick today.

BALA·DEVA: Bhima·sena has tricked you in battle and now he will survive!

DURYÓDHANA: But is it Bhima·sena who has tricked me?

BALA·DEVA: Then who has treated you in this way?

DURYÓDHANA: Listen.

It was the person who stole the Coral Tree
along with Indra's self-respect;
It was the person who just in play slept for
a thousand divine years in the ocean waters;
It was Krishna who suddenly entered into Bhima's
vehement mace,
Hari, who is loved by the whole world, who handed
me over to death, me who likes to fight fair.*

OFF STAGE: Clear the way, gentlemen. Clear the way!

BALA·DEVA: *(looking off stage)* Oh no! It is the honorable Dhrita·rashtra being announced. He has Gandhári and Dúrjaya with him and he's followed by the household. His heart is overwhelmed with grief. He is trembling with fear.* He is making his way over here. This is the man who

Is a mine of valor; whose vision was shared between
his hundred sons;
Is haughty with pride; has arms that reach down
like golden posts.

sṛṣṭo dhruvaṃ tri|diva|rakṣaṇa|jāta|śaṅkair
devair arāti|timir'|âñjali|tāḍit'|âkṣaḥ. [36]

tataḥ praviśati DHṚTARĀṢṬRO, GĀNDHĀRĪ, DEVYAU DURJAYAŚ *ca.*

DHṚTARĀṢṬRAḤ: putra, kv' âsi?

GĀNDHĀRĪ: ⌜puttaa, kahiṃ si?⌟

DEVYAU: ⌜mahā|rāa, kahiṃ si?⌟

DHṚTARĀṢṬRAḤ: bhoḥ, kaṣṭam!

vañcanā|nihataṃ śrutvā
sutam ady' āhave mama,
mukham antar|gat'|âsr'|âkṣam
andham andhataraṃ kṛtam. [37]

Gāndhāri, kiṃ dharase?

GĀNDHĀRĪ: ⌜jīvāvida mhi manda|bhāā.⌟

DEVYAU: ⌜mahā|rāa, mahā|rāa!⌟

RĀJĀ: bhoḥ, kaṣṭam, yan mam' âpi striyo rudanti.

pūrvaṃ na jānāmi gad"|âbhighāta-
rujām, idānīṃ tu samarthayāmi,
yan me prakāśī|kṛta|mūrdhajāni
raṇaṃ praviṣṭāny avarodhanāni. [38]

Surely the gods were concerned to protect their
highest heaven when they created him
With a cupped hand of malign darkness added
in his eyes for punishment.

Thereupon enters DURYÓDHANA*'s father* DHRITA·RASHTRA, *his mother* GANDHÁRI, *his* TWO WIVES *and his son* DÚRJAYA.

DHRITA·RASHTRA: Son, where are you?

GANDHÁRI: Where are you, my child?

THE TWO WIVES: Great chief, where are you?

DHRITA·RASHTRA: O this is too dreadful!

When I heard today that my son had been
struck down in the war by a trick,
My blind face was made more blind still by the tears
filling my eyes.

Gandhári, are you bearing up?

GANDHÁRI: I am still alive, sad though I am.

WIVES: Great chief, great chief!

DURYÓDHANA: Oh, this is too much, now that my wives are weeping too.

Before I was not conscious of the fractures from the
mace blow,
But now I really feel them,
Now that my wives have entered the battlefield
With the hair of their heads exposed.*

DHṚTARĀṢṬRAḤ: Gāndhāri, kiṃ dṛśyate Duryodhana|nāma|dheyaḥ kula|mānī?

GĀNDHĀRĪ: ⌜mahā|rāa, ṇa dissadi.⌟

DHṚTARĀṢṬRAḤ: kathaṃ na dṛśyate? ady' âsmy aham andho, yo 'ham anveṣṭavye kāle putraṃ na paśyāmi. bhoḥ Kṛtānta|hataka!

ripu|samara|vimardaṃ māna|vīrya|pradīptaṃ
suta|śatam ati|dhīraṃ vīram utpādya mānī
dharaṇi|tala|vikīrṇaṃ kiṃ sa yogyo na bhoktuṃ
sakṛd api Dhṛtarāṣṭraḥ putra|dattaṃ nivāpam? [39]

GĀNDHĀRĪ: ⌜jāda Suyodhaṇa, dehi me paḍivaaṇaṃ! putta|sada|viṇāsa|dutthidaṃ samassāsehi mahā|rāaṃ.⌟

BALADEVAḤ: aye, iyam atra|bhavatī Gāndhārī.

yā putra|pautra|vadaneṣv a|kutūhal'|âkṣī,
Duryodhan'|âstam|ita|śoka|nipīta|dhairyā,
asrair ajasram adhunā pati|dharma|cihnam
ārdrī|kṛtaṃ nayana|bandham idaṃ dadhāti. [40]

DHṚTARĀṢṬRAḤ: putra! Duryodhana! aṣṭādaś'|âkṣauhiṇī|mahārāja! kv' âsi?

DHRITA·RASHTRA: Gandhári, can you see him, the pride of our family, whom we know as Duryódhana?

GANDHÁRI: I cannot see him, great chief.

DHRITA·RASHTRA: How come you cannot see him? Now I am truly blind, when I cannot see my son as we look for him. O, Death, you vile thing,

Proud of producing a hundred sons, resolute
and brave,
Who crushed their enemy in war and were bright
with pride and valor,
Does not Dhrita·rashtra deserve to enjoy even once
The funeral oblation scattered on the ground
by a son?

GANDHÁRI: My dear Suyódhana, answer me! Comfort the great chief—he is in a state of shock at the loss of his hundred sons.*

BALA·DEVA: Oh, here is the honorable Gandhári.

Her eyes showed no keenness to see the faces of her
other sons and grandsons, but
Her fortitude has been consumed by her grief
at the downfall of Duryódhana.
This blindfold she wears as a token of devotion
to her lord
Has now been soaked continually by tears.*

DHRITA·RASHTRA: Son! Duryódhana! Great chief of eighteen armies! Where are you?

RĀJĀ: ady' âsmi mahā|rājaḥ?

DHṚTARĀṢṬRAḤ: putra|śata|jyeṣṭha! dehi me prativacanam!

DURYODHANAḤ: dadāmi khalu prativacanam. anena vṛttāntena vrīḍito 'smi.

DHṚTARĀṢṬRAḤ: ehi, putra! abhivādayasva mām.

RĀJĀ: ayam ayam āgacchāmi. *(utthānaṃ rūpayitvā patati)* hā dhik! ayaṃ me dvitīyaḥ prahāraḥ. kaṣṭaṃ bhoḥ.

hṛtaṃ me Bhīmasenena
gadā|pāta|kaca|grahe
samam ūru|dvayen' âdya
guroḥ pād'|âbhivandanam. [41]

GĀNDHĀRĪ: ⌜ettha, jādā!⌟

DEVYAU: ⌜ayye, imā mha.⌟

GĀNDHĀRĪ: ⌜aṇṇesaha bhattāraṃ.⌟

DEVYAU: ⌜gacchāmi manda|bhāā.⌟

DHṚTARĀṢṬRAḤ: ka eṣa, bhoḥ, mama vastr'|ântam ākarṣan mārgam ādeśayati?

DURJAYAḤ: ⌜tāda, ahaṃ Dujjayo.⌟

DURYÓDHANA: Today I am a great chief?

DHRITA·RASHTRA: Eldest of my hundred sons! Answer me!

DURYÓDHANA: I must answer.* This event has put me to shame.

DHRITA·RASHTRA: Come here, son! Speak to me.

DURYÓDHANA: Here, here I come. *(acts rising but falls back)* This is awful! It is a second blow. This is dreadful.

When Bhima·sena struck me with the mace
and took me by the hair today
He equally took both thighs and took away
my worship of my father's feet.*

GANDHÁRI: Here, my dear daughters!

THE TWO WIVES: Lady, here we are.

GANDHÁRI: Look for your husband.

THE TWO WIVES: I shall go. I feel so bad.

DHRITA·RASHTRA: Who is this? Who is pulling at the hem of my robe to lead my way?

DÚRJAYA: It's me, grandad, Dúrjaya.

DHṚTARĀṢṬRAḤ: pautra Durjaya, pitaram anviccha.

DURJAYAḤ: ⌜parissanto khu ahaṃ.⌟

DHṚTARĀṢṬRAḤ: gaccha! pitur aṅke viśramayiṣyasi.

DURJAYAḤ: ⌜tāda, ahaṃ gacchāmi.⌟ *(upasṛtya)* ⌜tāda, kahiṃ si?⌟

RĀJĀ: aye ayam apy āgataḥ. sarv'|âvasthāyāṃ hṛdaya|sannihitaḥ putra|sneho māṃ dahati. kutaḥ,

duḥkhānām anabhijñeyo
  mam' âṅka|śayan'|ôcitaḥ
nirjitaṃ Durjayo dṛṣṭvā
  kin nu mām abhidhāsyati? [42]

DURJAYAḤ: ⌜aaṃ mahā|rāo. bhūmīe uvaviṭṭho.⌟

RĀJĀ: putra, kim artham āgataḥ?

DURJAYAḤ: ⌜tuvaṃ cirāyasi tti.⌟

RĀJĀ: aho, asyām avasthāyāṃ putra|sneho hṛdayaṃ dahati.

DURJAYAḤ: ⌜ahaṃ pi khu de aṅke uvavisāmi.⌟

aṅkam ārohati.

DHRITA·RASHTRA: Grandson Dúrjaya, look for your father.

DÚRJAYA: But I'm tired!

DHRITA·RASHTRA: Go! You will be able to rest on your father's lap.

DÚRJAYA: I'm going, grandad. *(coming near* DURYÓDHANA*)* Daddy, where are you?

DURYÓDHANA: Oh no, he has come too. Whatever happens my love for my son fills my heart and burns me, because

He has no idea of suffering.
He loves to use my lap as his bed.
Seeing me beaten,
What will Dúrjaya say?

DÚRJAYA: Here's the great chief. He's sitting on the ground.

DURYÓDHANA: My son, what have you come for?

DÚRJAYA: Because you've been gone so long.

DURYÓDHANA: Even in this situation love for my son burns my heart.

DÚRJAYA: Just let me sit on your lap.

He climbs on DURYÓDHANA*'s lap.*

RĀJĀ: *(nivārya)* Durjaya! Durjaya! bhoḥ kaṣṭam!

hṛdaya|prīti|janano
  yo me netr'|ôtsavaḥ svayam,
so 'yaṃ kāla|viparyāsāc
  candro vahnitvam āgataḥ. [43]

DURJAYAḤ: ⌜aṅke uvavesaṃ kiṃ ṇimittaṃ tuvaṃ vāresi?⌟

RĀJĀ:

tyaktvā paricitaṃ, putra,
  yatra tatra tvay" āsyatām.
adya|prabhṛti n' âst' îdaṃ
  pūrva|bhuktaṃ tav' āsanam. [44]

DURJAYAḤ: ⌜kahiṃ ṇu khu mahā|rāo gamissadi?⌟

RĀJĀ: bhrātṛ|śatam anugacchāmi.

DURJAYAḤ: ⌜maṃ pi tahiṃ ṇehi.⌟

RĀJĀ: gaccha, putra, evaṃ Vṛkodaraṃ brūhi.

DURJAYAḤ: ⌜ehi, mahā|rāa, aṇṇesīasi.⌟

RĀJĀ: putra, kena?

DURJAYAḤ: ⌜ayyāe, ayyeṇa, savveṇa anta|ureṇa a.⌟

DURYÓDHANA: Dúrjaya! Dúrjaya! This is too much!

> He was the delight of my heart and a feast
> for my eyes.
> Through the lapse of time this moon has become
> a fire.

DÚRJAYA: Why are you stopping me from sitting on your lap?

DURYÓDHANA:

> My boy, give up the seat you loved and sit
> where else you may.
> After today this is not the seat you used to enjoy.

DÚRJAYA: Why? Are you going somewhere, great chief?

DURYÓDHANA: I shall follow after my hundred brothers.

DÚRJAYA: Take me there too.

DURYÓDHANA: Go, my boy, and say that to Wolf Belly.*

DÚRJAYA: Come on, great chief, they are looking for you.

DURYÓDHANA: Who are, my boy?

DÚRJAYA: Grandma and Grandad and the whole household.

RĀJĀ: gaccha, putra. n' âham āgantuṃ samarthaḥ.

DURJAYAḤ: ⌜ahaṃ tuvaṃ ṇaïssaṃ.⌟

RĀJĀ: bālas tvam asi, putra.

DURJAYAḤ: *(parikramya)* ⌜ayyā! aaṃ mahā|rāo!⌟

DEVYAU: ⌜hā hā mahā|rāo!⌟

DHṚTARĀṢṬRAḤ: kv' âsau mahā|rājaḥ?

GĀNDHĀRĪ: ⌜kahiṃ me puttao?⌟

DURJAYAḤ: ⌜aaṃ mahā|rāo bhūmīe uvaviṭṭho.⌟

DHṚTARĀṢṬRAḤ: hanta bhoḥ! kim ayaṃ mahā|rājaḥ?

yaḥ kāñcana|stambha|sama|pramāṇo,
loke kil' âiko vasudh"|âdhip'|êndraḥ,
kṛtaḥ sa me bhūmi|gatas tapasvī,
dvār'|êndrakīl'|ârdha|sama|pramāṇaḥ. [45]

GĀNDHĀRĪ: ⌜jāda, Suyodhaṇa, parissanto si?⌟

DURYÓDHANA: Go, my boy. I cannot come.

DÚRJAYA: I'll take you.

DURYÓDHANA: Don't be silly, my boy.

DÚRJAYA: *(stepping round him)* Ladies! Here's the great chief!

THE TWO WIVES: Oh no, oh no, the great chief!

DHRITA·RASHTRA: Where is he, the great chief?

GANDHÁRI: Where is my little boy?

DÚRJAYA: Here's the great chief, sitting on the ground.

DHRITA·RASHTRA: What, is this the great chief?

He was similar in height to a golden pillar.
The sole lord of sovereigns in the world, they said.
Now my son sits on the ground, miserable,
More like half a gate post high.

GANDHÁRI: My dear Suyódhana, are you tired out?

RĀJĀ: bhavatyāḥ khalv ahaṃ putraḥ.

DHṚTARĀṢṬRAḤ: k" êyaṃ, bhoḥ?

GĀNDHĀRĪ: ⌜mahā|rāa, aham a|bhīda|putta|ppaāiṇī.⌟

RĀJĀ: ady' ôtpannam iv' ātmānam avagacchāmi. bhos tāta, kim idānīṃ vaiklavyena?

DHṚTARĀṢṬRAḤ: putra, kathaṃ a|viklavo bhaviṣyāmi?

yasya vīrya|bal'|ôtsiktaṃ,
 saṃyug'|âdhvara|dīkṣitam
pūrvaṃ bhrātṛ|śataṃ naṣṭaṃ,
 tvayy ekasmin hate hatam. [46]

patati.

RĀJĀ: hā dhik! patito 'tra|bhavān. tāta, samāśvāsay' âtra|bhavatīm.

DHṚTARĀṢṬRAḤ: putra, kim iti samāśvāsayāmi?

RĀJĀ: a|parāṅ|mukho yudhi hata iti. bhos tāta, śoka|nigraheṇa kriyatāṃ mam' ânugrahaḥ.

tvat|pāda|mātra|praṇat'|âgra|maulir,
 jvalantam apy agnim a|cintayitvā,
yen' âiva mānena samaṃ prasūtas,
 ten' âiva mānena divaṃ prayāmi. [47]

DURYÓDHANA: Ma'm, I am certainly your son.

DHRITA·RASHTRA: Now, who is she?

GANDHÁRI: It's me, great chief, the mother of fearless sons.

DURYÓDHANA: I feel as if I was only born today. O father, don't be confused now.

DHRITA·RASHTRA: Son, how could I not be confused?

Overflowing with strength and heroism,
Consecrated for the rite of battle,
Your hundred brothers are already destroyed.
When you die, just you, everything is dead.

He collapses.

DURYÓDHANA: No! The honorable man has fallen! Father, comfort your queen.

DHRITA·RASHTRA: My son, just what comfort can I give?

DURYÓDHANA: Tell her I was killed in battle facing the enemy. Oh father, for my sake restrain your grief.

I have bowed the crown of my head to your feet.
Not even worrying about the blazing funeral pyre.
With the very same pride that I was born,
I go with pride to heaven.

DHṚTARĀṢṬRAḤ:

vṛddhasya me, jīvita|nisspṛhasya,
nisarga|sammīlita|locanasya
dhṛtiṃ nigṛhy' ātmani sampravṛttas
tīvraḥ samākrāmati putra|śokaḥ. [48]

BALADEVAḤ: bhoḥ kaṣṭam!

Duryodhana|nirāśasya,
nity'|âstam|ita|cakṣuṣaḥ
na śaknomy atra|bhavataḥ
kartum ātma|nivedanām. [49]

RĀJĀ: vijñāpayāmy atra|bhavatīm.

GĀNDHĀRĪ: ⌜bhaṇāhi, jāda.⌟

RĀJĀ:

namas|kṛtya vadāmi tvāṃ, yadi puṇyaṃ mayā kṛtam,
anyasyām api jātyāṃ me tvam eva jananī bhava. [50]

GĀNDHĀRĪ: ⌜mama maṇo|raho khu tue bhaṇido.⌟

RĀJĀ: Mālavi! tvam api śṛṇu.

bhinnā me bhrukuṭī gadā|nipatitair
vyāyuddha|kāl'|ôtthitair.
vakṣasy utpatitaiḥ prahāra|rudhirair
hār'|âvakāśo hṛtaḥ.
paśy' êmau vraṇa|kāñcan'|âṅgada|dharau

DHRITA·RASHTRA:

I am an old man, with nothing to live for.
My eyes have been closed from birth.
Sharp grief for my sons has welled up in me,
Undermined my resolve and trampled me.

BALA·DEVA: This is terrible!

I cannot bring myself to remind this honorable man,
Who has lost hope over Duryódhana,
Whose eye has now closed for ever,
That I am here.

DURYÓDHANA: Ma'm, may I ask you something?

GANDHÁRI: Just say, my dear.

DURYÓDHANA:

Making obeisance with my hands in prayer
  I say to you,
If I have acquired any merit,
May it be you who is my mother
In my next life as well.

GANDHÁRI: You have voiced just what I want.

DURYÓDHANA: Málavi! You listen to me as well.*

My forehead has been split with mace blows,
Inflicted in the course of a duel.
The place for a torque has been taken
By the drops of blood fallen on my chest.
Look at these two arms adorned well enough
Wearing wounds for golden armlets.

paryāpta|śobhau bhujau.
bhartā te na parāṅ|mukho yudhi hataḥ.
kiṃ, kṣatriye, rodiṣi? [51]

DEVĪ: * ⌜bālā esā saha|dhamma|cāriṇī rodāmi.⌟

RĀJĀ: Pauravi! tvam api śṛṇu.

ved'|ôktair vividhair makhair abhimatair
iṣṭaṃ. dhṛtā bāndhavāḥ.
śatrūṇām upari sthitaṃ priyaśataṃ.
na vyaṃsitāḥ saṃśritāḥ.
yuddhe 'ṣṭādaśa|vāhinī|nṛpatayaḥ
santāpitā nigrahe.
mānaṃ, mānini, vīkṣya me na hi rudanty
evaṃ|vidhānāṃ striyaḥ. [52]

PAURAVĪ: ⌜ekka|kida|ppavesa|ṇiccaā ṇa rodāmi.⌟

RĀJĀ: Durjaya, tvam api śṛṇu!

DHṚTARĀṢṬRAḤ: Gāndhāri, kin nu khalu vakṣyati?

GĀNDHĀRĪ: ⌜ahaṃ pi taṃ evva cintemi.⌟

RĀJĀ: aham iva Pāṇḍavāḥ śuśrūṣayitavyāḥ, tatra|bhavatyāś c' âmbāyāḥ Kuntyā nideśo vartayitavyaḥ. Abhimanyor jananī Draupadī c' ôbhe mātṛvat pūjayitavye. paśya, putra,

Your husband has been killed in battle, but
not with his back to the foe.
Why are you weeping, lady of warrior clan?

MÁLAVI: Look, I am a foolish girl, your lawful wife! Let me cry!

DURYÓDHANA: Páuravi! You listen to me as well.

We have sacrificed at the various permitted festivals
described in the Veda.
Our relatives have been supported.
The hundred beloved brothers have conquered
their enemies.
Our dependents have not been cheated.
The leaders of eighteen armies in battle
Have been sore pressed in defeat.
Proud woman, thinking about my pride,
For sure the wives of such people do not weep.

PÁURAVI: I have made one resolve—to enter the funeral pyre. I'll not cry!

DURYÓDHANA: Dúrjaya, you listen too!

DHRITA·RASHTRA: Gandhári, now what is he going to say?

GANDHÁRI: It's worrying me too.*

DURYÓDHANA: Be obedient to the Pándavas as you would to me, and follow the instruction of mother Kunti and those honorable people. Both Abhimányu's mother and Dráupadi you should honor like your own mother. Look, my son,

«ślāghya|śrīr, abhimāna|dīpta|hṛdayo
Duryodhano me pitā
tulyen' âbhimukhaṃ raṇe hata» iti
tvaṃ śokam evaṃ tyaja.
spṛṣṭvā c' âiva Yudhiṣṭhirasya vipulaṃ
kṣaum'|âpasavyaṃ bhujaṃ
deyaṃ Pāṇḍu|sutais tvayā mama samaṃ
nām'|âvasāne jalam. [53]

BALADEVAḤ: aho, vairaṃ paścāt|tāpaḥ saṃvṛttaḥ! aye, śabda iva.

sannāha|dundubhi|ninlāda|viyoga|mūke,
vikṣipta|bāṇa|kavaca|vyajan'|ātapatre
kasy' âiṣa kārmuka|ravo hata|sūta|yodhe
vibhrānta|vāyasa|gaṇaṃ gaganaṃ karoti? [54]

NEPATHYE:

Duryodhanen' ātata|kārmukeṇa
yo yuddha|yajñaḥ sahitaḥ praviṣṭaḥ,
tam eva bhūyaḥ praviśāmi śūnyam,
adhvaryuṇā vṛttam iv' âśvamedham. [55]

You must put aside grief and think like this:
"My father Duryódhana was killed by an equal
While facing his enemy in battle.
He was glorious and praiseworthy, his heart alight
with pride";
And when I am dead,
Actually touching Yudhi·shthira
On his long right arm in its sleeve,
Alongside Pandu's sons,
You should give me the water offering,
using my name.*

BALA·DEVA: Hmm, anger has changed into remorse! But what kind of noise is this?

There is a hush after the roll of battle drums
has stopped.
Arrows, armor, fly whisks and umbrellas are
scattered about.
Charioteers and soldiers lie dead. Who is twanging
their bow,
Scaring this throng of crows into the sky?

VOICE OFF STAGE:

The very same battle sacrifice I entered alongside
Duryódhana when his bow was strung,
I enter once more, now empty, like the horse sacrifice*
when the priest in charge has finished.

BALADEVAḤ: aye, ayaṃ guru|putro 'śvatthām" êta ev' âbhivartate. ya eṣaḥ,

sphuṭita|kamala|patra|spaṣṭa|vistīrṇa|dṛṣṭī,
rucira|kanaka|yūpa|vyāyat'|ālamba|bāhuḥ,
sa|rabhasam ayam ugraṃ kārmukaṃ karṣamāṇaḥ,
sa|dahana iva Meruḥ śṛṅga|lagn'|Êndra|cāpaḥ. [56]

tataḥ praviśaty AŚVATTHĀMĀ

AŚVATTHĀMĀ: *(pūrv'|ôktam eva paṭhitvā)* bhoḥ samara|saṃrambh' | ôbhaya | bala | jaladhi | saṅgama | samaya | samutthita | śastra | nakra | kṛtta | vigrahāḥ stok' | âvaśeṣāḥ śvās' | ânubaddha | manda | prāṇāḥ samara | ślāghino rājānaḥ. śṛṇvantu, śṛṇvantu bhavantaḥ!

chala|bala|dalit'|ôruḥ Kaurav'|êndro, na c' âhaṃ.
śithila|viphala|śastraḥ sūta|putraś ca, n' âham.
iha tu vijaya|bhūmau draṣṭum ady' ôdyat'|âsraḥ
sa|rabhasam aham eko Droṇa|putraḥ sthito 'smi. [57]

kim anayā mam' âpy a|pratilābha|vijaya|ślāghayā samara|śriyā? *(parikramya)* mā tāvat. mayi guru|nivapana|vyagre vañcitaḥ kila Kuru|tilaka|bhūtaḥ Kuru|rājaḥ. ka etac chraddhāsyati? kutaḥ,

BALA·DEVA: It is Ashva·tthaman, the son of our teacher,* making his way over here. See, 200

> His eyes are wide and clear like petals from
> a fully open lotus;
> His arms are hard and long like posts of shining gold.
> Drawing violently this dreadful bow,
> He looks like Mount Meru ablaze and
> with a rainbow clinging to its peak.

Thereupon enters ASHVA·TTHAMAN.

ASHVA·TTHAMAN: *(repeating what he has just said)* Ho, you chieftains, celebrated in battle! The opposing forces pouring together in the zeal of battle are the two oceans. The weapons are the crocodiles swept up in the clash, and they have dismembered your bodies. There are few of you left. Your life force is weak and hanging on your breath. Listen! You listen to me!

> It was the Kuru chief whose thighs have been crushed
> by a trick and not me.
> It was the charioteer's son* whose weapons were
> loose and ineffectual and not me.
> But it is me, the son of Drona, who now stands here
> alone on the field of their victory
> Waiting to see some action, my weapon raised aloft.

Maybe I have no use for the glory of battle without gaining 205
the praise of victory? *(walking about)* Not so! They say* the Kuru chief, the ornament of the Kurus, was tricked while I was offering funeral oblations to my father. Who could believe it? Weren't

udyat|prāñjalayo, ratha|dvipa|gatāś,
cāpa|dvitīyaiḥ karair
yasy' âikādaśa|vāhinī|nṛpatayas
tiṣṭhanti vāky'|ônmukhāḥ,
Bhīṣmo Rāma|śar'|âvalīḍha|kavacas,
tātaś ca yoddhā raṇe,
vyaktaṃ nirjita eva so 'py atirathaḥ
kālena Duryodhanaḥ. [58]

tat kva nu khalu gato Gāndhārī|putraḥ? *(parikramy', âvalokya)* aye, ayam abhihata|gaja|turaga|nara|ratha|prākāra|madhya|gataḥ samara|payodhi|pāra|gaḥ Kuru|rājaḥ. ya eṣaḥ,

maulī|nipāta|cala|keśa|mayūkha|jālair,
gātrair gadā|nipatana|kṣata|śoṇit'|ārdraiḥ
yāty astam astaka|śilā|tala|sanniviṣṭaḥ,
sandhy" âvagāḍha iva paścima|kāla|sūryaḥ. [59]

(upasṛtya) bhoḥ Kuru|rāja! kim idam?

RĀJĀ: guru|putra, phalam a|paritoṣasya.

AŚVATTHĀMĀ: bhoḥ Kuru|rāja, satkāra|mūlam āvarjayiṣyāmi.

RĀJĀ: kiṃ bhavān kariṣyati?

The commanders of eleven armies stood waiting
hanging on what he would say,
Holding up their cupped hands in respect, mounted
on chariots and elephants, bows to hand?
Bhishma, his armor licked by Párashu·rama's arrows,
and my father were fighters in the battle!
Clearly it was just time for Duryódhana to be beaten,
even though he was an excellent warrior.

So! Where has Gandhári's son gone! *(walking about and looking)* Ah, here is the Kuru chieftain. He has crossed over the ocean of battle and lies amid a dune of broken men and chariots, elephants and horses. See,

The net and hairgrips in his hair are loose and
slipped from his crown.*
His limbs are wet with the blood from wounds
inflicted by mace blows.
He is sinking down seated on the rock surface
of his mountain top
Like the sun in evening time plunged into the twilight.

(approaching him) Ho, Kuru chief! What is this?

DURYÓDHANA: Son of my teacher! This is the outcome of discontent. 210

ASHVA·TTHAMAN: O Kuru chief, I shall restore the basis for respect.

DURYÓDHANA: What are you going to do?

AŚVATTHĀMĀ: śrūyatām,

yuddh'|ôdyatam, Garuḍa|pṛṣṭha|niviṣṭa|deham,
aṣṭ'|ârdha|bhīma|bhujam, udyata|śārṅga|cakram
Kṛṣṇaṃ sa|Pāṇḍu|tanayaṃ yudhi śastra|jālaiḥ
saṅkīrṇa|lekhyam iva citra|paṭaṃ kṣipāmi. [60]

RĀJĀ: mā, mā bhavān evam!

gataṃ dhātry|utsaṅge
sakalam abhiṣiktaṃ nṛpa|kulaṃ.
gataḥ Karṇaḥ svargaṃ;
nipatita|tanuḥ Śantanu|sutaḥ.
śataṃ bhrātṝṇāṃ me
hatam abhimukhaṃ saṃyuga|mukhe,
vayaṃ c' âivam|bhūtā.
guru|suta, dhanur muñcatu bhavān. [61]

AŚVATTHĀMĀ: bhoḥ, Kuru|rāja!

saṃyuge Pāṇḍu|putreṇa
gadā|pāta|kaca|grahe
samam ūru|dvayen' âdya
darpo 'pi bhavato hṛtaḥ. [62]

RĀJĀ: mā, m" âivam! māna|śarīrā rājānaḥ. mān'|ârtham eva mayā nigraho gṛhītaḥ. paśya, guru|putra,

ASHVA·TTHAMAN: Listen!

Krishna is ready for the fight, his body mounted
on the back of Gáruda,
His four terrible arms clearly visible holding aloft
his bow and discus.
Like in a painting with crowded figures, using
a mass of weapons
I shall cast him and the children of Pandu
down in the fight.

DURYÓDHANA: No, not this! 215

An entire clan of consecrated rulers lies in the lap
of mother earth.
Karna has gone to heaven; the body of the son
of Shántanu has fallen.
My hundred brothers have been killed before me
in the maw of battle,
And I am reduced to this state. Son of my teacher,
let go of your bow!

ASHVA·TTHAMAN: Ha, Kuru chief!

When the son of Pandu struck you with the mace
and took you by the hair today
He equally took both thighs and took away
your pride as well.

DURYÓDHANA: No, no, not so! Chieftains are pride embodied. It was for the sake of pride that I took to coercion. Consider, son of my teacher,

yat kṛṣṭā kara|nigrah'|âñcita|kacā
dyūte tadā Draupadī,
yad bālo 'pi hatas tadā raṇa|mukhe
putro 'bhimanyuḥ punaḥ,
akṣa|vyāja|jitā vanaṃ vana|mṛgair
yat Pāṇḍavāḥ saṃśritā,
nanv alpaṃ mayi taiḥ kṛtaṃ, vimṛśa bho,
darp'|āhṛtaṃ dīkṣitaiḥ. [63]

AŚVATTHĀMĀ: sarvathā kṛta|pratijño 'smi!

bhavatā v" ātmanā c' âiva,
vīra|lokaiḥ śapāmy aham,
niśā|samaram utpādya
raṇe dhakṣyāmi Pāṇḍavān. [64]

BALADEVAḤ: etad bhaviṣyaty, udāhṛtaṃ guru|putreṇa.

AŚVATTHĀMĀ: Halāyudho 'tra|bhavān!

DHṚTARĀṢṬRAḤ: hanta, sākṣimatī khalu vañcanā.

AŚVATTHĀMĀ: Durjaya! itas tāvat.

pitṛ|vikrama|dāyādye
rājye bhuja|bal'|ârjite
vin" âbhiṣekaṃ rājā tvaṃ
vipr'|ôktair vacanair bhava. [65]

RĀJĀ: hanta, kṛtaṃ me hṛday'|ânujñātam. parityajanti me prāṇāḥ. ime 'tra|bhavantaḥ Śantanu|prabhṛtayo me pitṛ|pitāmahāḥ. etat Karṇam agrataḥ kṛtvā samutthitaṃ

How I dragged off Dráupadi as a gambling prize,
her hair twisted and held in my hand;
How again Abhimányu, still a young boy, a son,
was killed in battle;
How the Pándavas had to take refuge
in the wilderness with wild animals
because they had been tricked at dice.
For sure, think how little these ready men have done
to take pride from me.*

ASHVA·TTHAMAN: I am fully resolved!

To you and to myself and to the world of the heroes,
I swear
I will lead a night raid and I will burn up
the Pándavas in combat.

BALA·DEVA: It will happen! The teacher's son has spoken.

ASHVA·TTHAMAN: The honorable Plow Bearer!

DHRITA·RASHTRA: Oh no! This trickery has a witness.

ASHVA·TTHAMAN: Dúrjaya! Come here.

Without a consecration but through words
spoken by a brahmin,
Become the chief of a kingdom
Inherited through the conquests of your father,
Conquered by the strength of his arms.

DURYÓDHANA: Wonderful! What I want in my heart has happened. I can relinquish my life.* Here are the honorable forefathers of my father headed by Shántanu. Here my hundred brothers stand, Karna at their head. Here

bhrātṛ|śatam. ayam apy Airāvata|śiro|viṣaktaḥ kāka|pakṣa|dharo mah"|Êndra|kara|talam avalambya kruddho 'bhibhāṣate mām Abhimanyuḥ. imā Urvaśy|ādayo 'psaraso mām abhigatāḥ. ime mūrtimanto mah"|ârṇavāḥ. etā Gaṅgā|prabhṛtayo mahā|nadyaḥ. eṣa sahasra|haṃsa|prayukto māṃ netuṃ vīravāhī vimānaḥ Kālena preṣitaḥ. ayam ayam āgacchāmi. *(svargaṃ gataḥ.)*

yavanik" āstaraṇaṃ karoti.

DHṚTARĀṢṬRAḤ:

yāmy eṣa saj|jana|dhanāni tapo|vanāni.
putra|praṇāśa|viphalaṃ hi dhig astu rājyam. [66ab]

AŚVATTHĀMĀ:

yāto 'dya sauptika|vadh'|ôdyata|bāṇa|pāṇiḥ.
gāṃ pātu no nara|patiḥ śamit'|âri|pakṣaḥ. [66cd]

niṣkrāntāḥ sarve.

Ūrubhaṅgam avasitam.

śubhaṃ bhūyāt!

too is Abhimányu, riding on the head of Airávata, Indra's elephant. He has his side locks of hair* and is clinging to great Indra's hand. He is angry and is scolding me. Here are Úrvashi and other nymphs coming near. Here appear the great oceans. Here are the great rivers headed by the Ganges. Death has sent to fetch me a celestial vehicle, the carriage for heroes, pulled by a thousand swans. Here, here I come. *(He dies and goes to heaven.)*

The cloth is drawn.

DHRITA·RASHTRA:

Here I go to the penance grove, rich in good people. 230
Shame on the kingdom devalued by the loss
of its sons.

ASHVA·TTHAMAN:

Bow in hand, ready to slaughter those sleepers,
I am off now.
May the king protect the earth and
destroy all enemies.*

They all leave the stage.

"The Shattered Thighs" is completed.

May there be good fortune!

CHĀYĀ

The following is a Sanskrit paraphrase (chāyā) *of the Prakrit passages (marked with* ⌜corner brackets⌟ *in the play). References are to chapter and paragraph.*

How the Nagas were Pleased

1.10 ārya, iyam asmi!

1.12 ārya, katham na rodiṣyāmi? yadā tāto 'jjukā ca sthavira|bhāva|jāta|nirvedau kuṭumba|bhār'|ôdvahana|yogya idānīṃ tvam iti hṛdaya āropya tapo|vanaṃ gatau.

1.19 bho vayasya, na nirviṇṇa eva tvam etāvantaṃ kālam etayor jīvan|mṛtayor vṛddhayoḥ kṛta īdṛśaṃ vana|vāsa|duḥkham anubhavan? tat prasīda! idānīm api tāvad guru|jana|śuśrūṣā|nirbandhān nivṛty' êcchā|paribhoga|ramaṇīyaṃ rājya|saukhyam anubhūyatām.

1.22 aho! asya guru|jana|śuśrūṣ"|ânurāgaḥ!

1.22 bhavatu, evaṃ tāvad bhaṇiṣyāmi.

1.22 bho vayasya, na khalv aham kevalaṃ rājya|saukhyam uddiśy' âivaṃ bhaṇāmi. anyad api te karaṇīyam asty eva.

1.25 bho vayasya! atyanta|sāhasiko Mataṅga|deva|hatakas te pratipakṣaḥ. tasmiṃś ca samāsanna|sthite pradhān'|âmātya|samadhiṣṭhitam api na tvayā vinā rājyaṃ su|sthitam iti me pratibhāti.

1.28 bho vayasya, paśya paśya! eṣa khalu sara|saghana|snigdha|candana|van'|ôtsaṅga|parimilana|lagna|bahala|parimalo viṣama|taṭa|patana|jarjarī|kriyamāṇa|nirjhar'|ôccalita|śiśira|śīkar'|āsāra|vāhī prathama|saṅgam'|ôtkaṇṭhita|priyā|kaṇṭha|graha iva mārga|pariśramam apanayan romāñcayati priya|vayasyaṃ Malaya|mārutaḥ.

1.35 bho vayasya, āsannaṃ te priyaṃ nivedayati!

1.37 bho vayasya, etat khalu sa|viśeṣa|ghana|snigdha|pādap'|ôpaśobhitaṃ surabhi|havir|gandha|garbhit'|ôddāma|dhūma|nirgamam an|udvigna|mārga|sukha|niṣaṇṇa|śvāpada|gaṇaṃ tapo|vanam iva lakṣyate.

1.45 bho vayasya, kiṃ nu khalv eta īṣad|valita|kandharā niścala|mukh'|âpasarad|daradalita|darbha|garbha|kabalāḥ samunnamita|datt'|âika|karṇāḥ nimīlita|locanā ākarṇayanta iva hariṇā lakṣyante.

1.48 bho vayasya, ko nu khalv eṣa tapo|vane gāyati?

1.50 bho vayasya, etad dev'|āyatanaṃ paśyāvaḥ.

1.57 bhartṛdārike! ciraṃ khalu vāditam. na khalu te pariśramo 'gra|hastayoḥ?

1.58 hañje Caturike! bhagavatyāḥ purato vādayantyāḥ kuto mama pariśramaḥ?

1.59 bhartṛ|dārike, nanu bhaṇāmi, kim etasyā niṣkaruṇāyāḥ purato vāditena? iyantaṃ kālaṃ kanyakā|jana|duṣkarair niyam'|ôpavāsair ārādhayantyā na te prasādaṃ darśayati!

1.60 bho vayasya, kanyā khalv eṣā! kasmān na paśyāvaḥ?

1.63 bho vayasya! paśya paśya. eṣā na kevalaṃ vīṇayā karṇayor eva sukham utpādayati. anena vīṇā|vijñān'|ânurūpeṇa rūpeṇ' âkṣṇor api sukham utpādayati. kā punar eṣā? kiṃ tāvad devī? atha vā nāga|kanyakā? āho svid vidyādhara|dārikā? ut' āho siddha|kula|sambhav" êti?

1.66 diṣṭyā cirasya tāvat kālasya patitaḥ khalv eṣa gocare Manmathasya.

1.66 atha vā mam' âiva brāhmaṇasya.

1.67 bhartṛ|dārike! nanu bhaṇāmi kim etasyā niṣ|karuṇāyāḥ purato vāditena?

1.68 hañje! mā mā bhagavatīṃ Gaurīm adhikṣipa. adya kṛto me bhagavatyā prasādaḥ.

1.69 bhartṛ|dārike! kathaya tāvat kīdṛśaḥ sa prasādaḥ.

1.70 hañje, adya jānāmi svapna evam eva vīṇāṃ vādayantī bhagavatyā Gauryā bhaṇit" āsmi. «vatse, prituṣṭ" âsmi tav' âitena vīṇā|vijñān'|âtiśayena, anayā bāla|jana|durlabhay" â|sādhāraṇayā mam' ôpari bhaktyā ca. tad vidyādhara|cakravarty a|cireṇa te pāṇi|grahaṇaṃ nirvartayiṣyat'» îti.

1.71 bhartṛ|dārike, yady evaṃ, kasmāt svapna iti bhaṇasi? nanu hṛday'|êṣṭa eva devyā varo dattaḥ.

1.72 bho vayasya, avasaraḥ khalv asmākaṃ devī|darśanasya. tad ehi, praviśāvaḥ.

1.72 bhavati! satyam ev' âiṣā bhaṇati. vara ev' âiṣa devyā dattaḥ.

1.73 hañje? ko nu khalv eṣaḥ?

1.74 anay" ânyonya|sadṛśy" ākṛtyā eṣa sa bhagavatyāḥ prasāda iti tarkayāmi.

1.77 hañje, atisādhvasena na śaknomy etasya sammukhe sthātum!

1.79 bhavati, kim atra yuṣmākaṃ tapo|vana īdṛśa ācāraḥ, yen' âtithi|jana āgato vāṅ|mātreṇ' âpi na saṃbhāvanīyaḥ?

1.80 anurajyat" îv' âtr' âitasyā dṛṣṭiḥ! tasmād evaṃ tāvad bhaṇiṣyāmi.

1.80 bhartṛ|dārike, yuktaṃ bhaṇati brāhmaṇaḥ. ucitaḥ khalu te 'tithi|jana|satkāraḥ. tat kasmād etasmin mah"|ânubhāve pratipatti|mūḍh" êva tiṣṭhasi? atha vā tiṣṭha tvam! aham eva yath"|ânurūpaṃ kariṣyāmi.

1.80 svāgatam āryasya. āsana|parigraheṇ' âlaṅ|karotv imaṃ pradeśam āryaḥ.

1.81 bho vayasya, śobhanam eṣā bhaṇati! upaviśya muhūrtaṃ viśrāmyāvaḥ.

1.84 hā dhik parihāsa|śīle! m" âivaṃ kuru. kad" âpi ko 'pi tāpaso māṃ paśyet, tato mām a|vinīt" êti saṃbhāvayiṣyati.

1.92 arya! praṇamāmi.

1.94 yad gurur ājñāpayati.

1.98 dṛṣṭaṃ yat prekṣitavyam! idānīṃ madhy'|âhna|sūrya|santāpa|dviguṇita iva me jaṭhar'|âgnir dhamadhamāyati.* tan niṣkrāmāvaḥ. yen' âtithir bhūtvā muni|jana|sakāśāl labdhaiḥ kanda|mūla|phalair api tāvat prāṇa|dhāraṇaṃ kariṣyāmi.

2.2 ājñapt" âsmi bhartṛ|dārikayā Malayavatyā, «hañje Manoharike, adya cirayati bhrātā ma ārya|Mitrāvasuḥ. tad gatvā jānīhi, kim āgato na v" êti.»

2.2 kā punar eṣā ita ev' āgacchati?

2.2 kathaṃ, Caturikā!

2.4 hañje Caturike! kin nimittaṃ punas tvam evaṃ tvarita|tvaritam āgacchasi?

2.5 ājñapt" âsmi bhartṛ|dārikayā Malayavatyā, «hañje Caturike, kusum'|âvacaya|pariśrama|nissahaṃ me śarīraṃ śarad|ātapa|janita iva santāpo 'dhikataraṃ bādhate. tad gaccha tvam, bāla|kadalī|patra|parikṣipte candana|latā|gṛhe candra|maṇi|śilā|talaṃ sajjī|kurv» iti. anuṣṭhitaṃ ca mayā yath"|ājñaptam. tad yāvad gatvā bhartṛ|dārikāyai nivedayāmi.

2.6 yady evaṃ, tal laghu nivedaya, yen' âsyās tasmin gatāyāḥ santāpa upaśamaṃ gamiṣyati.

2.7 n' ēdṛśaḥ santāpa evam upaśamaṃ gamiṣyati! anyac ca vivikta|ramaṇīyaṃ candana|latā|gṛhaṃ paśyantyā adhikataraṃ bhaviṣyat' îti tarkayāmi.

2.7 tad gaccha tvam. aham api sajjaṃ śilā|talam iti bhartṛ|dārikāyai nivedayāmi.

2.11 hṛdaya! tathā nāma tadā tasmiñ jane lajjayā māṃ parāṅ|mukhī|kṛty' êdānīm ātmanā tasminn eva gatam as' îty aho te ātmambharitvam.

2.11 hañje, ādiśa me bhagavatyā āyatanasya mārgam.

2.12 nanu candana|latā|gṛhaṃ bhartṛ|dārikā prasthitā!

2.13 suṣṭhu tvayā smāritam. tad ehi, tatr' âiva gacchāvaḥ.

2.14 etu etu bhartṛ|dārikā.

2.16 aho asyāḥ śūnyahṛdayatvam! kathaṃ, tad eva devyā bhavanaṃ prasthitā.

2.16 bhartṛ|dārike, nanv itaś candana|latā|gṛham. tad ita ehi.

2.18 bhartṛ|dārike, etac candana|latā|gṛham. tat praviśya candra|maṇi|śilā|tale upaviśatu bhartṛ|dārikā.

2.20 bhagavan kusum'|āyudha, yena tvaṃ rūpa|śobhayā nirjito 'si, tasmin na kiñ cit tvayā kṛtam. māṃ punar an|aparāddhām abal" êti kṛtvā praharan kathaṃ na lajjase?

2.20 hañje, kasmāt punar etad ghana|pallava|niruddha|sūrya|kiraṇaṃ tādṛśam eva candana|latā|gṛhaṃ na me'dya saṃtāpa|duḥkham apanayati?

2.21 jānāmy aham atra kāraṇam! kin tu asambhāvanīyam iti bhartṛ|dārikā na tat pratipadyate.

2.22 ālakṣit" âsmy anayā! tath" âpi prakṣyāmi tāvat.

2.22 hañje, kiṃ tav' âitena? kathaya tāvat, kiṃ tat kāraṇam?

2.23 eṣa te hṛday'|êṣṭo varaḥ.

2.24 kasmin, kasmin saḥ?

2.25 bhartṛ|dārike, kaḥ «saḥ?»

2.27 bhartṛ|dārike, nanv etad asmi vaktu|kāmā, eṣa te hṛday'|êṣṭo varo devyā datta iti svapne prastute yas tat|kṣaṇam eva vimukta|kusuma|cāpa iva bhagavān makara|dhvajo bhartṛ|dārikayā dṛṣṭaḥ. sa te 'sya santāpasya kāraṇam. yen' âivaṃ svabhāva|śītalam api candana|latā|gṛhaṃ na te 'dya santāpa|duḥkham apanayati.

2.28 hañje, Caturikā khalu tvam. kiṃ te 'paraṃ pracchādyate. tat kathayiṣyāmi.

2.29 bhartṛ|dārike, nanv idānīm eva kathitam amunā var'|ālāpa|mātra|janitena sambhrameṇa. tan mā saṃtapyasva. yady ahaṃ Caturikā, tataḥ so 'pi bhartṛ|dārikām a|paśyan na muhūrtam apy anyasminn abhiramata ity, etad api may" ālakṣitam eva.

2.30 hañje, kuto ma iyanti bhāga|dheyāni?

2.31 bhartṛ|dārike, m" âivaṃ bhaṇa. kiṃ Madhu|mathano vakṣas|sthalena Lakṣmīm an|udvahan nirvṛto bhavati?

2.32 kiṃ vā su|janaḥ priyaṃ varjayitv" ânyad bhaṇituṃ jānāti? sakhi, ato'pi saṃtāpo 'dhikataraṃ māṃ bādhate, yat sa mah"|ânubhāvo vaṅ|mātreṇ' âpy a|kṛta|pratipattim a|dakṣiṇ" êti māṃ sambhāvayiṣyati.

2.33 bhartṛ|dārike, mā rudaḥ.

2.33 nanu bhaṇāmi mā ruda iti. ayaṃ khalu stana|paṭṭa|dattaś candana|pallava|raso 'mībhir avirala|patadbhir aśru|bindubhir uṣṇī|kṛto na te hṛdaya|santāpa|duḥkham apanayati.

2.34 sakhi, mā vīja. uṣṇaḥ khalv eṣa kadalī|dala|mārutaḥ.

2.35 bhartṛ|dārike, mā asya doṣaṃ kuru.

2.36 karoṣi ghana|candana|latā|pallava|saṃsarga|śītalam ap' îmam niḥśvāsais tvam eva kadalī|dala|mārutam uṣṇam.

2.37 sakhi, asti ko 'py asya duḥkhasy' ôpaśam'|ôpāyaḥ?

2.38 bhartṛ|dārike, asti, yadi sa ih' āgacchet.

2.41 bho vayasya, kasmin khalu gataṃ te dhīratvam?

2.46 evam adhīratvaṃ pratipadyamānen' ākhyāto 'nena hṛdayasya mahān āvegaḥ. tad evam ācakṣe.

2.46 bho vayasya, kasmāt tvam adya laghv eva guru|janaṃ śuśrūṣa-yitv" êh' āgataḥ?

2.49 bhartṛ|dārike, pada|śabda iva śrūyate!

2.50 hañje, mā īdṛśam ākāraṃ prekṣya ko 'pi hṛdayaṃ me tulayatu. tad uttiṣṭha. anena rakt'|âśoka|pādapen' âpavārite paśyāvaḥ ka eṣa iti.

2.52 bho vayasya, etac candana|latā|gṛham. tat praviśāvah.

2.56 bhartṛ|dārike, diṣṭyā vardhase! sa eva te hṛdaya|vallabhaḥ.

2.57 hañje, imaṃ prekṣya na śaknom' îh' âtyāsanne sthātum. kadā cid eṣa māṃ paśyet. tad ehi. anyato gacchāvaḥ.

2.58 atikātare! iha sthitām api kas tvāṃ paśyati? nanu vismṛto 'ntare rakt'|âśoka|pādapaḥ? tad ih' âiva tiṣṭhāvaḥ.

2.60 bho vayasya, eṣā sā candra|maṇi|śilā!

2.62 bhartṛ|dārike, «eṣā s" êty» ālāpaḥ śrūyate. tad avahite śṛṇuvaḥ.

2.64 bho vayasya, nanu bhaṇāmi eṣā sā candra|maṇi|śil" êti.

2.68 kā punar «eṣā» bhaviṣyati?

2.69 bhartṛ|dārike, yath" āvām apavārita|śarīre etaṃ paśyāvaḥ, tathā tvam apy etena dṛṣṭā bhaveḥ.

2.70 yujyata etat. kiṃ punaḥ praṇaya|kupitaṃ priya|janaṃ hṛdaye kṛtvā mantrayati?

2.71 mā īdṛśīm āśaṅkāṃ kuru. punar api tāvac chṛṇuvaḥ.

2.72 abhiramata eṣa etayā kathayā. bhavatu, etad ev' âsya vardhayiṣyāmi.

2.72 bho vayasya, tathā praruditā tvayā kiṃ bhaṇitā?

2.75 śrutam etac, Caturike. asti kim apy ataḥ paraṃ śrotavyam?

2.75 ehi, gacchāvaḥ.

2.76 bhartṛ|dārike, m" âivam. yena tvaṃ dṛṣṭā, so 'nyām uddiśy' âivaṃ bhaṇiṣyat' îti na me hṛdayaṃ pratyeti. tat kath"|âvasānaṃ tāvat pratipālayāvaḥ.

2.78 yad bhavān ājñāpayati.

2.78 bho vayasya, tvay" âiko varṇa ājñaptaḥ, mayā punar iha parvatāt pañca varṇā ānītāḥ. tad ālikhatu bhavān.

2.82 bho vayasya, a|pratyakṣam apy evam ālikhyata ity āścaryam.

2.85 Caturike, jātaṃ khalu kath"|âvasānam. tad ehi, ārya|Mitrāvasuṃ tāvat paśyāvaḥ.

2.86 haṃ. jīvita|nirapekṣa iv' âsyā ālāpaḥ.

2.86 bhartṛ|dārike! gat" âiva tasmin Manoharikā. ataḥ kadā cid bhartṛ|dārako Mitrāvasur ih' âiv' āgacchet.

2.91 bho vayasya, anena pracchādaya kadalī|patreṇ' êdaṃ citra|gataṃ karma. eṣa khalu siddha|yuvarājo Mitrāvasur ih' âiv' āgataḥ. kadā cid eṣa paśyet.

2.95 bhartṛ|dārike, āgataḥ khalv eṣa Mitrāvasuḥ.

2.96 hañje, priyaṃ me.

2.100 śroṣyāmi tāvat kiṃ tātena sandiṣṭam iti.

2.102 bhartṛ|dārike, kiṃ na kupyas' îdānīm?

2.103 hañje, mā tuṣya. kiṃ vismṛtaṃ ta etasy' ânya|hṛdayatvam?

2.105 bho, jānāmi bhavato na tāṃ varjayitv" ânyatra cittam abhiramata iti. tath" âpi yat kiñ cid bhaṇitvā visṛjyatām eṣaḥ.

2.106 hat'|āśa! ko v" âitan na jānāti?

2.109 samāśvasitu, samāśvasitu bhartṛ|dārikā!

2.110 bhoḥ! parādhīnaḥ khalv eṣaḥ. tat kim etena bhaṇatā? guru|janam asya gatv" âbhyarthaya.

2.114 kathaṃ pratyākhyāna|laghur Mitrāvasuḥ punar api mantrayate?

2.116 kiṃ mam' âitena daurbhāgya|kalaṅka|malinen' âtyanta|duḥkha|bhāgin" âdy' âpi śarīra|hatakena? yāvad ih' âiva rakt'|āśoka|pādape 'nay" âtimukta|latay" ôdbadhy' ātmānaṃ vyāpādayiṣyāmi. tad evaṃ tāvat.

2.116 hañje! paśya tāvan Mitrāvasur dūraṃ gato na v" êti. yen' âham ap' îto gamiṣyāmi.

2.117 yad bhartṛ|dārik" ājñāpayati.

2.117 anyādṛśam asyā hṛdayaṃ paśyāmi. tan na tāvad gamiṣyāmi. ih' âiv' âpavāritā paśyāmi kim eṣā pratipadyata iti.

2.118 bhagavati gauri! iha tvayā na kṛtaḥ prasādaḥ. tad anyasminn api tāvaj janmani yathā n' ēdṛśī duḥkha|bhāginī bhavāmi, tathā kuru.

2.119 paritrāyadhvaṃ! paritrāyadhvam! eṣā bhartṛ|dārik" ôdbadhy' ātmānaṃ vyāpādayati.

2.121 iyam aśoka|pādape.

2.124 hā dhik! ko nu khalv eṣaḥ?

2.124 muñca! muṃca me 'gra|hastam! kas tvaṃ nivārayitum? maraṇe 'pi kiṃ tvam ev' âbhyarthanīyaḥ?

2.127 bhavati, kiṃ punar asyā maraṇa|vyavasāyasya kāraṇam?

2.128 nanv eṣa eva te priya|vayasyaḥ!

2.130 bhavati, katham iva?

2.131 yā sā priya|vayasyena te k" âpi hṛdaya|vallabh" ālikhitā, tasyāṃ pakṣa|pātinā pratyākhyātasya Mitrāvasor «n' âhaṃ pratīcchām'» îti śrutvā jāta|nirveday" ānay" âivaṃ vyavasitam.

2.133 bhavati, yady evam, an|aparāddha idānīṃ priya|vayasyaḥ. atha vā yadi na pratyeti, svayam eva gatvā śilā|talaṃ paśyatu bhavatī!

2.134 muñca. muñca me 'gra|hastam.

2.137 eṣ" âsya hṛdaya|vallabhā!

2.138 Caturike, aham iv' ālikhitā!

2.139 bhartṛ|dārike, kiṃ bhaṇasi «aham iv' ālikhit"» êti? īdṛśam asya sādṛśyaṃ, yena na jñāyate kiṃ tāvad iha maṇi|śilā|tale bhartṛ|dārikāyāḥ pratibimbaṃ saṅkrāntam, uta tvam ālikhit" êti!

2.140 durjanī|kṛt" âsmy amun" êdaṃ citraṃ darśayatā.

2.141 bhoḥ, nirvṛtta idānīṃ gāndharvo vivāhaḥ. muñc' êdānīm asyā agra|hastam. eṣā k" âpi tvarita|tvaritam āgacchati.

2.143 bhartṛ|dārike, pratīṣṭā tvaṃ Jīmūtavāhanasya gurubhiḥ!

2.144 sampūrṇo manorathaḥ priya|vayasyasya; atha v" âtra|bhavatyāḥ. atha vā n' âitayoḥ,

2.144 mam' âiva brāhmaṇasya!

2.145 ājñapt" âsmi yuvarāja|Mitrāvasunā, yathā, «ady' âiva Malayavatyā vivāhaḥ. tal laghv enāṃ gṛhītv" āgacch'» êti. tad ehi, gacchāvaḥ.

2.146 gatā tvaṃ, dāsyāḥ putri, etāṃ gṛhītvā? priya|vayasyena punar atr' âiv' āsitavyam?

2.147 hat'|āśa! mā tvarasva! yuṣmākam api snāpanakam āgatam eva.

2.151 bho vayasya, āgataṃ snāpanakam.

3.2 nityaṃ yaḥ pibati surāṃ, janasya priya|saṅgamaṃ ca yaḥ karoti—mama tau dvāv eva devau Baladevaḥ Kāmadevaś ca.

3.3 sa|phalaṃ khalu mama Śekharakasya jīvitaṃ,

3.4 vakṣaḥ|sthale dayitā, datt'|ôtpala|vāsitā mukhe madirā, śīrṣe ca śekharaṃ nityam eva saṃsthitāni yasya.

3.5 are ko māṃ calayati?

3.5 avaśyam Navamālikā māṃ parihasati!

3.6 bhaṭṭaka, na tāvad āgatā Navamālikā.

3.7 prathama|pradoṣa eva Malayavatī|vivāha|maṅgalaṃ nirvṛttam. tat kasmād idānīṃ prabhāte 'pi n' āgacchati.

3.7 atha vā, amuṣmin Malayavatyā vivāha|maṅgal'|ôtsave sarva eva nija|praṇayinī|jana|sanāthaḥ siddha|vidyādhara|lokaḥ

Kusum'|ākar'|ôdyāne āpāna|saukhyam anubhavati. tat tasminn eva Navamālikā mām udīkṣamāṇā tiṣṭhati. tat tasminn eva gamiṣyāmi. kīdṛśo Navamālikayā vinā Śekharakaḥ?

3.9 etad udyānam. praviśatu bhaṭṭakaḥ.

3.12 śrutaṃ mayā, priya|vayasyaḥ Kusum'|ākar'|ôdyānaṃ gamiṣyat' îti. tad yāvat tatr' âiva gamiṣyāmi.

3.12 etad udyānaṃ. yāvat praviśāmi.

3.12 kasmāt punar ete duṣṭa|madhukarā mām ev' âbhidravanti.

3.12 bhavatu, jñātaṃ mayā! yan Malayavatyā bandhu|janena jāmātuḥ priya|vayasya iti sa|bahumānaṃ varṇakair vilipto 'smi. santāna|kusuma|śekharaṃ ca pinaddham. eṣo 'tyādaro me 'narthī|bhūtaḥ. kim idānīm atra kariṣyāmi? atha vā eten' âiva Malayavatyāḥ sakāśāl labdhena rakt'|âṃśuka|yugalena str" îva lambaṃ lambaṃ paridhāya uttarīya | kṛt' | âvaguṇṭhano gamiṣyāmi. paśyāmi tāvad dāsyāḥ putrā duṣṭa|madhukarāḥ kiṃ kariṣyant' îti.

3.14 are, ceṭa!

3.14 eṣā khalu Navamālikā, ahaṃ cirasy' āgata iti kupit" âvaguṇṭhanaṃ kṛtv" ânyato gacchati. tat kaṇṭhe gṛhītvā prasādayāmy enām.

3.16 aham ekeṣāṃ madhu|karāṇāṃ mukhāt katham api paribhraṣṭo 'nyasya duṣṭa|madhukarasya mukhe patito 'smi.

3.17 kathaṃ? kopena parāṅ|mukhī|bhūtā?

3.17 prasīda, Navamālike, prasīda!

3.19 ājñapt" âsmi bhartṛ | dārikāyā mātrā, «hañje Navamālike! Kusum' | ākar' | ôdyānaṃ gatv" ôdyāna | pālikāṃ Pallavikāṃ bhaṇa, adya sa|viśeṣaṃ tamāla|vīthikāṃ sajjī|kuru. Malayavatī| sahitena jāmātr" âtr' āgantavyam» iti. ājñaptā ca mayā Pallavikā. yāvad rajanī|virah'|ôtkaṇṭhitaṃ priya|vallabhaṃ Śekharakam anvicchāmi.

3.19 eṣa Śekharakaḥ.

3.19 katham? anyāṃ kām api striyam prasādayati!

3.20 Hari|Hara|Pitāmahānām api garvito yo na jānāti nantum, sa Śekharakaś caraṇayos tava, Navamālike, patati.

3.21 dāsyāḥ putra! matta|pālaka! kuto 'tra Navamālikā?

3.22 katham? aham iti kṛtvā mada|paravaśena Śekharakeṇ' ārya Ātreyaḥ prasādyate. yāvad alīka|kopaṃ kṛtvā dvāv apy etau parihasiṣyāmi.

3.23 bhaṭṭaka, muñca! muṃca etan. na bhavati Navamālikā. eṣā khalu Navamālikā roṣa|raktābhyāṃ nayanābhyāṃ paśyanty āgatā.

3.24 Śekharaka! kā nu khalv eṣā prasādyate?

3.25 ahaṃ manda|bhāgyāyāḥ putraḥ!

3.26 are kapila|markaṭaka! tvam api māṃ Śekharakaṃ parihasasi. are ceṭa! gṛhāṇ' êmam. yāvan Navamālikāṃ prasādayāmi.

3.27 yad bhaṭṭaka ājñāpayati.

3.28 prasīda, Navamālike, prasīda!

3.29 eṣa me 'pakramitum avasaraḥ.

3.30 kasmin, kasmin, kapila|markaṭaka, palāyase?

3.31 bhavati Navamālike, prasīda. mocaya mām.

3.32 yadi bhūmyāṃ śīrṣaṃ niveśya pādayor me patasi.

3.33 kathaṃ? rāja|mitraṃ bhūtvā, dāsyāḥ putri, pādayos te patiṣyāmi?

3.34 idānīṃ tvāṃ pātayiṣyāmi. Śekharaka, uttiṣṭh' ôttiṣṭha. prasannā khalv aham.

3.34 eṣa jāmātuḥ priya|vayasyas tvayā khalī|kṛtaḥ. etac chrutvā kadā cid bhaṭṭārako Mitrāvasuḥ kupyet. tad ādareṇa sammānay" âinam.

3.35 yan Navamālik" ājñāpayati.

3.35 ārya! tvaṃ priya|sambandhika iti kṛtv" âpahasitaḥ.

3.35 kiṃ satyam eva Śekharako mattaḥ, kṛtaḥ parihāsaḥ?

3.35 ih' ôpaviśatu sambandhikaḥ.

3.36 diṣṭy" âpagata iv' âsya mada|vegaḥ.

3.37 Navamālike, upaviśa tvam asya pārśvataḥ, yena dvāv api yuvāṃ samaṃ sammānayāmi.

3.39 ceṭaka, su|pūritaṃ khalv etac caṣakaṃ kurv accha|surayā.

3.41 Navamālike, pītvā caukṣitvā dehy etat!

3.42 yac Chekharaka ājñāpayati.

3.43 etan Navamālikā|mukha|saṃsarga|vardhita|rasaṃ Śekharakād anyena ken' âpy an|āsvādita|pūrvam. tat pib' âitat. kiṃ te 'taḥ paraṃ sammānaṃ karomi?

3.44 Śekharaka, brāhmaṇaḥ khalv aham.

3.45 yadi tvaṃ brāhmaṇaḥ, kva te brahma|sūtram?

3.46 tat khalv amunā ceṭen' ākṛṣyamāṇaṃ chinnam!

3.47 yady evaṃ, ved'|âkṣarāṇy api kati cid udāhara.

3.48 bhavati, sīdhu|gandhena mama ved'|âkṣarāṇi naṣṭāni. atha vā, kiṃ mama bhavatyā samaṃ vivādena? eṣa brāhmaṇaḥ pādayos te patati.

3.49 ārya, mā m" âivaṃ kuru! Śekharaka, satyaṃ brāhmaṇaḥ khalv eṣaḥ.

3.49 ārya, tvayā na kopitavyam. sambandhik'|ânurūpaḥ parihāsaḥ kṛtaḥ. Śekharaka, tvam ap' îmaṃ prasādaya.

3.50 aham ap' îmaṃ prasādayāmi.

3.50 marṣayatu, marṣayatv āryaḥ, yan mayā mada|para|vaśen' âparāddham. yen' âhaṃ Navamālikayā sah' āpānakaṃ gamiṣyāmi.

3.51 marṣitaṃ mayā. gaccha. yāvad aham api vayasyaṃ paśyāmi.

3.52 ārya, tathā.

3.54 atikrāntaḥ khalu brāhmaṇasy' âkāla|mṛtyuḥ. tad aham api matta|bālaka|jana|saṃsarga|dūṣita iha dīrghikāyā snāsyāmi.

3.54 eṣa khalu priya|vayasyo rūpiṇīm iva vara|lakṣmīṃ Malayavatīṃ avalamby' êta ev' āgacchati. tad ih' âiva sthāsyāmi.

3.59 hañje, na kevalaṃ darśanīyaḥ, priyam api bhaṇituṃ jānāti.

3.60 ayi pratipakṣa|vādini! satyam ev' âitat. kim atra «priya|vacanam?»

3.62 etv, etu bhartṛ|dārakaḥ.

3.65 etat kusum'|ākar'|ôdyānaṃ. praviśatu bhartṛ|dārakaḥ.

3.71 jayatu bhavān. svasti bhavatyai.

3.73 bho vayasya! laghv ev' āgataḥ, kin tu iyantaṃ kālaṃ vivāha|maṅgal'|ôtsava|milita|siddha|vidyādhar'|āpāna|darśana|kautūhalena paribhraman na lakṣitaḥ. tat priya|vayasyo 'pi tāvad etat paśyatu.

3.78 eṣā khalu tamāla|vīthikā. etac candana|latā|maṇḍapam, etac ca śarad'|ātapa|parikheditam iva tatra|bhavatyā vadanaṃ lakṣyate, tad iha sphaṭika|śilā|tale upaviśatu.

3.85 śrutaṃ tvayā, kathaṃ varṇit" êti?

3.86 Caturike, m" âivaṃ garvam udvaha. asmākam api madhye darśanīyo jano 'sty eva, kevalaṃ matsareṇa ko 'pi na varṇayati.

3.87 ārya, ahaṃ te varṇayāmi.

3.88 jīvito 'smi! karotu bhavatī prasādam, yen' âiṣa punar na bhaṇati īdṛśas tādṛśo markaṭ'|ākāra iti.

3.89 adya tvaṃ mayā vivāha|jāgareṇa nidrāyamāṇo nimīlit'|âkṣaḥ śobhamāno dṛṣṭaḥ. tad evam eva tiṣṭha.

3.91 yāvan nīlī|ras'|ânukāriṇā tamāla|pallava|rasena mukham asya kālī|kariṣyāmi.

3.98 bhavati, kiṃ te kṛtam?

3.99 nanu varṇito 'si!

3.100 dāsyāḥ putri! rāja|kulaṃ khalv etat! kiṃ te kariṣyāmi?

3.100 bhoḥ, yuṣmākaṃ purata ev' âhaṃ dāsyā dhītayā khalī|kṛto 'smi. kiṃ mam' êha sthitena? anyatra gamiṣyāmi.

3.102 kupitaḥ khalu mama ārya Ātreyaḥ. yāvad gatvā prasādayāmi.

3.103 hañje Caturike, kathaṃ mām ekākinīm ujjhitvā gacchasi?

3.104 evam eva ciram ekākinī bhava!

3.109 eṣa khalu siddha|yuvarājo Mitrāvasuḥ ken' âpi kāry'|ântareṇa kumāraṃ preksitum āgataḥ.

4.44 hā putra Śaṅkhacūḍa! kathaṃ vyāpādyamānaḥ kil' âdya tvaṃ mayā draṣṭavyaḥ?

4.47 hā putraka Śaṅkhacūḍa! kathaṃ vyāpādyamānaḥ kil' âdya tvaṃ mayā prekṣitavyaḥ?

4.47 anena mukha | candreṇa virahitam andhakārī | bhaviṣyati pātālam.

4.49 hā putraka! kathaṃ te '|dṛṣṭa|sūrya|sukumāraṃ śarīraṃ nirghṛṇa|hṛdayo Garuḍa āhārayiṣyati?

4.53 hā putraka! tiṣṭha. muhūrtam api tāvad vadanaṃ te prekṣiṣye.

4.54 ehi, kumāra! kiṃ tav' âitayā bhaṇantyā? putra|sneha|mohitā khalv eṣā na rāja|kāryaṃ jānāti.

4.56 ānītaḥ khalu mayā vadhya|śilā|samīpaṃ Śaṅkhacūḍaḥ. yāvad etad vadhya|cihnaṃ rakt'|âṃśuka|yugalaṃ dattvā vadhya|śilāṃ darśayāmi.

4.58 kumāra! Śaṃkhacūḍa! eṣa svāmina ādeṣa iti kṛtv" êdṛśam api niṣṭhuraṃ mantryate.

4.60 nāga|rājo Vāsukir ājñāpayati!

4.62 «etad rakt'|âṃśuka|yugalaṃ paridhāy' āroha vadhya|śilāṃ, yena rakt'|âṃśuka|cihn'|ôpalakṣitaṃ Garuḍo gṛhītv" āhāra|karaṇāya neṣyati.»

4.64 Śaṅkhacūḍa, gṛhāṇ' âitat.

4.66 hā vatsa! etat khalu tad vadhya|cihnaṃ vasanaṃ, yena bibheti me hṛdayam.

4.67 āsannā khalu Garuḍasy' āgamana|velā. tal laghv apakrāmāmi.

4.69 hā jāta! hā putraka! hā manoratha|śata|labdha! kutra tvāṃ punaḥ prekṣiṣye?

4.73 putraka, kathaṃ samāśvasimi? kim eka|putra iti kṛt'|ânukampena nivartito 'si nāga|rājena? hā kṛtānta|hataka, katham idānīṃ tvayā nirghṛṇa|hṛdayen' âivaṃ vistīrṇe jīva|loke mama putraka eva smṛtaḥ? sarvathā hat" âsmi manda|bhāginī.

4.77 hā putraka! Śaṅkhacūḍa! durlabhaḥ saṃstambhaḥ. yad" âiva nāga|loka|parirakṣakeṇa Vāsukinā svayaṃ parityakto 'si, tadā kas te paritrāṇaṃ kariṣyati?

4.79 Garuḍa! Vinatā|nandana, vyāpādaya mām! ahaṃ ta āhāra|nimittaṃ parikalpitā.

4.84 hā putraka! ahaṃ punas tava maraṇa|bhītā sarvam eva Garuḍa|mayaṃ paśyāmi.

4.86 putraka, punaḥ punar evaṃ bhaṇa!

4.88 putraka, ciraṃ jīva!

4.90 pratihataṃ khalv etat. tvam api me Śaṅkhacūḍa|nirviśeṣaḥ putraka eva. atha vā Śaṅkhacūḍād adhikataraḥ, ya evaṃ bandhu|jana|parityaktaṃ mama putrakaṃ śarīra|pradānena rakṣitum icchasi.

4.108 kathaṃ? paścimam asya vacanam?

4.108 putraka, tvām ujjhitv" ânyatra me pādau na prasarataḥ. tat tvayā saha gamiṣyāmi.

5.10 pratihataṃ khalv a|maṅgala|vacanam!

5.11 anena dur|nimittena vepata iva me hṛdayam.

5.15 mahā|rāja, yadi tatr' âpi n' âsti, tat kv' êdānīṃ gato mama putrakaḥ, yen' âivaṃ cirayati?

5.17 ahaṃ punar muhūrtakam apy ārya|putram a|paśyanty anyad eva kim apy āśaṅke.

5.26 putrakasy' êva me etac cūḍā|ratnam.

5.27 m" âivaṃ bhaṇa!

5.31 Sunanda, api nāma kadā cid etāvatyā velayā śvaśura|kulam eva gato me putrako bhaviṣyati. tad gaccha, jñātvā laghv ev' âsmākaṃ nivedaya.

5.42 mahā|rāja, eṣa ko 'pi prarugṇa|vadana ita eva tvarita|tvaritam āgacchan hṛdayaṃ me ākulī|karoti. taj jñāyatāṃ tāvat, ka eṣa iti.

5.46 a|vidhave, dhīrā bhava! na khalu ta īdṛśī ākṛtir vaidhavya|duḥkham anubhavati.

5.47 amba, tav' âiṣ" āśīḥ.

5.57 hā putraka! kiṃ tvayā kṛtam?

5.58 hā, kathaṃ satyī|bhūtam eva me duś|cintitam.

5.62 vatsa, uttiṣṭh', ôttiṣṭha. mā rudihi. vayam api kiṃ Jīmūtavāhanena vinā jīvāmaḥ? tat samāśvasihi tāvat.

5.63 hā āryaputra! kutra tvaṃ mayā draṣṭavyaḥ?

5.68 hā putraka Jīmūtavāhana! yasmai te guru|jana|śuśrūṣāṃ varjayitv" ânyat sukhaṃ na rocate, sa katham idānīṃ pitaram ujjhitvā svarga|saukhyam anubhavituṃ prasthito 'si?

5.70 tāta, dehi me ārya|putrasya cūḍā|ratnaṃ, yen' êdaṃ hṛdaye kṛtvā jvalana|praveśen' ātmanaḥ santāpam apanayāmi.

5.72 mahā|rāja, tat kiṃ pratipālyate?

5.75 sarvathā devatānāṃ prasādena jīvantam eva me putrakaṃ drakṣyāmi.

5.76 dur|labhaṃ khalv etan mama manda|bhāgyāyāḥ.

5.110 jāte, muhūrtakam api tāvad virama. ebhir a|virata|patadbhir aśru|bindubhis te nirvāpyate 'yam agniḥ.

5.119 mahā|rāja, kṛt'|ârth" âsmi. a|kṣata|śarīrasy' âiva putrakasya mukhaṃ dṛṣṭam.

5.120 yat satyam ev' ārya|putraṃ paśyanty apy a|saṃbhāvanīyam iti kṛtvā na pratyemi.

5.125 hā putraka! kathaṃ vāṅ|mātreṇ' âpi tvayā na sambhāvit" âsmi.

5.126 hā ārya|putra! kathaṃ guru|jano 'pi tvay" ôpekṣitavyaḥ?

5.133 hā putraka, paśyatām ev' âsmākaṃ kṛtānta|hataken' âpahriyase.

5.135 pratihataṃ khalv a|maṅgalam. na rodiṣyāmi. jāte, samāśvasihi tāvat. varam iyatīṃ velāṃ bhartus te mukhaṃ dṛṣṭam.

5.136 hā ārya|putra! kiṃ karomi manda|bhāgyā?

5.137 vatse, m" âivaṃ kuru. pratihataṃ khalv etat!

5.140 ati|duṣkara|kāriṇī khalv aham. y" ēdṛśam apy ārya|putraṃ paśyantī ady' âpi jīvitaṃ na parityajāmi.

5.141 nṛśaṃsa! katham idānīṃ tvay" âitad āpūryamāṇa|nava|rūpa|yauvana|śobham ev' âitad|avasthaṃ putrakasya me śarīraṃ kṛtam?

5.159 dhanyā khalu sā, yā Garuḍa|mukha|patitam apy a|kṣata|śarīram eva putrakaṃ drakṣyati.

5.163 hā kin nu khalv etad vartate?

5.163 paritrāyadhvaṃ. paritrāyadhvam. eṣa me putrako vipadyate.

5.164 hā ārya|putra, parityaktu|kāma iva lakṣyase.

5.170 hā vatsa! hā guru|jana|vatsala! hā Jīmūtavāhana! kutr' âsi mayā punar draṣṭavyaḥ?

5.173 hā ārya|putra, kutra māṃ parityajya gato 'si? nirghṛṇe Malayavati, kim etad draṣṭavyam ity etāvatīṃ velāṃ jīvit" âsi?

5.176 bhagavanto lokapālāḥ! amṛtena siktvā putrakaṃ me jīvayata.

5.181 putraka Śaṅkhacūḍa, laghu sajjaya. duḥkham khalv asmābhir vinā bhrātā te vartate.

5.187 bhagavati Gauri, tvay" ājñaptaṃ, «vidyādhara | cakravartī te bhartā bhaviṣyat'» îti. tat kathaṃ mama manda | bhāgyāyās tvam apy alīka|vādinī saṃvṛttā?

5.195 bhagavatyāḥ prasādena.

5.197 diṣṭyā pratyujjīvita ārya|putraḥ.

The Shattered Thighs

100 utsarat', āryāḥ. utsarata!

105 putraka, kv' âsi?

106 mahā|rāja, kutr' âsi?

110 jīvit" âsmi manda|bhāgā.

111 mahā|rāja, mahā|rāja!

115 mahā|rāja, na dṛśyate.

118 jāta Suyodhana, dehi me prativacanam! putra | śata | vināśa | duḥsthitaṃ samāśvāsaya mahā|rājaṃ.

128 atra, jāte!

129 ārye, ime svaḥ.

130 anveṣethāṃ bhartāram.

131 gacchāmi manda|bhāgā.

133 tāta, ahaṃ Durjayaḥ.

135 pariśrāntaḥ khalv aham.

137 tāta! ahaṃ gacchāmi.

137 tāta, kutr' âsi?

140 ayaṃ mahā|rājo. bhūmyām upaviṣṭaḥ.

142 tvaṃ cirāyas' îti.

144 aham api khalu te aṅke upaviśāmi.

148 aṅke upaveśaṃ kin nimittaṃ tvaṃ vārayasi?

150 kutra nu khalu mahā|rājo gamiṣyati?

152 mām api tatra naya.

154 ehi, mahā|rāja, anviṣyase.

156 āryay", āryeṇa, sarveṇ' ântaḥ|pureṇa ca.

158 ahaṃ tvāṃ neṣyāmi.

160 āryāḥ! ayaṃ mahā|rājaḥ!

161 hā hā mahā|rājaḥ!

163 kutra me putrakaḥ?

164 ayaṃ mahā|rājo bhūmyām upaviṣṭaḥ.

167 jāta, Suyodhana, pariśrānto 'si?

170 mahā|rāja, aham a|bhīta|putra|pradāyinī.

183 bhaṇa, jāta.

185 mama mano|rathaḥ khalu tvayā bhaṇitaḥ.

188 bālā eṣā saha|dharma|cāriṇī rodimi.

191 eka|kṛta|praveśa|niścayā na rodimi.

194 aham api tad eva cintayāmi.

NOTES

Bold *references are to the English text;* ***bold italic*** *references are to the Sanskrit text. An asterisk (*) in the body of the text marks the word or passage being annotated.*

How the Nagas were Pleased

1.1 **Cupid**, or Kama, "love/passion," is bodiless because his body was burned away by Shiva, angry at Kama's attempt to distract him by love for Párvati from his asceticism. The episode described in this verse is the penultimate moment in the Buddha's struggle for Awakening, in which he was assailed by threat and temptation by Mara, "death," the figure who in Buddhism represents all obstruction on the spiritual path. We should note that the Tibetan translation of "How the Nagas were Pleased" contains a verse that precedes this one. It does not occur in any surviving Sanskrit source, but HAHN argues that it was a part of the original *nandī* (opening invocation) of the play and translates it thus: "May this handful flowers [sic] protect you! / It was bound by Mara's daughter Rati / at the time of the Buddha's (decisive) meditation. / She was excited because she expected / to see her beloved there. / (The flowers) were encircled by bees, / their wings agitating in their longing for honey, / and their feet set them to trembling / so that the pollen fell down in rich quantities / from their stamen." (HAHN 1991: vii)

1.3 **By Cupid ... protect you**: the impact of the Buddha's strength on each group of witnesses is being described here, along with the Buddha's indifference. Kama, the god of love, fires arrows that are tipped with flowers, not points, and this characteristic is alluded to repeatedly throughout the love scenes of the play.

1.30 **Elephants from the four quarters**: there is a mythical elephant assigned to each of the cardinal points.

1.39 **The tree** was on occasion used to create cloth by ascetics. Peeling too much bark could kill the tree.

1.39 The "**Sama Veda**" is one of the three principal Vedas, or divisions of brahmanical scripture, and contains primarily verses redacted from the "Rig Veda" for the purpose of ritual chanting.

1.45 **Darbha grass**: sacred grass used in ceremonial.

1.47 **Lyre strings**: the *vipañci vīṇā* is, according to the *Naṭyaśāstra*, a kind of bow-harp with nine strings. If so, its nearest modern relative is the saung of Burma and Northern Thailand.

1.47 **Ornaments**: ***gamaka*** refers to the technical grasp of the variety of manners of playing notes or groups of notes.

1.49 The **kákali mode** is one in which the words are sung softly.

1.51 The **tamála tree**, *Xanthochymus pictorius*, has dark bark and white flowers. The ethos expressed here is that a married woman should not be viewed by strangers, but an unmarried girl would be fair game.

1.54 ***gaura*** is a light yellowish color. In this verse the heroine uses Sanskrit for the only time in the play.

1.56 ***tattva-*** em. : *sattva-* G

1.56 While other translators, following the guidance of Shiva·rama, take this as a reference to an aspect of instrumental playing, ***vyañjana*** are "consonants/syllables" and this is a reference to her singing in Sanskrit, rather than the usual Maharashtri, the preferred Prakrit for high-class ladies when uttering verse (or song) and which is notorious for its lack of consonants! We should note that instrumental, rather than vocal, "**clarity**" would be at odds with the *kākalī* mode mentioned at 1.49.

1.56 **Cow tail**: a kind of rhythmic variation which begins fast and gradually reduces tempo. The other two are the "uniform" (*samā*) and "in a stream" (*sroto|gatā*).

1.56 **Essence, flood and sequential**: these last three are speculative translations of the Sanskrit terms, which are usually left untranslated by translators, and in some cases entirely omitted! These are methods of accompaniment to singing, and respectively involve matching the rhythm of the song (***tattva***), fast and independent playing (***ogha***), and filling in pauses in the song (***anugata***).

1.65 **Hari** is a name for Indra, who was cursed such that his body be covered with a thousand vaginas by the sage Gáutama when he caught Indra lusting after his wife, Ahálya. The curse was later commuted to eyes. The moon is designated as **carrying a hare** (***śaśabhṛt***) since, in South Asia, the markings on the moon are said to resemble the outline of a hare. The **dank nether region** is the abode of the Nagas.

1.74 **Each for the other:** ⌜*aṇṇoṇṇa*⌟ (*anyonya*) is a difficult reading to interpret and we should note an alternative, *-ananya*, which would mean "unique."

1.87 **The crown**: in a Buddhist context the crown of the head, *uṣṇīṣa*, is the swelling on top of the head that is familiar on statues of the Buddha. This and the following signs are all "characteristics of a great person" (*mahā/puruṣa/lakṣaṇa*) and are indicators of the highest spiritual or political destiny. Similarly, **the hair between his eyebrows** catches the eye because it is white.

1.98 *dhamadhamāyati* em. : *damadamāyati* G

2.20 The **Lord** addressed here is Kama, the god of love.

2.27 **His Lordship**: again the Lord referred to here is Kama, whose banner shows the *makara*, a semi-mythological creature somewhat resembling a crocodile or dolphin.

2.31 **Slayer of Madhu** refers to Vishnu, who killed the demon Madhu who had stolen the Vedas from Brahma·deva. **Lakshmi** is the wife of Vishnu. The episode is related in the 'Peace' book (*Śāntiparvan*) of the "Maha·bhárata."

2.43 **How can you say … in public**: I have translated the adverb "without qualification/openly/bluntly/in public" (*nirvyājam*) twice, as both qualifying the hero's lovesickness, in the sense that, of all lovesick people, he is openly feeble rather than making any attempt to disguise his state, and also as qualifying the companion's statement (the last being the interpretation preferred by others). The ambiguity increases the comic irony of the verse.

2.50 **Ashóka tree**: *Saraca indica*, a small erect evergreen tree with dark green foliage, bearing heads of fragrant red flowers.

2.57 **Her thigh shaking**: a standard "sign" indicating intense emotion.

2.74 **As if weeping**: Indian folklore has it that moonstone weeps moisture under the influence of the moon.

2.77 The **pigment** (*manaś/śilā*) is formed of red arsenic. He wants small chunks that he can use like chalk.

2.80 In order to derive the pun about the moon, the compound *śobh"/âdharasya* needs also to be read as *śobhā/dharasya*.

2.91 **Drawing**: G's reading, ⌜***kamma***⌟ (*karma*), is glossed by Shiva·rama as follows: *kriyata iti karma likhitaṃ vanitā/rūpam ity arthaḥ*. Other editions read *kanyakām* here.

2.107 *iha* em. : *iva*

2.116 ⌜***pi***⌟ accepted from G's variant readings.

2.116 **Atimúkta vine**: a form of jasmine.

2.132 **It's she who is … mine of jewels**: a pleasingly complex punning metaphor: Málayavati's grace and beauty is explained by her royal lineage which is on a par with the birth of the moon from the ocean waters in which many jewels were hidden, and like the rising of the boat-like sliver of the new moon (which crescent rises on its "back" in South Asia) over the sea, all punning on the genesis of his drawing of his "moon," i.e. Málayavati, from the minerals/jewels he used to make his drawing.

2.141 A **marriage of mutual affection**, or *gāndharva* marriage, is based on spontaneous mutual affection without consultation of relatives.

3.2 **Kama·dev(a)** is Kama, or Cupid, the god of love. **Bala·deva** is associated with drinking alcohol.

3.12 **Santána** flowers come from one of the five Kalpa trees of Indra's heaven.

3.20 **Hari, Hara or Pita·maha**: these are alternative names for the three major Hindu deities, Vishnu, Shiva and Brahma.

3.23 Although *edaṃ* can mean "he, she" or "it, this," and so by a slight change of punctuation (⌜***muñca. edaṃ na …***⌟ to ⌜*muñca edaṃ. na …*⌟) we could understand "Let her go. It isn't Nava·málika," I have stuck for better or worse to my policy of following GANAPATI SHASTRI's interpretation as expressed by his *chāyā*.

3.26 **Ginger** from the scattered powders, presumably.

3.35 At this point Shékharaka turns in mischief to extracting an apology from Atréya for having called him "the prince of drunks." **Our dear master**: Shiva·rama glosses **sambandhikaḥ* as *sambandhimitram*, i.e. "*sambandhika* means a friend who is connected [to]…" in this case someone who is "dear" to the speaker, in other words Shékharaka's employer. The excuse of joking at the expense of "relations" is a valid one, and the practice is still in vogue at modern weddings in South Asia.

3.41 **Give it back**: G's reading, ⌜***cokkhia***⌟ (*caukṣitvā*), implies a causative denominative verb derived from *cukṣā*, "pure/clean." Shiva·rama glosses as follows: *caukṣitvā pavitrī/kṛtya, priyā/mukh'/ôcchiṣṭam hi pavitram*, "*caukṣitvā* means 'making it clean.' The means of cleaning is its being spat back out from the mouth of his beloved"!

3.44 **I'm actually a brahmin**: this joke revolves around the prohibitions incumbent on a brahmin regarding his need to preserve his ritual purity. Both the alcohol and its being handled and shared (let alone used as mouthwash) by low caste persons all destroy that purity.

3.58 The verse is a double entendre, referring to a standard three-fold penance of body, speech and mind, but ambiguously subverted by the suggestion that the "penance" he describes is his obsession with his beloved. "**Hmm**" renders ***huṃ***, a mantra frequently used in ritual and/or meditative contexts.

3.113 The **enemy** is Matánga.

3.128 The **mental defilements** are the fundamental dispositions whereby human beings remain unenlightened. They are formulated variously most simply as greed, hatred and delusion, but in more sophisticated discussions as attachment, anger, pride, ignorance, false views and doubt.

3.130 **I shall enlighten you there**: the pun is that he would like to "enlighten" him in the sense of a Buddhist "awakening" (*bodhi*), rather than just explain himself.

3.131 The day lotus opens its petals during the day, and closes them at night. The verse as a whole marks the end of the day in the place of the traditional praise to the setting sun.

4.4 The practice appears to be that every day **for ten days** after the wedding the bride's family send a pair of **red garments** for the lucky couple to wear.

4.7 **On this first day of the festival**: i.e. the first day of the Dipávali (Diwali) festival in the autumn month of Kárttika at the end of the monsoon.

4.65 **Thus, taking them ... his head**: in other editions a version of this stage direction is placed in the mouth of Shankha·chuda as an explicit statement of acceptance.

4.72 Other editions have here a verse, in the mouth of Shankha·chuda, as follows:

yair atyanta/dayā/parair na vihitā
bandhy" ârthinām prārthanā,
yaiḥ kāruṇya/parigrahān na gaṇitaḥ
sv'/ârthaḥ par'/ârthaṃ prati,
ye nityaṃ para/duḥkha/duḥkhita/dhiyas,
te sādhavo 'staṃ gatā.
mātaḥ, saṃhara bāṣpa/vegam adhunā.
kasy' âgrato rudyate?

"They are all gone, those good people whose minds are always pained by the pain of others, who being deeply compassionate do not make vain the entreaties of the needy, who, because they take up compassion do not count their own need against the need of others. Mother, stop this flood of tears. Before whom are you now weeping?"

4.79 **Vínata**: the mother of Gáruda.

4.92 A **dog-cooker** is a *caṇḍāla* or untouchable. The consumption of dog flesh, being from a despised and polluting animal, is disgusting and unacceptable for any member of caste society. **Vishva·mitra**, a sage, was forced to consume dog flesh that he stole from a *caṇḍāla*'s hut at night. When the *caṇḍāla* found him, he scolded him as a high caste man for the impropriety of eating such food. A lengthy debate on the issue evolves between them, Vishva·mitra arguing that he should be allowed to take just the dog's ass. Eventually he wins and retreats with the morsel. Regarding the second line, a poor **Gáutama** brahmin, lost from his caravan, was given shelter by **Nadi·jangha**, the lord of the cranes, and sent on his way to further help. Subsequently returning the same way, Gáutama killed the lord of the cranes for food on his journey. When discovered, Gáutama himself was executed by *rākṣasa*s (demons) for the injustice, but subsequently revived by Indra at the request of the revivified crane. Both stories are to be found in the 'Peace' book (*Śāntiparvan*) of the "Maha·bhárata." **Tarkshya** is a name for Gáruda.

4.104 *Vināyaka* is a name for both Gáruda and Ganésha. In order to derive the "secondary" reading concerning Shiva, some of the puns in this verse require breaking the compound words in ways different from those that are shown in the printed text. Specifically, *ahinā hāreṇa*, and */âsthi/kapālaṃ*. Ganésha would be delighted by this appearance because Shiva is his father.

4.109 **Gokárna**: a temple and pilgrimage place to Shiva on the coast near Karwar.

4.122 The terrifying flavor of this verse comes from the comparison of Gáruda's arrival to the events at the end of the world.

4.130 **Curling Shesha up into a circle**: other texts read *saṃsmaran*, "remembering" rather than ***saṃharan***, "drawing up." Shesha is the thousand-headed Naga who holds up the universe and acts as a couch for Vishnu inbetween the periods of universal creation. Gáruda's elder brother is Áruna, the charioteer of the sun.

4.131 **By the merit ... to help others**: the form of this wish is familiar in the Buddhist context where "dedication of merit" for the benefit of others is formalized in ritual.

4.135 **A rain of flowers**: the flowers are blown from the **parijáta** tree, one of the five trees of heaven produced at the churning of the ocean. The model for this miraculous occurrence is the death of the Buddha, the archetypal bodhisattva in all Buddhist traditions.

5.42 **Shattered** (⌜***paruṇṇa***,⌟ *prarugṇa*): an oblique reference to Práruja, a creature in the "Maha·bhárata" that is killed by Gáruda: "your Práruja-ed face."

5.60 **Great being** is a standard epithet applied to spiritually advanced people, particularly bodhisattvas. The term occurs several times always weighted with this sense and particularly in the pun at 5.81.

5.78 At this point some recensions end Act Five, Act Six opening with a change of scene.

5.94 The **svástika**, an equilateral cross with each arm bent at ninety degrees (to left or right), is an ancient symbol of good fortune, as its name implies. It is attested from the Indus Valley period (third millenium BCE) onwards and came to be used as an auspicious sign in Hindu, Jain and Buddhist traditions. Members of the magician clan have the sign on their chest. This positive heritage has been overshadowed by its adoption by the Nazi and contemporary neo-Nazi groups in the twentieth century.

5.98 Because the Lokalóka mountain range ("**ends of the world**") rings the universe and separates it from the unfathomable outer darkness, it represents the limit of the visible universe.

5.102 **A region even lower than the dank nether region**: i.e. a region of hell, disposed beneath the lower region, *pātāla/tala*, occupied by the Nagas.

5.103 **This is a bodhisattva I have murdered**: in *jātaka* stories, depicting previous lives of the Buddha, the hero is designated the bodhisattva. More generally, a bodhisattva is any Buddhist hero or ideal character who is dedicated to the achievement of Buddhahood and is thus depicted exemplifying the requisite virtues for this. The virtue of giving, often in the form of extreme self-sacrifice, is therefore the theme of numerous exemplary stories, and thus, in a Buddhist context, people who sacrifice themselves for others are usually considered to be bodhisattvas. This is the moment of realization, even conversion, in which Gáruda realizes the evil nature of his conduct, see 5.150 [26].

5.113 The **mare's fire** is a submarine fire located near the south pole, so called because it is supposed to resemble a mare's face. It bounds the ocean, burning off the excess water.

5.143 The analysis of the body offered here is a version of a standard Buddhist bodily analysis the purpose of which is to create an attitude of dispassion.

5.149 The **measured number** of beings refers presumably to the Naga-a-day policy agreed with Vásuki.

5.169 "By the merit I have accrued today by protecting a snake through the gift of my own body, in every birth may I in this very way acquire a body in order to help others." = 4.131 [25].

5.172 Buddhist readers will recognize the allusion here to the six perfections (*pāramitā*) or practical virtues cultivated by the bodhisattva pursuing the spiritual path in Mahayana Buddhism. These are: giving (*dāna*), morality (*śīla*), forbearance (*kṣānti*), effort (*vīrya*), meditative states (*dhyāna*) and understanding (*prajñā*). Here, Harsha alludes to the perfection of meditative states in the form of compassion, *karuṇā*, one of the four "immeasurable states" (*apramāṇa*), a popular Buddhist meditation subject.

5.178 The **Lord of the hungry ghosts** is the god of Death, Yama. *Preta* can also mean "spirit of the dead," but in a Buddhist context *preta* usually means the inhabitant of a specific lower realm of beings characterized by extreme hunger and thirst. I have given preference to the latter meaning in the light of the author's apparent Buddhist intent. In this connection we can note that **Shakra** is the frequent designation for Indra in Buddhist texts.

5.184 Cf. 1.87 [18], of which this verse is an adaptation.

5.204 'The Beginning' (*Ādiparvan*) of the "Maha·bhárata" relates the story of the enmity of Gáruda and the snakes (*Āstikaparvan*). The snakes, coveting ambrosia, agreed to release Gáruda's mother from her slavery to their own mother, if he should bring it to them. This he did but tricked them out of it at the last moment after his mother was released. In frustration they licked the bed of *kuśa* grass on which he had placed the ambrosia and the sharp grass blades cut their tongues in two.

5.206 **Lake Mánasa** is located beside Mount Kailása, the abode of Gauri, and is frequented by migrant geese.

5.208 There is a standard list of seven "treasures/jewels" possessed by an emperor that occurs frequently in Buddhist sources: a discus, an elephant, a horse, a gem, a woman, an entrepreneur and a minister or viceroy.

5.211 Alongside the verbal play between *vinata* and ***vinīta*** here, Gáruda (***Vainateya***) has not only been disciplined insofar as his behavior is controlled, but also in the sense that he has accepted the discipline of Buddhist conduct, a development regularly denoted by terms cognate with *vinaya* (in this case *vinīta*).

5.216 This verse is not present in other recensions.

The Shattered Thighs

1 There is no *nāndī*, benedictory verse, in this or a number of other play texts as preserved in the South Indian performance tradition. The present verse 1, "May the illustrious Késhava...," might be considered the *nāndī* were it not that this stage direction indicates that a *nāndī* has already been recited. Interpretation of the description of the opening actions of a performance in the *Nāṭyaśāstra* and of this variation from the North Indian textual pattern is not agreed. An interesting and constructive exploration of this complex debate is offered in TIEKEN 2001.

2 **Késhava** is a name for Krishna, ally of the Pándavas. **Árjuna** is the third of the Pándava chiefs. **Drona's son** is Ashva·tthaman. As the verse indicates, the rest are Kurus or their allies, who are the opponents of the Pándavas in the "Maha·bhárata" war.

14 **Decoction of enmity**: variant: "a house of hostility" (*vairasyāyatanam*) D

23 **Clinging to a single sword:** variant: "wearing arrows as his only jewels" (*ratnaikasāyakadharaṃ*) G

23 **The ladies of the family handing down a son-in-law:** the groom is greeted by the unwidowed married women of the bride's house on the day of the wedding.

24 For **axes,** *paraśu,* G reads *Hāṭaka,* a geographical designation implying in context, "slingshots from Hátaka."

28 **Madhúka**: *Bassia latifolia* "the honey tree," the seeds and blossoms of which are used in the production of arrack, an alcoholic drink.

32 **The authority of a chief** or "their own authority" (*ātma/bal'/ādhānam*) D

35 G's manuscript reads "second [soldier]" but proposes, in a note, emending to "third [soldier]" and this is followed by D.

36 This verse makes references to the exploits of Árjuna. In order: Indra advised Árjuna to practice asceticism to propitiate Shiva in order to acquire from him the weapons to kill Bhishma and Drona. He was so successful that Shiva fought with him disguised as a hunter (*kirāta*). **Oath-bound confederates** is an allusion to an episode related in 'Drona' (*Droṇaparvan*), the seventh book of the "Maha·bhárata" in which Árjuna defeated Trigárta and his brothers who had sworn an oath to kill him. Árjuna assisted Agni, the fire god, in destroying the Khándava forest in defiance of Indra, who as god of rain tried to put out the fire. In gratitude Agni gave Árjuna the bow, Gándiva. Árjuna assisted Indra in defeating the armored demon(s) in dispute over the unfairly distributed wealth arising from the churning of the ocean.

41 **Plow-bearing**: Bala·rama used a plow as a weapon.

42 **Beautiful** (*cāru*): variant: "heated" (*tapta*) G

44 **His eyes bulging from his face in fury**: variant: "whose face has eyes filled with the fire of anger in (every) glance" (*krodh'/âgnik'/âkṣ'/ānanaḥ*) D

47 **A deft step:** the *Nāṭyaśāstra* has an entire chapter (11) devoted to *cārī* movements. The essence of the *cārī* is that the foot, shank and hip are moved simultaneously. Some thirty-two *cārī*s are enumerated and defined. They are the basis for stage fighting (11.5). In understanding this passage we should bear in mind the ubiquity

of "martial dance" in Indian martial arts, from the *Kalarippayattu* traditions of Kerala to the *Aki Kiti* kick fighting of Nagaland.

47 **The lord of men**: i.e. Duryódhana.

50 **first soldier**: not in G and B, supplied in D

58 **Son of the Wind**: Bhima was the son of the wind god, Vayu.

59 **As if the all-pervasive Wind had ... given him strength**: Vayu, wind, is considered to be the basis or element of movement in the body, and is "all-pervasive" (*sarva/gati*).

63 **Blessed Island-born Vyasa...**: G suggests this speech should be in the voice of the second soldier.

64 **Eyes filled with contempt**: variant: "The eyes of Bala·rama, veiled by his garland..." (*mālā/saṃvṛta/locanena*) D

66 **His lovely crest is shivering**: variant: "Whose crest is waving and loosened..." (*cala/vilulita/mauliḥ*) D

75 **In its mouth the remains of Saubha ... the forces of my foes**: the *Bhāgavata Purāṇa* describes a battle between the Shalvas and Vrishnis in which Bala·rama kills the king of the former and destroys his city Saubha with his plow. On another occasion Bala·rama wished to bathe in the Kalíndi, or Yámuna, and ordered the river to flow to him. When it did not he "dragged" it to him with his plow.

78 **Vásuki**, the serpent king, was employed by the gods and titans as a rope to coil around Mándara mountain and thus twirl it to churn up the ocean and release, among other things, ambrosia.

89 **Bhima has fulfilled his vow:** During the dice game which started the "Maha·bhárata" war Duryódhana patted his thigh in a provocative request for Dráupadi to sit on his lap, at which Bhima swore to break those same thighs.

94 **Reverberate**: G suggests *pratīsāriṇā*, "to throw in succession or in return."

94 **The terrible lac house ...**: Bhima had rescued himself and the other Pándavas from the burning house of lac built for their destruction by Duryódhana. **Váishravana's abode** is Gandha·mádana, a fragrantly forested mountain to the east of Meru. Bhima had gone to Gandha·mádana mountain to acquire flowers for Dráupadi and fought with the *gandharva*s there. Bhima had met **Hidímba the demon lord** in the forest where he slew him. Subsequently he married Hidímba's sister, Hidímbi, who transformed herself into the appearance of a beautiful woman and they had a son, Ghatótkacha, who is the subject of another one act play by Bhasa.

99 **It was the person ... who likes to fight fair**: reference is made to exploits of Krishna. One of the five trees of heaven, the Coral Tree appeared from the churning of the ocean and was appropriated by Indra, though subsequently taken from him by Krishna.

101 **He is trembling with fear**: not in G

113 **The hair of their heads exposed**: in mourning the practice is to undo the hair, which is otherwise dressed close to the scalp.

118 **Comfort the great chief ...**: G has the variant: "Greet the great chief. He is unhappy and grieved by the loss of his hundred sons." (⸢*putta/sada/viṇāsa/dukkhidaṃ mahā/rāaṃ ca manda/bhāaṃ*⸣ (⸢*saṃbhāvehi*⸣ conj.); Skt.: *putra/śata/vināśa/duḥkhitaṃ mahā/rājaṃ ca manda/bhāgam*).

120 **This blindfold she wears ... soaked continually by tears**: Gandhári swore to wear a blindfold out of respect for her husband's blindness.

124 **I must answer**: variant: "I shall tell him a different story" (*anyaṃ dadāmi khalu vṛttāntam*) G. I follow D here.

127 While not consistent with the details of the fight rendered here, in the "Maha·bhárata" proper, after Bhima has laid Duryódhana low, he touches his victim's head with his foot—a dramatic insult to the injured man. This is presumably a reference to that action.

153 **And say that to Wolf Belly**: "and speak to Wolf Belly," G.

186 **Málavi! You listen to me as well**: the parallel for the exchange with his wives is to be found in the case of Pandu's wives, Kunti and Madri, in 'The Beginning' (*Ādiparvan*), the first book of the "Maha·bhárata," who vie for the privilege of sati on their husband's death.

188 ***devī***: thus all editions, but from context it must designate Málavi.

194 All Duryódhana's statements to family members are nuanced but the comments by his parents here express their concern at what demands Duryódhana will make upon the coming generation of Kurus, i.e. whether he will instruct his son to continue the dynastic rivalry that has destroyed his generation of the Kuru clan.

196 The **water offering** is made by the deceased's heir before the lighting of the pyre. The significance of the reference to **Yudhi·shthira's sleeve** is that a warrior's arms are bared for combat, but if clothed imply peace.

199 The **horse sacrifice** is a major sacrificial rite concerned with ensuring royal offspring and latterly establishing universal monarchy. G's text reads that the sacrificial area is "not empty" (*a/śūnya*) i.e. "still crowded."

200 **The son of our teacher**: i.e. of Drona.

204 **The charioteer's son**: i.e. Karna, foster son of Ádhiratha, who was cursed by his teacher Párashu·rama to the effect that the skills he had learned from him by deceit would be made useless by having ineffectual weapons.

205 **They say** not in G.

208 **The net and hairgrips ...**: his hair had been dressed for battle with a containing net held in place by hairgrips (*mayūkha*, "peg"). Note the secondary resonance of ***mayūkha/jāla***, which can also mean "net of rays," with the final image of the setting sun. This is not a pun as such because, although it is the sense most translators take as primary, this compound is an attributive instrumental in

the plural signifying the plurality of the net and hairgrips, whereas if this compound were to be translated as a simile referring to his disheveled hair looking like rays of light, etc. it would need to be a singular *bahuvrīhi* compound qualifying *eṣaḥ*. Translating in such a way also ignores the protocol of hair, whereby loosed hair indicates disarray, pathos or mourning, which is the whole point of this description of the demise of a great hero.

220 These are all events that are related earlier in the "Maha·bhárata." **A gambling prize** …: the dice game was the main cause of the "Maha·bhárata" war, resulting as it did in the humiliation of Dráupadi and her Pándava husbands. **Abhimányu** …: on the thirteenth day of the war Árjuna's son Abhimányu, though too young to fight on his own, was allowed to break a crucial formation of the Kuru army, upon which, against the plan, he was isolated from his own side, and, against the rules of war, surrounded and killed by the Kuru army. **The Pándavas had to take refuge** …: as a result of the second dice game with the Káuravas, the Pándavas were exiled to the wilderness for twelve years. This is the subject of the entire third book of the "Maha·bhárata."

228 **I can relinquish my life**: variant: "my life is as if departing" (*parityaljant" îva*) D

228 **Side locks of hair**: this is the typical manner of dressing the hair for boys and men of the kshatriya class.

231 **May the king protect the earth and destroy all enemies**: this line of benediction is ascribed to Bala·deva in D.

PROPER NAMES, EPITHETS, AND TITLES

How the Nagas were Pleased

ADEPTS (*siddha*), "those who are accomplished (in magical power)," a mythical class of beings

ATRÉYA the brahmin companion of the Hero, Jimúta·váhana. Herein the Companion, q.v.

BODHISATTVA an epithet for the Buddha-to-be, referring to him prior to his enlightenment, including in previous lives, when he was set on the path to Awakening

CHÁTURIKA a maid to Málayavati, the Heroine

COMPANION (*vidūṣaka*), a fool or jester, usually a brahmin who speaks in *Śaurasenī* and is companion to the Hero, here called Atréya

CONQUEROR (*Jina*), an epithet of the Buddha

CUPID = Kama, the god of love

DHÁNADA "giver of wealth," a name for Kubéra, the lord of riches and guardian of the northern quarter

GÁRUDA king of the birds and enemy of snakes, Nagas. The son, along with Áruna and Áruni, of Káshyapa and Vínata

GAURI "brilliant, golden," a name for Párvati, a goddess, consort of Shiva

HARI a name for Vishnu/Krishna

HÍMAVAT "snowy," a name for the Himálaya mountains

INDRA chief of the thirty(-three) lower gods in heaven

JIMÚTA·KETU King of the Magicians and father of the Hero, Jimúta·váhana

JIMÚTA·VÁHANA the Hero, son of the Magician king, Jimúta·ketu

KAILÁSA a mountain in the Himálaya, abode of Kubéra and Shiva

KAMA "love," the Indian deity associated with love, passion and lust. In the hagiography of the Buddha prior to his enlightenment he is said to have tempted him with his voluptuous and enticing daughters

KÁSHYAPA father of Gáruda

KÁUSHIKA the head of the hermitage featured in Act One

LAKSHMI the wife of Vishnu, who appeared from the ocean when it was churned by the gods and demons

LOKALÓKA "the world and the non-world," a mountain range that circles the known universe and separates it from the outer darkness

MAGICIANS (*vidyā/dhara*), a class of semi-divine beings

MÁLAYAVATI the Heroine, the daughter of the Adept king, Vishva·vasu

MÁNDARA the mountain used by the gods and *ásura*s to churn the ocean

MANO·HÁRIKA a maid of Málayavati, the Heroine

MARA "death," in Buddhism the personification of obstructions to the spiritual path

MATÁNGA "elephant, he who wanders at will/willfully," enemy of the state, an insubordinate tributary prince who attempts to usurp Jimúta·váhana's authority

MERU the mountain at the center of the continent of India, around which the sun and planets revolve. It is made of gold and the Ganges river flows from heaven down to its peak and therefrom through India

MITRA·VASU brother of Málayavati and son of Vishva·vasu

NAGA "serpent," a class of beings who are snakes or serpents but who can disguise themselves as human beings. The Buddhist ordination ceremony demands that candidates affirm that they are not Nagas to prevent infiltration of the monastic community. If they cannot so affirm the ordination is abandoned

NAVA·MÁLIKA a maid to Málayavati, the Heroine

SHAKRA an alternative name for Indra

SHANKHA·CHUDA a Naga whose turn it is to be eaten by Gáruda

SHANDÍLYA the personal name of the ascetic featured at the end of Act One near whose hermitage the Hero and Heroine meet

SHÉKHARAKA the personal name of the Rogue (*viṭa*), a member of Mitra·vasu's household

SUNÁNDA the personal name of the doorman

TARKSHYA a name for Gáruda, though also used for his father and elder brother

VÁSAVA = Indra q.v.

VÁSUKI chief of the Nagas, who agrees to sacrifice one Naga subject per day to Gáruda

VÍNATA mother of Gáruda and wife of Káshyapa

VISHVA·VASU King of the Adepts and father of Málayavati and Mitra·vasu. He does not appear in the play

YAMA the lord of death and the underworld

The Shattered Thighs

This glossary is provided to give orientation for the reader unfamiliar with the personnel of the "Maha·bhárata" as they appear in "The Shattered Thighs." It includes all the proper names and epithets used in this translation, and incidentally provides some indication of the complex dynastic currents that underlie the "Maha·bhárata" war. Information about episodes rather than people is supplied where relevant in the notes to the translation. Place names and the proper names of inanimate objects are included here.

ABHIMÁNYU the son of Árjuna and Subhádra

AIRÁVATA the elephant mount of Indra

ÁRJUNA "white," the third of the Pándava brothers

ASHVA·TTHAMAN "having the strength of a horse," son of Drona

BALA·DEVA an alternative name for Bala·rama

BALA·RAMA "powerful Rama," the elder brother of Krishna by Dévaki and the eighth manifestation of Vishnu. Plays a neutral role in the "Maha·bhárata" battle

BHIMA "terrifying," second of the five Pándavas, "fathered" by the god Vayu, "the wind"

BHIMA·SENA "having a terrifying army," an epithet of Bhima

BHISHMA "dread," a son of Shántanu who sided with the Kurus. He is an uncle to Pandu and Dhrita·rashtra

CHITRÁNGADA the name of Bhima's mace, meaning literally "decorated with a variety of bands"

DHRITA·RASHTRA "whose realm is stable, regent," blind Kuru patriarch, father of one hundred sons, including Duryódhana, and husband of Gandhári. He was born to Vichítra·virya and Ámbika, fathered by Vyasa

DRÁUPADI "daughter of Drúpada (the king of the Panchálas)," the wife of the five Pándava brothers

DRONA "vessel," the father of Ashva·tthaman and teacher of both the Pándavas and the Kurus

DÚRJAYA "hard to beat," the young son of Duryódhana

DURYÓDHANA "hard to fight," the chief of the Kurus and eldest son of Dhrita·rashtra

GÁNDIVA Árjuna's bow

GANDHÁRA an ancient Himalayan kingdom of North-West India. The king of Gandhára is Shákuni, the brother of queen Gandhári

GANDHÁRI "lady of Gandhára," the wife of Dhrita·rashtra and mother of his hundred sons, the Kurus

GÁRUDA the king of the birds and the mount of Vishnu. The enemy of snakes

Golden Peak (*Hemakūṭa*), the name of one of several mountain ranges that divide the world, north of the Himalayas

Hátaka a country and nation mentioned in the "Maha·bhárata"

Hari a name for Krishna

Hidímba a large evil-smelling cannibal demon killed by Bhima

Indra the divine king of the Vedic pantheon and divine father of Árjuna

Island-born Vyasa (*Dvaipāyana Vyāsa*) a name for Vyasa

Janárdana "delighter of people," a name of Krishna

Jayad·ratha "whose chariots are victorious," the king of Sindh and brother by marriage to Duryódhana

Kailása a Himalayan mountain, the residence of the gods Kubéra and Shiva

Kalíndi the river Yámuna, whose waters run from the Kalínda mountain

Karna "ear," half brother of the Pándavas by Kunti and the sun god Surya, fighting alongside Duryódhana with the Kurus

Késhava "long-haired," a name for Krishna

Khándava "gladed/gorged/honeycombed," a forest in Kuru·kshetra burned by Árjuna and Krishna

Kripa uncle of Ashva·tthaman, brother-in-law to Drona and teacher of the Kurus

Krishna "black," god, a manifestation of Vishnu and the younger brother of Bala·rama. He assists the Pándavas

Kunti "daughter of Kunti·bhoja," the wife of Pandu and mother of Yudhi·shthira, Bhima and Árjuna, the three eldest of the Pándavas, and of Karna

Kuru ancestor of both Pandu and Dhrita·rashtra. His name is used as the patronymic of Dhrita·rashtra and his descendants

KURUS (*Kaurava*) the sons of Dhrita·rashtra and opponents of the Pándavas in the "Maha·bhárata" war

MÁLAVI "lady of the Málava people," a wife of Duryódhana

MÁNDARA a sacred mountain employed by the gods and *ásura*s to churn the ocean

MERU the mountain at the center of the Indian continent in traditional cosmology

PÁNDAVAS the five sons of Pandu: Yudhi·shthira, Bhima, Árjuna, Nákula and Saha·deva

PANDU "white," the brother of Dhrita·rashtra, son of Vyasa. Married to Kunti and Madri and human father of Árjuna

PÁRASHU·RAMA "Rama with the axe," the sixth manifestation of Vishnu

PARTHA "son of Pritha," a name for Árjuna

PLOW BEARER (*Halāyudha*), a name for Bala·rama, bearing on his use of a plow as a weapon

PRITHA another name for Kunti

RAMA herein the text's abbreviation of Bala·rama

SAMANTA·PÁNCHAKA the name for the battlefield, taken from a ford in Kuru·kshetra

SHÁNTANU "healthy," the father of Bhishma and a descendant of Kuru.

SHARÁSA "bow," one of the sons of Dhrita·rashtra

SAUBHA the city of King Shalva, sacked by Bala·rama

SHIVA "auspicious/destroyer," one of the major Hindu deities

SUYÓDHANA "fighting well," an alternative name for Duryódhana

ÚRVASHI "dawn," a heavenly nymph

VÁISHRAVANA a name for Kubéra, the god of wealth and ruler of the northern quarter

VÁSUKI the king of the serpents

VEDA "knowledge," the revealed scripture of brahmanical and Hindu religion

VISHNU "worker, preserver," one of the major Hindu deities

VÍDURA "wise," an uncle to both sets of brothers, Kurus and Pándavas, and younger brother of Dhrita·rashtra and Pandu. Dispenses advice to the Pándavas and Dhrita·rashtra

VYASA "the compiler," the seer who arranged the Veda and composed the "Maha·bhárata" and appears in the latter as father of Pandu and Dhrita·rashtra

WOLF BELLY (*Vṛkodara*) a name for Bhima

YADU older brother of Puru, head of Yádava lineage

YÁMUNA a river tributary of the Ganges

YUDHI·SHTHIRA "steady in battle," the eldest of the five Pándavas

INDEX

Sanskrit words are given in the English alphabetical order, according to the accented CSL pronuncuation aid. They are followed by the conventional diacritics in brackets.

THE CLAY SANSKRIT LIBRARY

Current Volumes

For further details please consult the CSL website.

1. The Emperor of the Sorcerers (*Bṛhatkathāślokasaṃgraha*) (vol. 1 of 2) by *Budhasvāmin.* Sir James Mallinson
2. Heavenly Exploits (*Divyāvadāna*) Joel Tatelman
3. Maha·bhárata III: The Forest (*Vanaparvan*) (vol. 4 of 4) William J. Johnson
4. Much Ado about Religion (*Āgamaḍambara*) by *Bhaṭṭa Jayanta.* Csaba Dezső
5. The Birth of Kumára (*Kumārasaṃbhava*) by *Kālidāsa.* David Smith
6. Ramáyana I: Boyhood (*Bālakāṇḍa*) by *Vālmīki.* Robert P. Goldman
7. The Epitome of Queen Lilávati (*Līlāvatīsāra*) (vol. 1 of 2) by *Jinaratna.* R.C.C. Fynes
8. Ramáyana II: Ayódhya (*Ayodhyākāṇḍa*) by *Vālmīki.* Sheldon I. Pollock
9. Love Lyrics (*Amaruśataka, Śatakatraya & Caurapañcāśikā*) by *Amaru, Bhartṛhari & Bilhaṇa.* Greg Bailey & Richard Gombrich
10. What Ten Young Men Did (*Daśakumāracarita*) by *Daṇḍin.* Isabelle Onians
11. Three Satires (*Kalividambana, Kalāvilāsa & Bhallaṭaśataka*) by *Nīlakaṇṭha, Kṣemendra & Bhallaṭa* Somadeva Vasudeva
12. Ramáyana IV: Kishkíndha (*Kiṣkindhākāṇḍa*) by *Vālmīki.* Rosalind Lefeber

13. The Emperor of the Sorcerers (*Bṛhatkathāślokasaṃgraha*) (vol. 2 of 2) by *Budhasvāmin*. Sir James Mallinson
14. Maha·bhárata IX: Shalya (*Śalyaparvan*) (vol. 1 of 2) Justin Meiland
15. Rákshasa's Ring (*Mudrārākṣasa*) by *Viśākhadatta*. Michael Coulson
16. Messenger Poems (*Meghadūta, Pavanadūta & Haṃsadūta*) by *Kālidāsa, Dhoyī & Rūpa Gosvāmin*. Sir James Mallinson
17. Ramáyana III: The Forest (*Araṇyakāṇḍa*) by *Vālmīki*. Sheldon I. Pollock
18. The Epitome of Queen Lilávati (*Līlāvatīsāra*) (vol. 2 of 2) by *Jinaratna*. R.C.C. Fynes
19. Five Discourses on Worldly Wisdom (*Pañcatantra*) by *Viṣṇuśarman*. Patrick Olivelle
20. Ramáyana V: Súndara (*Sundarakāṇḍa*) by *Vālmīki*. Robert P. Goldman & Sally J. Sutherland Goldman
21. Maha·bhárata II: The Great Hall (*Sabhāparvan*) Paul Wilmot
22. The Recognition of Shakúntala (*Abhijñānaśākuntala*) (Kashmir Recension) by *Kālidāsa*. Somadeva Vasudeva
23. Maha·bhárata VII: Drona (*Droṇaparvan*) (vol. 1 of 4) Vaughan Pilikian
24. Rama Beyond Price (*Anargharāghava*) by *Murāri*. Judit Törzsök
25. Maha·bhárata IV: Viráta (*Virāṭaparvan*) Kathleen Garbutt
26. Maha·bhárata VIII: Karna (*Karṇaparvan*) (vol. 1 of 2) Adam Bowles
27. "The Lady of the Jewel Necklace" and "The Lady who Shows her Love" (*Ratnāvalī & Priyadarśikā*) by *Harṣa*. Wendy Doniger

28. The Ocean of the Rivers of Story (*Kathāsaritsāgara*) (vol. 1 of 7)
by *Somadeva*. Sir James Mallinson
29. Handsome Nanda (*Saundarananda*)
by *Aśvaghoṣa*. Linda Covill
30. Maha·bhárata IX: Shalya (*Śalyaparvan*) (vol. 2 of 2)
Justin Meiland
31. Rama's Last Act (*Uttararāmacarita*) by *Bhavabhūti*.
Sheldon Pollock. Foreword by Girish Karnad
32. "Friendly Advice" (*Hitopadeśa*) by *Nārāyaṇa* &
"King Víkrama's Adventures" (*Vikramacarita*). Judit Törzsök
33. Life of the Buddha (*Buddhacarita*)
by *Aśvaghoṣa*. Patrick Olivelle
34. Maha·bhárata V: Preparations for War (*Udyogaparvan*) (vol. 1 of 2)
Kathleen Garbutt. Foreword by Gurcharan Das
35. Maha·bhárata VIII: Karna (*Karṇaparvan*) (vol. 2 of 2)
Adam Bowles
36. Maha·bhárata V: Preparations for War (*Udyogaparvan*) (vol. 2 of 2)
Kathleen Garbutt
37. Maha·bhárata VI: Bhishma (*Bhīṣmaparvan*) (vol. 1 of 2)
Including the "Bhagavad Gita" in Context
Alex Cherniak. Foreword by Ranajit Guha
38. The Ocean of the Rivers of Story (*Kathāsaritsāgara*) (vol. 2 of 7)
by *Somadeva*. Sir James Mallinson
39. "How the Nagas were Pleased" (*Nāgānanda*) by *Harṣa* &
"The Shattered Thighs" (*Ūrubhaṅga*) by *Bhāsa*.
Andrew Skilton

To Appear in 2009

Bhatti's Poem: The Death of Rávana (*Bhaṭṭikāvya*)
by *Bhaṭṭi*. OLIVER FALLON

"Bouquet of Rasa" & "River of Rasa" (*Rasamañjarī & Rasataraṅgiṇī*)
by *Bhānudatta*. SHELDON POLLOCK

Garland of Past Lives (*Jātakamālā*) (vol. 1 of 2) by *Āryaśūra*
JUSTIN MEILAND

Garland of Past Lives (*Jātakamālā*) (vol. 2 of 2) by *Āryaśūra*
JUSTIN MEILAND

Gita·govínda: Love Songs of Radha and Krishna (*Gītagovinda*)
by *Jayadeva*. LEE SIEGEL. Foreword by SUDIPTA KAVIRAJ

How Úrvashi Was Won (*Vikramorvaśīya*) by *Kālidāsa*
VELCHERU NARAYANA RAO & DAVID SHULMAN

Little Clay Cart (*Mṛcchakaṭikā*) by *Śūdraka*.
DIWAKAR ACHARYA. Foreword by PARTHA CHATTERJEE

Maha·bhárata VI: Bhishma (*Bhīṣmaparvan*) (vol. 2 of 2)
ALEX CHERNIAK

Maha·bhárata XII: Peace (*Śāntiparvan*) (vol. 3 of 5) Part Two:
"The Book of Liberation" (*Mokṣadharma*). ALEX WYNNE

Maha·bhárata XIV: The Horse Sacrifice (*Āśvamedhikaparvan*)
GREG BAILEY

On Self-Surrender, Compassion, and the Mission of a Goose:
Sanskrit Poetry from the South (*Ātmārpaṇastuti, Dayāśataka & Haṃsasaṃdeśa*) by *Appaya Dīkṣita* and *Vedāntadeśika*.
YIGAL BRONNER & DAVID SHULMAN

Princess Kadámbari (*Kādambarī*) (vol. 1 of 3)
by *Bāṇa*. DAVID SMITH

The Quartet of Causeries (*Caturbhāṇī*)
by *Śūdraka, Śyāmilaka, Vararuci & Īśvaradatta*.
CSABA DEZSŐ & SOMADEVA VASUDEVA

Seven Hundred Elegant Verses (*Āryāsaptaśatī*)
by *Govardhana*. FRIEDHELM HARDY